General Yamashita's Dream Book:

How To Successfully Find Hidden Treasure In The Philippines

By Aquila Chrysaestos

Published by New Generation Publishing in 2013

Copyright © Aquila Chrysaestos 2013

First Edition

The author asserts the moral right under the Copyright, Designs and Patents Act 1988 to be identified as the author of this work.

All Rights reserved. No part of this publication may be reproduced, stored in a retrieval system or transmitted, in any form or by any means without the prior consent of the author, nor be otherwise circulated in any form of binding or cover other than that which it is published and without a similar condition being imposed on the subsequent purchaser.

www.newgeneration-publishing.com

All rights reserved. No part of the publication may be reproduced, stored in a retrieval system, or transmitted in any form or by any means, electronic, mechanical, photocopying, recording, or otherwise, without the written prior permission of the author.

Information available in the book provided "as is". The author makes no representations or warranties either expressed or implied as to the accuracy of the information in these pages or its fitness for any purpose whatsoever. The author cannot be held responsible for any loss, accident, injury, or death which may occur from any reader's misunderstanding or modifying published data in this book.

The author cannot guarantee that the interpretation of the treasure symbols published in this book can be error free, and that the explanations given should be used for general guidance only.

The author makes no representations or warranties either expressed or implied as to the accuracy of the information given by manufactures of products listed on featured website links listed in this book. The author does not have any commercial connection with any of these companies, and has supplied data to encourage you the reader to research into new and modern treasure hunting techniques, and seek out new technologies that will speed up treasure detection when carrying out your own field operations. The author is not trying to promote new products or suggest that the reader should purchase any of these products shown on the following featured pages of this book.

The views of individuals are not necessarily shared by the author of this book.

This book is dedicated to my son Joshi and a message to him:

Go and live your dreams no matter what others may say and become a living legend doing what you want to achieve in life, with the spirit of adventure and love for humanity in your heart pushing you forward, and you **will** win through my son.

All my love to you always.

Dad x

Contents   Page

Introduction   11

1.00 **Operation "Golden Lily"**	14
2.00 **Main Players Involved In Operation "Golden Lily" (1937-45)**	17
2.10 **Hirohito Emperor Showa of Japan**	18
2.20 **Prince Yasuhito Chichibu**	21
2.30 **Prince Takahito Mikasa**	23
2.40 **Prince Takeda Tsunehisa**	24
2.41 Prince Takeda Tsunehisa Treasure Symbols Page 1	25
2.42 Prince Takeda Tsunehisa Treasure Symbols Page 2	26
2.43 Prince Takeda Tsunehisa Treasure Symbols Page 3	27
2.50 **General Tomoyuki Yamashita**	28
2.51 Japan Surrenders	29
2.52 General Yamashita's Trial	32
2.53 Inside Manila Court House: Yamashita's Trial	33
2.54 The Execution	34
2.55 Yamashita's Trial: The Conclusion	37
2.56 Yamashita's Driver	39
2.57 **Why was "Golden Lily" Renamed "Yamashita's Gold"?**	41
2.58 General Yamashita Treasure Symbols Page 1	47
2.59 General Yamashita Treasure Symbols Page 2	48
2.60 General Masaharu Homma	49
2.61 Americans Surrender on Corregidor Island	51
2.62 Corregidor Island	52
2.63 **Homma: Bataan Death March**	53
2.64 Homma's Trial And Conviction	55
2.65 General Homma Treasure Symbols Page 1	58
2.66 General Homma Treasure Symbols Page 2	59
2.67 General Homma Treasure Symbols Page 3	60
2.68 "Golden Lily": Roles Other People Played	61
3.00 **Japanese Military Involvement**	62
3.10 **The Japanese Engineering Battalion**	63
3.20 The Japanese Engineering Battalion Treasure Symbols Page 1	64
3.30 The Japanese Engineering Battalion Treasure Symbols Page 2	65
3.40 The Japanese Engineering Battalion Treasure Symbols Page 3	66
3.50 **The Tanaka Detachment**	67
3.60 Colonel Tanaka Toru Treasure Symbols Page 1	68
3.70 Colonel Tanaka Toru Treasure Symbols Page 2	69
3.80 Colonel Tanaka Toru Treasure Symbols Page 3	70
3.90 Advanced Japanese Landings in December 1941	71
4.00 **Japanese Military Numbers On The 30th September 1944**	73
4.10 Are Imperial Japanese Treasure Sites In The Philippines Real?	74
4.20 Marcos: Does He Have The Largest Treasure Recovery In History?	84
4.30 Japanese Imperial Treasure Site Markings For The Philippines (Dated 1943-45)	89

4.40 Partial List of Known Japanese Imperial Treasure Burial Sites On The Philippine Islands	91
4.50 The Famous Marcos Head Statue	94
4.60 Japanese Imperial Treasure Maps	95
4.70 What Is The Key To Unlock The Map?	96
4.80 What was a 555 or a 777 site?	97
4.90 A Basic Treasure Map: (Origin Not Known)	98
5.00 **How Did The Japanese Engineers Excavate The Tunnels?**	100
5.10 Imperial Treasure Vault Construction	102
5.20 Why Were The Imperial Sites Dug In This Manner?	104
5.30 Teresa 2 Imperial Site # 5	107
5.40 Teresa 2 Imperial Treasure Site Map # 5 (1943)	109
5.50 Teresa 2: The Buried Hoard Explained	109
5.60 Teresa 2 Top And Side View Detail	110
5.70 Teresa 2: How The Site Was Excavated In 1974	111
5.80 A Basic Japanese Treasure Map Explained	113
5.90 The Clock Face Reveals Its Secret	115
6.00 **Treasure And Compass Map Layout Explained**	116
6.10 Clock Face Examples	118
6.20 Lucky Japanese Symbols	119
6.30 Sakura Music And Words	122
6.40 Japanese Writing Explained	123
6.50 Japanese Writing: A Brief History	124
6.60 Hiragana Script	125
6.70 Hiragana Script Symbols	126
6.80 Katakana Script Symbols	127
6.90 The Japanese Calendar Used During WWII	131
7.00 **Basic Japanese Numbers**	132
7.10 The Lucky Seven Gods Of Japanese Mythology	133
7.20 The No. 7 Treasure Symbols	135
7.30 Korean Writing	136
7.40 The Hangeul Alphabet	138
7.50 A Basic Tick List To Go Treasure Hunting In The Philippines	140
7.60 Some Of The Relevant Treasure Hunting Laws Regarding The Philippines	141
7.70 DENR Relevant Treasure Hunting Laws	143
7.80 Weather Recovery Time Window	145
7.90 Typhoon And Monsoon Season	147
8.00 **The Search And Recovery Agreement (Sample)**	148
8.10 Finding Buried Treasure	151
8.20 Excavation Considerations	155
8.30 Basic Equipment For Treasure Hunting Activities	157
8.40 Basic Detection Equipment	158
8.50 A Useful Digital Watch	160
8.60 The Casio Watch: How Does It Work?	162
8.70 A Basic Metal Detector	164
8.80 An Inexpensive Data Logger To Show You 3D Images Underground Prior To Excavation	166
8.90 Detector Used in The Philippines Whites TM 808™	167

9.00 **The "ABC" of Generic Japanese Treasure Symbols And Relevant Documentation**	168
9.01 Arrow Signs	169
9.02 Bird Treasure Signs	170
9.03 Box Treasure Signs	171
9.04 The Secret Of The Cemented Box Revealed!	172
9.05 Buddha Treasure Signs	173
9.06 **Bridge Treasure Sign**	175
9.07 Broken Ceramics and Glass Markers	177
9.08 Broken Ceramics and Glass Examples	178
9.09 The Carabao Secret	179
9.10 Cone Shape Mountain	181
9.11 Concrete Steps And Hidden Gold Bars	182
9.12 **Diamond Symbols**	183
9.13 Fall Rock In Cave	184
9.14 Footprints Explained: My Left Foot	185
9.15 My Right Foot	186
9.16 Two Feet	187
9.17 Crossed Feet	187
9.18 **Two Feet With Treasure Symbols**	188
9.19 Gate Guard	189
9.20 Gold Treasure Signs	190
9.21 Gold Bar Types	191
9.22 Calculations For Estimating The Weight Of A Gold Bar	194
9.23 Heart-Shaped Rocks And Treasure Signs	196
9.24 **Heart-Shaped Rock Photo**	197
9.25 Heart Treasure Signs Example 1	198
9.26 Heart Treasure Signs Example 2	199
9.27 Heart-Shaped Rock As Part Of A Treasure Site	200
9.28 Heart Treasure Signs On Rocks	202
9.29 Korean Heart Treasure Sign	202
9.30 **Hollow Rock Treasure: A Photographic Example**	203
9.31 Hollow Rock Treasure: Diagrams And Symbols	204
9.32 Hollow Rock Treasure: Photographic Examples A & B	205
9.33 Hollow Rock Treasure: Photographic Examples C	206
9.34 Pink Concrete: How To Break It	207
9.35 Pink Concrete: Using Acid	208
9.36 **Pink Concrete: Use Thermite**	209
9.37 Pink Concrete: "The Solution"	210
9.38 Pink Concrete: Using Dexpan	211
9.39 The Pulley Secret Explained	213
9.40 Rock Tunnel Maps Explained	214
9.41 Rock Analysis By Water	215
9.42 **Rice Field Treasure Symbols**	216
9.43 River And Waterfall Burial Locations	217
9.44 Waterfall Photograph: Spot The Treasure Clues	218
9.45 Waterfall Photograph: Symbols Revealed	218
9.46 River Burial Locations And Clues	219
9.47 River Digging And Water Treasure Symbols	221

9.48 **Sun And Spoke Treasure Symbols Explained**	223
9.49 Snake Symbols	224
9.50 Tree Markers And Treasure Signs	225
9.51 Trees With Eyes	228
9.52 Triangle, Dead and Bonsai Tree Markers	228
9.53 Turtle Treasure Signs	230
9.54 **Photographic Analysis Of Stone Turtles**	232
9.55 More Photographic Analysis Of Stone Turtles	233
9.56 Photographic Analysis Of A Stone Turtle Shell	234
9.57 Treasure Faces	235
9.58 How To Find Treasure Inside Tunnels	236
9.59 How To Find Secret Tunnel And Cave Entrances	237
9.60 **Construction of A Japanese Treasure Tunnel System (Luzon)**	239
9.61 Types of Tunnel Layouts	240
9.62 Feel Your Way To Find Gold Deposits	241
9.63 Examples Of Excavated Treasure Shafts	243
9.64 An Actual Treasure Site Found In Rizal (2006)	245
9.65 Triangle Treasure Signs	247
9.66 **Treasure Mound Shape Identification**	248
9.67 Tunnel Signs	249
9.68 Mirror Images	250
9.69 Mirror Images Underground	251
9.70 The Riddle Of Broken Rocks	252
9.71 Pyramid-Shaped Rock	254
9.72 **Water Well Secret No.1**	255
9.73 Water Well Secret No.2	256
9.74 Water Pump Secret	257
9.75 "X" Marks the Spot Symbols	258
9.76 "Z" Symbol Meanings	259
10.00 **Hidden Dangers: Toxic Gas**	260
10.10 Japanese Germ Warfare	261
10.20 Sarin Gas	264
10.30 Methane Gas (CH4)	265
10.40 Hydrogen Cyanide (HCN)	267
10.50 Mustard Gas (C4 H8Cl12S)	269
10.60 Poison Gas Symbols	271
10.70 Itchy Skin	272
10.80 Grey Powder And Danger Signs	275
10.90 Black Water	278
11.00 **Japanese "Katashiro" (to curse a human being)**	285
11.10 Booby Traps and Japanese Bombs	287
11.20 Booby Trap Signs	288
11.30 The German-Made Teller Mine	289
11.40 The Italian-Made Thermos Bomb	289
11.50 German-Made Stick Grenade	290
11.60 Japanese Stick Grenade, Japanese Hand Grenade & Japanese Knee Mortar Grenade	290
11.70 Land Mines Used By The Japanese Forces	291
11.80 Booby Traps in Tunnels and Shafts	292

11.90	Imperial Japanese Bombs Used During WWII	294
12.00	**Explosive Danger Signs**	296
12.10	Water Traps	297
12.20	Water Trap Solution No.1	298
12.30	Water Trap Solution No.2	298
13.00	**Where Did The Japanese Bury The Gold And Precious Items That They Looted?**	300
13.10	Untouched Treasure Sites Compiled Over Twenty Years Of Research By: Mr G. Santchez	301
13.20	Philippine Map Showing Buried Gold Deposits	303
13.30	Sea Treasure Sites	307
13.40	Locations Of Japanese Ships Sunk During WWII	309
13.50	The Imperial Japanese Navy Symbols	312
13.60	How Do I Apply For A Treasure Hunter's Permit To Dive On Ship wrecks?	313
13.70	List Of Japanese Prisoner of War Camps In The Philippines During WWII	317
13.80	Airfields Occupied By The Japanese During WWII	319
13.90	Japanese Airfields In Use On The 30th September 1944	320
14.00	**Building Up A Picture Of A Beach Treasure Site**	321
14.10	Do Not Assume Anything Until You Have The Whole Picture!	322
14.20	Why Did The Japanese Military Bury Gold Deposits On Beaches?	326
14.30	Markers And Clues To Look For On Beach Sites	328
14.40	Our Beach Treasure Site	330
14.50	Treasure Site Layouts	331
14.60	The Pentagon Treasure Deposit Layout	332
14.70	Types Of Pentagon Markers	333
14.80	An Example Of A 5 Arrow Pentagon Deposit Marker	334
14.90	Pentagon Treasure Site Layout	335
15.00	**Lightning And Gold Theory**	337
15.10	An Example Of Lightning & Gold Theory	339
15.20	Does Buried Gold Give Off An Aura?	341
15.30	An Infrared Image Of Buried Gold From Known Treasure Sites	343
15.40	Spiritual Activity At Potential Treasure Sites	345
15.50	What About This "Orb" Picture?	347
15.60	Orbs That Spell Danger And Disaster	349
15.70	Japanese Military Isuzu Type 94 6-Wheeled Transport Truck	351
15.80	Why Is this Information Important to a Treasure Hunter?	352
15.90	How Do I Tell If A Buried Truck Is Under The Ground?	353
16.00	**Analysis of Sliding Rock Treasure Markings**	354
16.10	River Rock Treasure Analysis	355
16.20	Treasure Items Recovered In The Philippines	356
16.30	Recovered Gold Bars	357
16.40	Gold Bars And A Small Buddha	358
16.50	More Recent Finds	359
16.60	Treasure Supposedly Found In The Mountains South Of Cagayan de Oro	361
16.70	Nickel Babbit Bars Found	366
16.80	I Found Some Metal Is It Valuable?	367

16.90 Counterfeit Johnson Matthey Platinum Bars	369
17.00 **Specific Gravity Table For Metals**	371
17.10 I Can't Melt The Metal!	372
17.20 A Recovered Gold Certificate	373
17.30 A Recovered J.P.MORGAN Gold Bullion Liberty Bond	374
17.40 Historic U.S. Gold Certificates (1934)	376
17.50 Woodrow Wilson Series 1934 Gold Certificate	377
17.60 Recovered Woodrow Wilson Series 1934 Gold Certificates	377
17.70 When Were Gold Certificates Used?	378
17.80 Wells Fargo U.S. Dollar Notes	380
17.90 Can These Old U.S. Notes Be Redeemed?	381
18.00 **Japanese Treasure Maps and locations: Panabo Del Norte: Nr Davao, Mindanao**	383
18.10 Untouched Treasure Site: Southern Mindanao	384
18.20 Japanese Treasure Map of Southern Cotabato Mindanao	385
18.30 The Arsanai Japanese Flag Map Dated 27th August, 1944. Real or Fake?	386
18.40 Japanese Treasure Map: Location Unknown	387
18.50 Another Japanese Treasure Map: Location Unknown	388
18.60 Imperial Japanese Korean Treasure Symbols 1 For Davao Region Mindanao	389
18.70 Imperial Japanese Korean Treasure Symbols 2 For Davao Region Mindanao	390
18.80 Japanese Military Map Symbols 1	391
18.90 Japanese Military Map Symbols 2	392
19.00 **Japanese Characters For Geographical Features 1**	393
19.10 Japanese Characters For Geographical Features 2	394
19.20 General Observations Taken From A Japanese Topographical Map Of 1940	395
19.30 **112 Japanese Treasure Symbols Showing Distance**	397
19.40 **336 Japanese Treasure Symbols Showing Direction**	401
Conclusion	411
Bibliography	413
Appendix	414

Introduction

When you plan to write a book on treasure hunting and start researching then compiling your thoughts on paper, you realise how large the subject matter really is, particularly in relation to reading and understanding the meaning of treasure symbols. This subject is much more comprehensive and deeper than just knowing what one symbol may mean. You the treasure hunter must know the subject "Treasure Hunting in the Philippines" intimately before you start on your own fascinating treasure hunting adventure.

I still receive monthly emails from Filipino treasure hunters wanting me to read and decipher treasure symbols still found today carved on rocks and trees all over the many islands that make up the Philippines. They ask me for detailed symbol explanations, and how the meanings I give relate to their particular site and geographic area in question. I explain at length that the symbols can only be decoded if we know which code writer was assigned to a particular Japanese Officer or Battalion who carved the symbols and for what reason.

As you see on subsequent pages of this book, each Japanese general or Battalion had a unique set of treasure code books, and used these coded symbols wherever they were stationed or "visited" during the Second World War. The same symbol can have many meanings, therefore it is very important to know which code book was used and by whom in order to have the correct meaning and avoid any misunderstandings.
With this in mind, I have written this book to help treasure hunters understand what has been buried in the Philippine Islands, how it was buried by the Japanese during the Second World War, and how to decipher the many treasure symbols written by various Japanese and Korean code writers for the Japanese military generals and naval admirals occupying different islands during the Japanese military occupation of 1942-1945.

With ease of reading in mind, I have broken the book down into 19 sections where each section complements the other and answers most of the questions I asked myself six years earlier when I was introduced to treasure hunting activities being carried out in Northern Luzon at the time of my visit. Many of the questions I had could not be answered by anyone that I knew personally, therefore it was then that I decided to carry out my own research by travelling to the Philippines again and again to see for myself several burial sites and to work with native treasure hunters. This book has been compiled from my experiences as well as those of many other Filipino treasure adventurers of which I am greatly thankful.

In many sections of this book I have included external website links to information relating to this subject matter which has been added to the various sections of this book. My objective is to aid you in reaching the ultimate goal of finding your own treasure and achieving a successful recovery.

I have also supplied approximate Global Satellite Positions of treasure sites or towns, cities or areas that are known to have been near or occupied by the Japanese forces during WWII. This information must be verified by you the reader as to its accuracy and relevance if you decide to pursue your treasure hunting activities at these identified cities and town locations.

Use this book for field reference as you visit potential sites, so that you gain a much deeper understanding of what you should know compared to what you think you know. Please remember that no one person is an expert on this subject, we are all students with open minds and should always strive to learn more about this very interesting time in Philippine history.

Never become arrogant into thinking that you know everything there is to know about the resourcefulness and cunning of the Japanese military stationed in the Philippines during the Second World War.

They were masters of construction and used all of the materials at their disposal to camouflage, conceal, and bury vast riches inside caves, tunnels, mine shafts, bunkers, and secret treasure vaults on land and hide many tons of war loot in coastal sea caves, sunken shipwrecks and submarines in natural bays where the depth of the water was over 300 feet deep.

Please Remember
Lack of local knowledge and ignorance regarding hidden booby traps and poisonous gas traps could get you injured or even killed. Therefore, I have supplied as much information on treasure hunting dangers in sections 10, 11, and 12 of this book for you to take note and digest before you get yourself into any trouble.

Always expect the unexpected, and apply caution to any treasure hunting excavation or activity. If your gut feeling tells you **"Don't do it"** then don't, remember your actions may injure others in your treasure hunting group, or even locals living in the surrounding area of your treasure site. So please always beware of obvious and hidden dangers below and above the ground and always *work safely*.

Yamashita gold legends are still very much alive in the Philippines today as they were in the closing months of 1945. Many sites have been left as they were all those years ago untouched and forgotten in time and space, now awaiting present discovery. As the price of gold, silver, copper and platinum escalate due to man's greed for cheaper money supply, more individuals and groups will want to explore the Philippines for this hidden wealth and to dig frantically hoping to unearth lost riches.

In September 2012, while flying from Amsterdam to Heathrow, London, I sat beside an Australian called Trevor Johnston, managing director of Asia Pacific Commodities based in Hong Kong. He told me that gold demand will outstrip supply in Southeast Asia in the coming months, and the price will climb to an astonishing $3000 USD in the next two years. He advised me to buy as much gold as I could afford now before this commodity went skyward.

If the demand for gold and other precious metals reaches a point where demand is so massive, gold mining companies and speculators will look for other ways to retrieve these precious commodities quickly. They will turn to buried treasure deposits where the investment to recover will be far cheaper than spending millions of dollars on a new gold mine venture. The Philippines has many treasure vaults awaiting discovery. All the country needs is the investment from these money men to unlock these vaults and recover what has been stored underground for over half a century.

1.0 Operation "Golden Lily" (*Kin No Yuri*) 1937-1945 A Brief History

After Japan's full-scale invasion of China on 7th July 1937, Emperor Hirohito appointed one of his brothers, Prince Chichibu, to head a secret organization called Kin No Yuri "Golden Lily" (taken from one of the Emperor's poems) whose function was to ensure that all stolen *"war booty"* riches were to be properly accounted for. Putting an Imperial prince in charge guaranteed that everyone, even the most senior commanders, would follow strict orders regarding the collection and transportation of gold bullion, jewels, golden Buddhas, ancient religious artifacts, foreign currency, precious metals, and other valuable items, to designated ports, and forward bound to Japan.

The Emperor also posted his cousin, Prince Tsuneyoshi Takeda, to the Kwantung Army staff in Manchuria, and later as his personal liaison officer to the Saigon headquarters of Field Marshall Count Hisaichi Terauchi, to supervise looting and ensure that the proceeds were shipped to Japanese mainland in areas under Terauchi's total control.

He ordered Admiral Masahura, then overall military commander of the Philippines, before General Yamashita and other Admirals and generals, that all war treasure booty taken from the occupied territories of Java, Sumatra, Singapore, Malaysia, Thailand, Burma, Northern India, and the Dutch East Indies be collected and shipped directly to the Philippine Islands when the Americans had blockaded shipping routes to mainland Japan in late 1943.

Although assigned to Saigon, Takeda worked almost exclusively in the Philippines as second in command to Prince Chichibu, Hirohito's brother. Emperor Hirohito named his uncle, Prince Yasuhiko Asaka, deputy commander of the Central China Area Army, in which he commanded the final assault on Nanking, the Chinese capital, between 2nd of December and 6th of December 1937, and allegedly gave the order to "kill all captives".

The Japanese removed some 6000 tons of gold from Chiang Kai-shek's treasury and many riches from the homes and offices of the leaders of Nationalist China.

By the spring of 1942, the Japanese Imperial forces had captured all South-East Asia, including the Philippines and Indonesia, and the work of "Golden Lily" increased many times over. In addition to the monetary assets of the Dutch, British, French and Americans in their respective colonies, "Golden Lily" operatives absconded with as much of the wealth of the overseas Chinese populations as they could find.

Japanese soldiers tore gold gilt from Buddhist temples, stole solid gold Buddha's from Burma, sold opium to the local populations and collected gemstones from anyone who had any. The gold was then melted down into 75 kg ingots at a big Japanese-run smelter in Ipoh, Malaya and marked with its degree of purity and weight. Prince Chichibu and his staff inventoried all this plunder and put it aboard large merchant ships, usually disguised as hospital ships with large green crosses painted on the side, bound for mainland Japan.

A lot of gold and gems were lost through American Naval submarine warfare, sinking Japanese merchant ships transporting plunder back to Japan. By early 1943, it was only possible for the Japanese to break through the Allied blockade around the main Philippine islands by using submarines. Prince Chichibu moved his headquarters from Singapore to Manila and ordered all treasure shipments from Singapore and Malaya to make their way to Manila, General Santos, Subic Bay, Davao and other "safe" Philippine ports for subsequent reburial.

At the end of the war the Imperial Family's plan was simply to withdraw all their forces from occupied Asia, except the Philippines which would remain under Japanese colonial rule under the banner "Asia for Asians", headed by Judge Jose Laurel as president of a Philippine puppet-type government. This would enable Japan to have a military presence in the country in order to excavate the stolen riches at leisure with little interference from other foreign governments, both near and far. It was always the intention of Emperor Hirohito that all the wealth stored underground in the Philippines would be recovered to only benefit the Imperial Japanese Family who would become immensely rich as a result when the hostilities were over.

There was no plan to share this vast stolen wealth with the Japanese people, indeed it was a plan conceived by greed, and by evil men who would never see this treasure fully recovered in their lifetimes.

From 1942 to 1945, Takeda and Chichibu supervised the building of 175* "Imperial" storage sites to hide the treasure until the war ended. Thousands of slave laborers and prisoners of war dug tunnels and fortified cave systems with reinforced concrete hundreds of feet underground. When the gold was successfully transferred into the new vaults, all the workers, including Japanese Officers, tunnel engineers and prisoners, were invariably buried alive when the entrances and ventilation holes were sealed up on the orders of Prince Chichibu or Prince Takeda once they were satisfied the work and the tunnel engineers' maps were correct and accurate. These locations were secret and only known to the members of the Japanese Imperial Family.

Each Imperial treasure site on land was booby-trapped to some degree. All "Golden Lily" site maps are elaborately encoded to hide exact location, depth of treasure, air vents, secret entrances to be used later for safe recovery and location of booby traps (e.g. large aerial bombs, sand traps, poison gases, tripwires etc) noted and recorded. In Manila itself, "Golden Lily" excavation teams constructed treasure caverns in the dungeon of the old Spanish Fort Santiago, within Fort McKinley (now Fort Bonifacio), the former American military headquarters, and under the foundations of Manila Cathedral.

A high-ranking Japanese intelligence officer who worked with Prince Chichibu during the war stated in 1968 that Japan had hidden 100 billion dollars worth of treasure in the Philippines alone. Because of the difficulty in recovery techniques at that time, it would take a very dedicated team more than one-hundred years to recover it all.

"Go-Shichi no Kiri": The Japanese House Crest. The Japanese Imperial Crest or Mikado's Seal is the Private symbol of the Imperial Family dating back to as early as the twelfth century.

* Robert Curtis stated to Tomas Cyran in his book *In Search of Gold* that he was in possession of 175 copies of these Imperial maps.

2.00 Main Players Involved In Operation "Golden Lily" (Kin No Yuri) 1937 - 1945

In the following section I have written brief descriptions of the main Japanese players involved in Operation "Golden Lily" during 1937 to the end of the Second World War.

This is not a complete comprehensive list. However, other authors have written so much about this subject I suggest if you want to find out more in-depth knowledge about "Golden Lily" both past and present refer to the reading material listed on this very subject in the appendix of this book.

I will now concentrate on six of the main Japanese "Golden Lily" characters, namely:

    2.10 **Hirohito Emperor Showa of Japan**
    2.20 **Prince Yasuhito Chichibu**
    2.30 **Prince Takahito Mikasa**
    2.40 **Prince Takeda Tsunehisa**
    2.50 **General Tomoyuki Yamashita**
    2.60 **General Masaharu Homma**

On the following pages I have given a brief explanation of the roles each of these people played in operation "Golden Lily", and the treasure code symbols used by Prince Takeda and Generals Yamashita and Homma. It is essential that you, the treasure hunter, have some background history on the main players and how they were involved in "Golden Lily".

It is important to know where they "visited" during their time in the Philippines during 1942-45, which will become self-evident as you read about these characters in turn.

The treasure code books that were used by the 12th and 18th Engineering Battalion and Colonel Tanaka Toru are also listed in the section of the book together with a brief history about their movements during the invasion of the Philippines. See sections:

    3.10) **The Japanese Engineering Battalion**
    3.20) **The Tanaka Detachment**

2.10 Hirohito Emperor Showa of Japan

We begin with Hirohito. He was born in Tokyo on 29th April 1901, the eldest son of Crown Prince Yoshihito. His father became emperor when Hirohito was only eleven years old.

Hirohito Emperor Showa of Japan (1901-1989)[1]

In 1921, Hirohito went on a six-month tour of Europe, becoming the first member of the Japanese Imperial Family to travel abroad. He married an Imperial princess called Nagako in 1924, and they had seven children. Hirohito became emperor at the young age of twenty-five when his father died in 1926.

The emperor was regarded as a divine God by many Japanese, but in reality he had little power, with civilian matters of state, and increasingly military officials decided national policy. He reluctantly supported the invasion of Manchuria and the war against China, and

---

[1] This photographic image was published before December 31st 1956, or photographed before 1946 and not published for 10 years thereafter, under jurisdiction of the Government of Japan, considered to be **public domain** law of Japan. According to article 23 of old copyright law of Japan and article 2 of supplemental provision of copyright.

attempted to encourage cooperation with Britain and the United States of America.

However, he had no choice but to approve the Japanese attack on Pearl Harbor that led to war between Japan and the United States in December of 1941. Despite his lack of enthusiasm over the decision to go to war, he was pleased with the Japanese military and naval successes that followed.

By the spring of 1945, the defeat of Japan seemed imminent. The Japanese government was deeply divided between military leaders who wanted the war to continue and the civilian population who wanted to negotiate for peace. Emperor Hirohito had decided to choose the peace option.

Following the atomic bomb attacks on Hiroshima and Nagasaki, Hirohito insisted to his ministers and military chiefs of staff that Japan surrender, and on the 15th August 1945 he made a radio broadcast announcing the end of the war. This was the first time the people of Japan had heard the voice of their emperor.

Some allied leaders wanted to try Hirohito in an international court as a war criminal. General Douglas MacArthur, who was in charge of the United States' occupying forces in Japan, felt it would be easier to introduce democratic reforms if Hirohito stayed in office. Hirohito nonetheless repudiated his divine status.

Douglas MacArthur and Emperor Hirohito: their first meeting at the U.S. Embassy Tokyo, 27th of September, 1945.[2]

---

[2] Photograph by U.S. Army photographer Lt. Gaetano Faillace. This image is a work of a U.S. Army soldier or employee, taken or made during the course of the person's official duties. As a work of the U.S. federal government, the image is in the **public domain.**

In the book *Gold Warriors*, the authors Sterling and Penny Seagrave state that the reason Hirohito was not tried for war crimes by MacArthur was simply because a business deal was done with Hirohito so that the U.S. government could have a large share of the plundered loot taken by Japan during operation "Golden Lily" during the war years.

President Truman, General MacArthur and John Foster Dulles and a few others knew about billions of dollars worth of gold, silver, precious stones, foreign bank notes, bonds, and religious artifacts.

MacArthur is reputed to have set up a special trust fund for Hirohito at the Sanwa Bank, and also set up a secret M-Fund to fund political right wing activists that would support U.S. foreign policy.

By the end of the war, Hirohito, according to historian James Mackay, had over $100 million hidden away in foreign currency and gold deposited in bank accounts in Switzerland ($20M USD), South America ($35M USD), and Portugal ($45M USD), and other amounts in Spain and in the Vatican bank in Rome.

In the post-war years, Hirohito travelled throughout Japan to see the progress of reconstruction and to win popularity for the Imperial Family. He also represented Japan abroad. He was very interested in marine biology and published numerous scholarly works in this particular field.

Hirohito died of cancer on the 7th of January 1989 at the Imperial Palace in Tokyo and was succeeded by his son Akihito.

2.20 Prince Yasuhito Chichibu

Prince Yasuhito Chichibu (1902-1953)
"Golden Lily" Code Name: Chako. Brother to the Emperor of Japan.[3]

Prince Yasuhito Chichibu, also known as Prince Yasuhito, was the second son of Emperor Taishō and a younger brother of the Emperor Shōwa.

As a member of the Japanese Imperial Family, he was the patron of several sporting, medical, and international exchange organizations. Before and after World War II, the English-speaking prince and his wife attempted to foster good relations between Japan and the United Kingdom and enjoyed a good rapport with the British Royal Family.

As with other Japanese Imperial princes of his generation, he was an active-duty career officer in the Japanese Imperial Army. Like all members of the Imperial Family, he was exonerated from all criminal prosecutions before the Tokyo tribunal held by Douglas MacArthur.

---

[3] This photographic image was published before December 31st 1956, or photographed before 1946 and not published for 10 years thereafter, under jurisdiction of the Government of Japan, considered to be **public domain** law of Japan. According to article 23 of old copyright law of Japan and article 2 of supplemental provision of copyright.

Military Career

Prince Chichibu received his commission as a second lieutenant in the infantry in October 1922 and was assigned to the First Imperial Guard Division. He was promoted to first lieutenant in 1925 and became a captain in 1930 after graduation from the Army War College. He received a promotion to the rank of major and was assigned to command the Thirty-First Infantry Division stationed at Hirosaki, Aomori in August 1935.

In August 1937, Prince Chichibu was appointed battalion commander of Thirty-First Infantry Regiment and promoted to lieutenant colonel in 1938, then finally to colonel in August 1939. During the war, he was involved in combat operations, and was sent to Manchukuo before the Nomonhan incident and to Nanjing after the Nanjing massacres occurred.

"Golden Lily" Treasure Activities

In a book about Yamashita's gold, authors Peggy and Sterling Seagrave postulated that Prince Chichibu led from 1937 to 1945 what the authors called the "Golden Lily" (*Kin no yuri*) Operation. By which members of the Imperial household allegedly were personally involved in stealing treasures from countries invaded by Japan during World War II. It was known that Prince Chichibu would visit the Philippines for periods of six months. This time would coincide with the dry season when he would visit Manila. In 1942 he was living the high life in General MacArthur's penthouse suite situated at the Manila Hotel. He was seen in various geographical regions in the spring of 1943, and positively identified in Nueva Viscaya during the winter of 1944/45 when he met his cousin Prince Takeda on the Pingkian river bridge to survey yet another Imperial treasure site which was going to be excavated below the concrete foundations of the bridge and where gold bullion would be buried and re-concreted over.

When the wet season began, Chichibu would fly to Singapore in order to help ease his tuberculosis. These sightings and treasure burial visits of the prince are contrary to official versions, as told in the memoirs of Princess Chichibu (Setsuko). According to her, the prince retired from active duty after being diagnosed with pulmonary tuberculosis in June 1940, and spent most of World War II convalescing as major general at his villa in Gautama, Shizuoka province, on the eastern foot of Mount Fuji and never really recovered from his illness.

2.30 Prince Takahito Mikasa

Prince Takahito Mikasa (1915 -)

Prince Mikasa is the fourth and youngest son of Emperor Taishō and Empress Teimei. He is a younger brother of Emperor Shōwa (Hirohito) and the only surviving paternal uncle of Emperor Akihito. With the death of his sister-in-law, Princess Takamatsu (Kikuko), on the 17th of December 2004, Prince Mikasa became the oldest living member of the Japanese Imperial Family.

Military Career

Prince Mikasa was promoted to lieutenant (first class) in 1937; to captain in 1939; and to a full major in 1941.

"Golden Lily" Treasure Activities

In the summer of 1942, Prince Mikasa accompanied Prince Chichibu while they toured potential treasure sites around Manila. They were especially interested in Manila Cathedral, Fort Santiago, San Augustin Church, Ft. McKinley, and Santo Tomas University. These sites were to be linked by a tunnel network 90 feet underground with treasure vaults constructed under these historic buildings. He had little involvement with "Golden Lily" during the rest of WWII. He served in Nanjing China from 1943 to 1944, and then served as a staff officer in the Army Section of the Imperial General HQ in Tokyo until Japan surrendered in August 1945.

2.40 Prince Takeda Tsunehisa

Prince Takeda Tsunehisa was the eldest son of Prince Kitashirakawa Yoshihisa and thus the brother of Prince Kitashirakawa Naruhisa. In 1902, he served in the House of Peers and on the 30th of November 1903 graduated from the 15th class of the Imperial Japanese Army Academy.

Prince Takeda Tsunehisa
(1884 - 1973) "Golden Lily"
Code Name: Kimsu Murakusi.
First Cousin to the Emperor of Japan.[4]

Military Career

In 1904, Prince Takeda was appointed as a major general in the Imperial Japanese Army. He served with distinction in the Russo-Japanese War of 1904-1905 in the Imperial Guards Division and was awarded the Order of the Golden Kite (5th class) for bravery in combat. He graduated from the 22nd class of the Army War College in 1910.
On his return to Japan after the Russo-Japanese War, Emperor Meiji authorized Prince Tsunehisa to start a new princely house in March 1906, largely to provide a household with suitable status for his sixth daughter Princess Tsune-no-miya (Masako). Prince Takeda married Princess **Masako** in 1908, who gave him a son and a daughter.

The treasure code book Prince Takeda used was called the **"Masako Code"** to honour his wife's namesake as seen in section 2.41. Many of these codes can also be found on official Imperial treasure maps of the time.

---

[4] This photographic image was published before December 31st 1956, or photographed before 1946 and not published for 10 years thereafter, under jurisdiction of the Government of Japan, considered to be **public domain** law of Japan. According to article 23 of old copyright law of Japan and article 2 of supplemental provision of copyright.

2.41 Prince Takeda Tsunehisa Treasure Symbols
Page 1

IMPERIAL JAPANESE MASAKO CODE

PRINCE TAKEDA TSUNEHISA

LOCATIONS: VISITED ALL 175 SITES ON THE ISLANDS
CODE: BLUE: LENGTH, WEIGHTS
DURATION: 1942-45   CODE: YELLOW: TREASURE

Symbol	Meaning	Symbol	Meaning
↓	UP TO 4 METERS	⚲	UP TO 3 METERS
ℯ↱	1-7 METERS WITH CAVE	⌐	5 METERS WITH CAVE
→	UP TO 100 METERS	o→	UP TO 25 METERS
o→	UP TO 1-7 METERS	o→	UP TO 1-5 METERS
⌒	5 METERS WITH CAVE	⊙→	INSIDE TUNNEL
⛉	UP TO 7 METERS	⌣	MAIN ENTRANCE TO TREASURE
→	50-100 METERS	>	ARROW WAY
5※	BURIED GOLD	⊙	TREASURE UNDER
▭	TREASURE ON SPOT	6	TREASURE UNDER
✕	MILLION DEPOSIT	7M	TREASURE UNDER WATER
⸑	TREASURE UNDER	∨∽T	UP & DOWN TREASURE

2.42 Prince Takeda Tsunehisa Treasure Symbols
Page 2

IMPERIAL JAPANESE MASAKO CODE
PRINCE TAKEDA TSUNEHISA
LOCATIONS: VISITED ALL 175 SITES ON THE ISLANDS

DURATION: 1942-45   CODE: YELLOW: TREASURE

Symbol	Meaning	Symbol	Meaning
·X·)	TREASURE UNDER	⟨	TREASURE DOWN
萬	JEWELRIES	卍	ANTIQUE
7 ☼	BURIED GOLD	+ ○ / □	MONEY
X |	TREASURE UNDER	♂	JEWELRIES
ᒼ	TREASURE ON SPOT	≢ ⁊	BAR & MONEY
⊠	DIAMONDS	▬●▬	GOLD
⇟	GOLD	▭○▭	TREASURE ON SPOT
⟿	TO TREASURE	3	OBJECT UNDERNEATH
⟼∞	DEPOSIT IN SPRING	△	GOLD ON ONE SIDE OF TREE/ROCK
⊗ ⊠	TREASURE UNDER	✕	ON LINE OF TREASURE
° ⑧ ○	GOLD UNDER OBJECT	🐍	TREASURE IN WATER

2.43 Prince Takeda Tsunehisa Treasure Symbols
Page 3

IMPERIAL JAPANESE MASAKO CODE
PRINCE TAKEDA TSUNEHISA

LOCATIONS: VISITED ALL 175 SITES ON THE ISLANDS
CODE: GREEN: DIRECTIONS   CODE: RED: DANGER
DURATION: 1942-45   CODE: YELLOW: TREASURE

Symbol	Meaning	Symbol	Meaning
⊂)G8	IN TUNNEL	N₀I	UNDER A TREE
Z	START HERE	→→→	POINTS DOWN TO GOLD
⌒ ▫	TREASURE OPPOSITE	◊ ▢	PYRAMID GOLD UNDER
D	DEPOSIT UNDERNEATH	⊞	BOMB
⊕	POISON GAS	≩	SIGN OF DEATH
✾	BOOBYTRAP	H	DANGER
J	U/GROUND TUNNEL	⋎	TUNNEL GOING DOWN

2.50 General Tomoyuki Yamashita

General **Yamashita Tomoyuki** was a general of the Imperial Japanese Army.
He was born in a small town called Kochi on the 8th of November 1885. After passing the Cadet's Academy on the 26th June 1906, he attended the military staff college between 1913 and 1916.

General Tomoyuki Yamashita (1885-1946)

Despite his great ability, he fell into disagreement with the Showa Emperor when he took compassion on the rebel officers of the February 26th incident in 1936.

He also clashed with the Prime Minister, General Tojo Hideki and his supporters. Yamashita insisted that Japan should end the conflict with China and keep peaceful relations with the United States and with the United Kingdom, which earned him an unimportant post in the Kwantung Army.

In 1941 he was placed in the command of the Twenty-Fifth Army. In the Malayan campaign, his 30,000 soldiers successfully forced 10,000 British Soldiers in Singapore to surrender. The national Japanese hero was, however, sent to far-away Manchuria again.

In 1944, when the war situation was critical for Japan, when Saipan fell into the American hands in July 1944, Tojo and his cabinet resigned, and a new government was formed. Out of sheer desperation, General Yamashita assumed the command of the Fourteenth Army Group to defend the Philippines, replacing Lieutenant General Shigenori Kuroda who was known as a womanizer and liked to drink; he had not contributed significantly to the war effort, and was therefore replaced by a much more able general. General Yamashita arrived in Manila on the 7th of October 1944 with orders to stop the American advance at any cost, or Japan would be the next to fall.

2.51 Japan Surrenders

General Akira Mutō is seen on the left and General Yamashita can be seen on the right of this picture.

General MacArthur and the U.S. army landed on Leyte only ten days after his arrival in Manila. Then the Imperial forces suffered severe defeats in Leyte, where 60,000 Japanese died, out of 200,000 troops who defended the entire archipelago. He tried to rebuild his army but was forced to retreat from Manila to the mountains of northern Luzon.

The first atomic bomb was dropped on Hiroshima, Japan on the 6th of August 1945, and the second device was dropped on Nagasaki only three days later. Because of the terrible devastation these "new atomic weapons" caused, Emperor Hirohito had to order a total end to the war on August the 14th 1945 via radio broadcasts to the Japanese nation accepting total surrender. Only in charge for eight short months, General Yamashita was given orders to surrender to the advancing American forces.

On the 2nd of September 1945, General Yamashita and his surrender party totaling twenty-one people surrendered near Kiangan, Northern Luzon to a Major General William H. Gill, then commander of the 32nd Infantry Division, and a special detachment of Company "I" Second Battalion, 128th United States Infantry.

The Japanese solders surrender in the mountains and hills north of Baguio, Northern Luzon.

Today, 2012: There are still small deposits of looted gold buried in the mountainous area of Kiangan. Here we can see four approximate locations to the east of the town. Three of which seem to be buried in a straight line, awaiting discovery.

Baguio was the site of the formal surrender of General Tomoyuki Yamashita and Vice Admiral Okochi. It is where they gave up the entire Imperial Japanese Armed Forces to American authorities at the High Commissioner's Residence (now the United States Ambassador's Residence) in Camp John Hay on September 3rd, 1945, marking the end of World War II.

The photograph above shows General Tomoyuki Yamashita seated in the middle on the near side of the table. Seated on the opposite side, second from left, is Lieutenant General Jonathan M. Wainwright, U.S. Army. Toward the right end of the table, immediately to the left of Gen. Yamashita's head, are Commodore Norman C. Gillette, USN, Deputy Commander, and Philippine Sea Frontier.[5]

During the Japanese occupation, Camp John Hay became a major depository of looted gold. This treasure was dumped into deep pits in the surrounding grounds and another smaller cache under the United States Ambassador's building where the old wine cellars were converted into treasure vaults and secretly sealed up. If this was indeed the case then General Yamashita in the picture above would have been sitting on top of a massive gold hoard buried by his own men when this building had become his headquarters earlier on in the war.

General Tomoyuki Yamashita (center) having a meal with fellow Japanese officers inside New Bilibid prison before his trial.[6]

---

[5] This photograph image above is a work of a sailor or employee of the U.S. Navy, taken or made during the course of the person's official duties. As a work of the U.S. federal government, the image is now in the **public domain**.

[6] This photographic image was published before December 31st 1956, or photographed before 1946 and not published for 10 years thereafter, under jurisdiction of the Government of Japan, considered to be **public domain**.

2.52 General Yamashita's Trial November 1945

The First day of the trial outside Manila court house, Below General Yamashita salutes General MacArthur, the "American Hero", as they enter the building.[7]

A month later, on the 7th December, exactly four years to the day after the attack on Pearl Harbour and only one month after his 66th birthday, General Tomoyuki Yamashita was convicted of war crimes in Manila during the closing days of WWII that he did not order or commit.

He was not physically in Manila, he did not give the orders to slaughter men, women and children.

(Yamashita)**

"Golden Lily": A Secret History (Part One)

See:
http://www.youtube.com/watch?v=dn8tY0RQeuU&feature=related

(Yamashita)**
"Golden Lily": A Secret History (Part Two)

See:
http://www.youtube.com/watch?v=iKWBChQsq3Q&feature=related

---

[7] This photographic image was published before December 31st 1956, or photographed before 1946 and not published for 10 years thereafter, under jurisdiction of the Government of Japan, considered to be **public domain** law of Japan. According to article 23 of old copyright law of Japan and article 2 of supplemental provision of copyright.

2.53 Inside Manila Court House: Yamashita's Trial

Outside the court room circa Nov. 1945[8]

General Yamashita inside Manila Court House with his attorneys Sanberg and Reel.[9]

---

[8] (Photograph Source: Family of Harry E. Clarke).

[9] Source: United States National Archives (ARC 292613).

2.54 The Execution

An American military commission tried Yamashita on war crimes charges, and the trial was publicized greatly in the Philippines; Yamashita symbolized the Japanese officers that the Filipinos came to blame for the war time atrocities, and the press build up swayed the public opinion against the Japanese general. The military commission found him guilty of this trumped up charge and stated:

"That he deliberately planned to massacre and exterminate a large part of the civilian population of Batangas Province as a result of which more than 25,000 men, women, and children all unarmed noncombatant civilians, were brutally mistreated and killed".

He was found completely *guilty* of all charges.

The hurried trial and execution, despite backing of the United States Supreme Court, led to accusations that he was wrongfully charged for his crimes, possibly driven by MacArthur's *personal vendetta* against him as revenge for the atrocities committed against the citizens of Manila during the last days of Japanese occupation.

There was no concrete evidence linking Yamashita to these atrocities, and none were presented during the trials; instead, any form of evidence, including hearsay, diaries of unidentified persons, and statements of absent persons were accepted and presented at the court, which went against the basic laws of evidence in the American judicial system of law and order.

According to Major George Guy, one of Yamashita's attorneys:

"There was not one word or one shred of credible evidence to show that General Yamashita ever ordered the commission of even one of the acts with which he was charged or he ever had any knowledge of the commission of any of these acts, either before they took place, or after their commission."

However, the judges presiding over the military commission insisted that as the supreme commander of the Japanese forces, Yamashita was indeed guilty because as the commander in control of the troops, he was fully responsible for the organized and systematic acts of atrocities upon the people of the Philippines.

On behalf of their client, Yamashita's assigned six attorneys filed for appeal, first at the Supreme Court of the Commonwealth of the Philippines and then the United States Supreme Court. The Supreme Court of the Commonwealth of the Philippines turned down their request for appeal.

The United State Supreme Court judges discussed the case. Even though Justice Wiley Rutledge and Justice Frank Murphy wrote opinions noting that they had reasons to believe an appeal should be granted, the majority of justices voted to deny the appeal process.

Rutledge said the trial had been: **"No trial in the tradition of the common law and the US Constitution"**, while Murphy said that Generals Homma and Yamashita were "taken without regard to the due process of law"; together, they commented that such an execution of Yamashita would be *"legalized lynching"*. Regardless of this statement, the US Supreme Court found "an unlawful breach of duty by General Yamashita as an army commander to control the operations of members of his command by "permitting them to commit" the extensive and widespread atrocities".

The Court further "pre-supposes that violations of the law of war are to be avoided through the control of the operations of war by commanders who to some extent are responsible for their subordinates".

With that the US Supreme Court denied the request for an appeal. As a last-ditch effort, Colonel Harry E. Clarke, Sr., Yamashita's chief defense counsel, filed for clemency at the desk of President Harry Truman. The president declined to act upon it.

Yamashita had a terrible sense of what was coming to him, and to show his gratitude for all his attorneys had done for him General Yamashita gave each one personal items that meant much to him as a military officer.

Clarke was given a tea service that General Yamashita carried though Manchuria, China, Malaya, Japan, and the Philippines, as well as Yamashita's military ribbons.

Lieutenant Colonel Gordon Feldhaus received Yamashita's general staff fourragere chord and one of his three-star insignias. Lieutenant Colonel Walter Hendricks received the cordovan saber belt and the other three-star insignia and Captain Frank Reel and Captain Milton Sandberg received his sets of brush pens. And finally Guy, a cavalry officer, received Yamashita's gold ceremonial spurs.

General Yamashita was sentenced on the 7th December 1945. Weeks before Yamashita's death sentence was to be carried out, the case came to MacArthur for review. MacArthur stated that:

"It is not easy for me to pass penal judgment upon a defeated adversary in a major military campaign. I have reviewed the proceedings in a vain search for some mitigating circumstances on his behalf. I can find none." After digging into deeper details on the philosophical basis on why he believed he was responsible for the action of his troops, he approved the sentence; why this was the case is still a mystery.

Following the Supreme Court decision, an appeal for clemency was made by Colonel Harry E. Clarke, Sr., to U.S. President Harry S. Truman. Truman, however, *declined to intervene* and left the matter entirely in the hands of the military authorities. In due course, General MacArthur confirmed the sentence of the Commission.

At Los Baños Prison Camp, 30 miles (48 km) south of Manila, on the 23rd of February 1946, General Tomoyuki Yamashita was hanged. After climbing the thirteen steps leading to the gallows, he was asked if he had a final statement. General Yamashita replied through a translator:

"As I said in the Manila Supreme Court that I have done with my all capacity, so I don't feel ashamed in front of the Gods for what I have done when I have died. But if you say to me "you do not have any ability to command the Japanese Army" I should say nothing for it, because it is my own nature. Now, our war criminal trial going on in Manila Supreme Court, so I wish to be justified under your kindness and right. I know that all your American and American military affairs always have tolerant and rightful judgment. When I have been investigated in Manila court, I have had a good treatment, kind full attitude from your good-natured officers who all the time protected me. I never forget what they have done for me even if I had died. I don't blame my executioner. I'll pray the Gods bless them. Please send my thankful word to Col. Clarke and Lt. Col. Feldhaus, Lt. Col. Hendrix, Maj. Guy, Capt. Sandburg, Capt. Reel, at Manila court, and Col. Arnard. I thank you."

2.55   Yamashita's Trial: The Conclusion

The hasty arranged trial is often questioned about its legal status when General Yamashita was accused of his soldiers' crimes that he had never ordered or had prior knowledge of. Japanese communication lines had been disrupted by the U.S. Army at this time. It is now believed that the "scheduled" judgment was General Mac Arthur's private revenge for the occupier of *"his"* Philippines. Mac Arthur later regretted hanging Yamashita, and agreed after the event that Yamashita should not have been put on trial for war crimes he had **not** ordered or even committed when the Japanese Army and the general had retreated from Manila into the mountain regions of Northern Luzon.

As the Americans advanced into Manila in early February, an estimated 25,000+ men women, children and babies were slaughtered by drunken Japanese soldiers and sailors under the command of **Rear Admiral Sanji Iwabuchi** who disobeyed Yamashita's orders to leave Manila *unharmed* and head north to the hills of Baguio. This man disobeyed direct orders from his senior commanding officer and allowed his men commit mass murder.

How could a man like Yamashita be hanged for war crimes that had been committed by others? The general was physically over 250 kilometers (155 miles away) north of Manila at the time the killings took place. The sailors under the command of **Admiral Iwabuchi**, where never brought to trial by the Americans or indeed by the Filipino government. Iwabuchi managed to escape the American forces, and returned to Japan via submarine.

Why didn't Mac Arthur extradite Iwabuchi to face a war crimes trial in Manila after the war when the evidence of his crimes against humanity was so overwhelming? The reason was simple this man was ***not actively involved in land based Golden Lily operations,*** and of no interest to Mac Arthur or indeed the Office of Strategic Services at this time.

Note:

General Akira Mutō: In October 1944, he was appointed chief of staff of the Japanese Fourteenth Area Army under General Tomoyuki Yamashita. He was accused of having conducted a campaign of slaughter, torture and other atrocities against the Filipino civilian population, prisoners of war and civilian internees, by ordering "guerrilla containment".

After the surrender of Japan, Mutō was arrested by the American occupation authorities and charged with war crimes before the International Military Tribunal for the Far East. He was convicted for atrocities against civilians and prisoners of war in both China and the Philippines, and was executed by hanging on 23rd of December 1948. Was he the real reason General Yamashita was executed for war crimes against the Filipino people after all was he following Yamashita's orders, or was he a renegade who ordered these atrocities without the knowledge of Yamashita? We will never know the real truth now lost in time and **space.**

2.56 Yamashita's Driver

Severino Santa Romana, a member of the U.S. Office of Strategic Services, had gleaned from Major Kijomi Kashi, aged 31 at the time, who had been General Yamashita's personal driver during his service in the Philippines that had driven Yamashita to several locations where millions of dollars of gold bullion had been buried during the last year of the war. Much later, Severino Santa Romana would successfully recover gold from twelve treasure vaults and become a secret CIA agent and the gatekeeper of the **Black Eagle Trust Fund**.

Santa Romana started a rumour that Kijomi had in fact committed suicide when being held in Bilidad prison.
This was in fact a lie; the Major had agreed to show Santa and his team where he took Yamashita, and revealed a dozen treasure locations in exchange for his life and a large bribe. Kijomi returned to his family in Japan after the war, but over the next fifty-seven years he would return many times to the Philippines to secretly recover treasure from Imperial sites and smaller officer stashes.

A number of these "secret" recoveries were made at Clark Air Force Base, with the full knowledge of the U.S. government at the time. According to Sterling and Peggy Seagrave, in their book *Gold Warriors*, Kijomi Kashi's last successful recovery was in 2002 at the ripe old age of eighty-eight. He and his team recovered 2 metric tons of gold biscuit bars that were eventually shipped out of the Philippines, hidden inside a steam roller and hoisted aboard a Japanese freighter that was docked in Subic Bay, which later sailed for mainland Japan.

In the spring of 1945 General Yamashita ordered his driver to travel in his staff car to Dingalan Bay to oversee the unloading of a Japanese ship laden with treasure. If Kijomi had stayed with Yamashita in the mountains of Kiangan Luzon then his fate may have followed that of General Yamashita's. In reality Kijomi profited greatly from the spoils of war and died a very rich man.

It is now obvious that the American government did not want Yamashita to tell the world about "Golden Lily" and the vast amounts of gold buried in the Philippines, and the subsequent recoveries that were to begin from information gathered by Romana when he tortured Major Kashi.

General Yamashita was made the *scapegoat* and his knowledge about Imperial treasure site locations and "Golden Lily" activity had to die with him. This secret was only known to few high-ranking American military officers and the U.S. President Truman.

According to Sterling and Peggy Seagrave, in their book *Gold Warriors*, in late 1945, the Americans were to steal vast amounts of plundered gold from Imperial sites in the Philippines for their own covert uses with the help of Hirohito, in exchange for war crimes immunity, and a large share in the buried plunder.

The American government made sure that American POWs could not demand financial compensation against the Japanese Imperial Family for mistreatment during the Second World War, a sickening betrayal by a corrupt government that did not care about the suffering of their own American POWs during the Japanese conflict.

"The greed of man has no bounds, and will always corrupt those who seek it".

2.57 Why Was "Golden Lily" Renamed "Yamashita's Gold"?

President Marcos coined this phase in 1969, when a large treasure deposit was found under the main flag pole of Camp Aquinaldo in the Philippines.
His army excavated the site and recovered **over 2,000 metric tons** of gold bars and hundreds of precious stones.

In 1970 the Cosmopolitan Magazine wrote an article describing the Marcos couple as the wealthiest in Asia. Marcos himself said that he had recovered "Yamashita's" treasure. The myth was born, but in reality General Yamashita had nothing to do with treasure. He was too busy trying to defend the Philippines from the advancing American forces.

General Yamashita did however observe the progress of twelve Imperial sites in the last ten months of the war. Driven there by his driver Major Kojima Kashi, as mentioned previously, he was taken to Baguio in the west of Luzon, to Bambang in the centre and Aparri at the northern tip of the island. He was ordered by Prince Chichibu to speed up the burial of treasure simply because MacArthur had already landed in Leyte.

"Golden Lily" Treasure Activities

The Treasure was never Yamashita's; it was by definition "Imperial Treasure", arguably belonging to the Imperial Japanese family. He may have had a small stash of gold hidden away somewhere in Northern Luzon, but this misconception that he "owned" all of the thousands of tonnes of gold buried between 1943-45 in the Philippines by the Japanese Imperial forces is totally unfounded, and totally absurd.

Soon after the "Yamashita's Gold" article appeared in the Cosmopolitan magazine, Marcos tried to ban any further reporting, fearing that the countries that had lost so much from the Japanese occupation could still lay claim to the treasure that was stolen from them. He knew that international law had stated at all stolen treasures and antiquities must be returned to the countries of origin. This law was still in force when he discovered the gold and precious stones at Camp Aquialdo, and this "*international ruling*" only ended in 1985.

The Yamashita "Singapore Treasure Connection"

General Yamashita's name has been linked with buried treasure in the Philippines since the early 1970s and possibly earlier. However, some people speculate that hidden treasure was also buried in Malaysian jungles and even underneath the Syonan Jinja in Singapore during Japanese military occupation that started in early 1942 and lasted three and half years.

The "plundered gold" is believed to have been anything from gold bullion to religious statues. The idea was that these stolen riches from Asia would help finance Japan's war effort, since Japan at this time was poor in raw materials such as iron ore, copper, nickel and other metals needed to manufacture aircraft, tanks, and ships to feed the war effort.

The gold would help pay for these metals if the Japanese could not find them in countries they had invaded. This gold had to be transported from the continent back to Japan, via the South China Sea. Most of the stolen gold from Southeast Asia was first shipped to the port of Singapore, where it was then relayed to the Philippines. From the Philippines the gold was intended to be shipped to the Japanese home islands. Most of this treasure ended up being buried in the Philippines because of the American shipping blockade of the South China Sea and constant US Navy patrols of known shipping routes from Singapore to the Japanese mainland.

If gold bullion could not be shipped from Singapore to Japan because of this blockade, then Yamashita had no choice but to bury it underneath Syonan Jinja, where the Japanese Shinto shrine would guard the treasure.

There is, however, a theory that General Yamashita may have given orders to bury plundered gold and religious artifacts very close to a Japanese Jinja Shrine situated at Mac Ritchie Reservoir in Singapore (GPS: Lat: 1°20'29.66"N: Long: 103°49'56.44"E). In the closing months of the war as Japan's military efforts to win an outright victory became more futile.

Syonan Jinja Japanese Shrine In Singapore

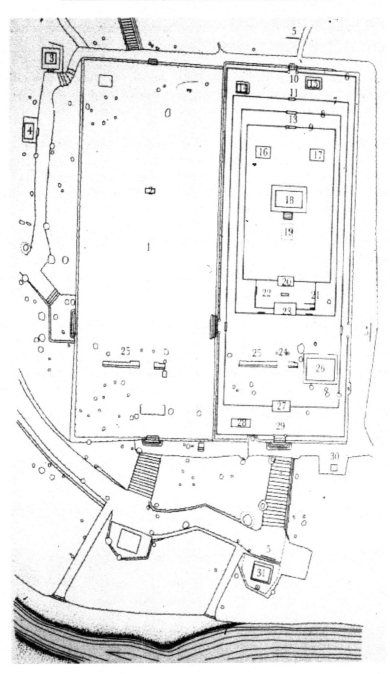

Buried in the dense jungle of the MacRitchie Catchment Area, are the ruins of Syonan Jinja, a Japanese Shinto Shrine dating back to World War II, built by POWs to commemorate Japanese soldiers who died fighting in the invasion of Singapore.

Syonan Jinja was the location of many Japanese religious and cultural ceremonies. The original structure, built during the Japanese Occupation (1942-1945), was a temple with no walls.

Raised from the ground by a stone platform graduated with a few steps, the sloping temple roof rested on pillars that stood at regular intervals round the perimeter of the platform. It is believed that during rituals worshippers would drink from a huge granite ceremonial fountain located outside the shrine.

A Shinto ceremony took place here every New Year's Day for the few years that the shrine existed. This was marked by the sounding of the temple bell, the arrival of devotees and the presence of a Shinto priest presiding over rituals.

Syonan Jinja was destroyed when the Japanese Occupation ended in 1945. Crumbling granite steps that once led to the shrine are visible, as well as the stone fountain. Of the temple building itself, there is a low stone wall that runs one length of the building and several square pits in the ground that probably once supported pillars. Nowadays the jungle vegetation has covered most of temple ruins.

The Failed British Treasure Hunt

In late 1981, an Indonesian gardener named Mr. Sappari, who worked at the reservoir during the occupation years, suggested that something very valuable had been buried close to the Jinja Shrine. He stated that just before the defeat looked imminent in 1945, several Japanese soldiers in trucks drove up to the reservoir and undertook what Sappari described as "a lot of burial activity".

Could this be the lost treasure belonging to Sultan Ibrahim who lived in the Sultan of Johor Palace prior to the invasion of Singapore by Imperial Japanese forces?

In Early 1942, the Sultan of Johor Palace was used by General Yamashita as his headquarters during the invasion of Singapore because of the five-story tower which gave him far-reaching views of northern Singapore in which he used to view his successful planned attack against the British forces in early February. Transporting such plundered treasure from the Palace to the Shrine would have been relatively easy, simply because the distance from the Palace to the Syonan Jinja Japanese Shrine is only five kilometers, a very short journey indeed made by Japanese military trucks.

In 1947, the British administration had hired Sappari and several other labourers to dig deep at the suspected end of reservoir, paying them a sizeable sum for their efforts – and their secrecy. Sappari commented in 1981:"It was hard work. We worked on several spots, digging a total of 21 holes to a depth of 7 meters. But we found nothing."

It seems that British Military Intelligence must have been aware that several burials did take place in this area, but the precise locations were not accurate enough to secure successful recoveries. These deposits are still buried in overgrown jungles at depths of up to 7 meters and will be now under the current water table. The locations of two deposits have already been recently identified in late 2011 by this author.

Several targets are scattered around the old site of the Syonan Jinja Shrine today, awaiting discovery and will require a ground-penetrating radar to locate them now under the boggy ground. A large floating barge will be required to take the weight of an earth excavator in order to dig the muddy water around these long-lost treasures with safety and ease.

Note: Then there is Batam and other neighbouring Riau islands in Indonesia. It was rumoured that several high-ranking Japanese Officers escaped from Singapore just ahead of the British forces in 1945 and hid out for a while on these nearby islands, together with a large slice of stolen treasure.

The treasure symbols on the next two pages are *reputed* to belong to the Yamashita treasure code book. This code book would not have hundreds of treasure codes, simply because General Yamashita was only in the Philippines for a period of eight months. His task was to defend the islands from the advancing Americans, and not to bury treasure as previously stated. He oversaw some of the "Imperial" burials but was not active in the design and supervising the construction stages of these treasure sites or indeed handling massive amounts of treasure.

He would attend the closure of the finished sites with at least one of the Imperial princes once the vaults deep underground had been filled with precious booty.

As I have stated previously, the Yamashita code book would have been used to mark small burials of war booty taken from local people or churches, banks, and security houses holding gold bars, coins, currency notes, and rich historical religious artefacts as his troops advanced through the Philippines, looting as they advanced.

2.58 General Yamashita Treasure Symbols Page 1

IMPERIAL JAPANESE 25TH ARMY TREASURE SYMBOLS

GENERAL TOMOYUKI YAMASHITA

LOCATIONS: FORT Mc KINLEY, MANILA, IPO, BULACAN, CAMP JOHN HAY, BAGUIO, BAMBANG, BAGABAG, AND KIANGAN, N. LUZON.

DURATION: 1944-45   CODE: YELLOW: TREASURE

△	TREASURE MIDDLE OF ROCK OR TREES	♡	RICH OBJECT BURIED
↓	POINTS TO TREASURE	⌐•⌐	GOLD INSIDE ROCK
▭	TREASURE IN BOX	⊥ (on base)	GOLD UNDER A ROCK OR TREE
⌒•	TREASURE UNDER	⌐	MONEY DEPOSIT
荵	BURIED GOLD BARS	ヲ古	DIAMONDS
□ E B	BOXES OF GOLD	E B	BOX OF GOLD BARS
┼ □	MONEY	K1A	IMAGE OF BUDDHA
⁊•	SILVER COINS	Is	JADE, TOPAZ, RUBY
⊥	GOLD	央金	GOLD
ô	JEWELS	⊙ (with legs)	DIAMONDS
∧	UNCUT DIAMONDS	△	SILVER DEPOSIT

2.59 General Yamashita Treasure Symbols Page 2

IMPERIAL JAPANESE 25TH ARMY TREASURE SYMBOLS

GENERAL TOMOYUKI YAMASHITA

LOCATIONS: FORT McKINLEY, MANILA, IPO, BULACAN, CAMP JOHN HAY, BAGUIO, BAMBANG, BAGABAG, & KIANGAN, N.LUZON.
CODE: GREEN: DIRECTIONS   CODE: RED: DANGER
DURATION: 1944-45   CODE: YELLOW: TREASURE

Symbol	Meaning	Symbol	Meaning
〜〜〜	TREASURE UNDER	↓	POINTS TOWARDS TREASURE
(arrow/bird shape)	GOLD SIDE OF TREE / ROCK	A	PYRAMID CENTER TREASURE
ナ	TREASURE UNDER	(sword shape)	POINTS TO TREASURE
☼	CLOSE TO GOLD	△ △	CLEAR DEPOSIT IN TRIANGLE OF TREES OR ROCK
(snake shape)	POINTS TO GOLD	宇	TREASURE
∫	FOOT OF MOUNTAIN	←→	TREASURE DIVIDED
25A	CAVE	∿	SIDE BY SIDE
ツ=1	GO THROUGH	7	PROCEED DIGGING
A∨	TREASURE UNDER WALL	ρ)A	TUNNEL
ξ	BOOBYTRAP	Q (with dots)	BOOBYTRAP
ε₃	BOOBYTRAP	⌒•	BOOBYTRAP

Very recently in 2011, a war diary belonging to a close aide to General Yamashita has been found. The diary has daily entries from 1942-1945. In the rear of the diary the writer lists 500 smaller treasure sites all situated in the Philippines, and in the back pages three treasure maps were found for large treasures, written in Kanji, situated in Mindanao. This diary was found in an old library in a small town called Kochi. A coincidence I think not! Now a treasure hunter is studying this diary, and plans to excavate some of these burial sites in the Philippines.

2.60 General Masaharu Homma

General Masaharu Homma (1888-1946)[10]

Masaharu Homma, a general in the Imperial Japanese Army, was noted in the history books for his role in the invasion and occupation of the Philippines during World War II, in which he earned the nickname, **The Tiger of Manila**.

Homma, who was also an amateur painter and playwright, was also known as the Poet General. Some said at the time, not a really a tough and decisive general, to some he was too soft with his men, and needed to be a hardened taskmaster to gain more respect from the soldiers under his command.

Military Career

In 1937, Homma was appointed aide-de-camp to Prince Chichibu, the brother of Emperor Hirohito. He accompanied the prince on a *"diplomatic tour"* of Europe which ended in Germany. There he

---

[10](This photographic image was published before December 31st 1956, or photographed before 1946 and not published for 10 years thereafter, under jurisdiction of the Government of Japan, considered to be **public domain** law of Japan. According to article 23 of old copyright law of Japan and article 2 of supplemental provision of copyright.

attended the infamous Nuremberg rally and met Adolf Hitler, with whom the prince tried to boost relations, following the Anti-Comintern Pact of 1936.

With the start of the Pacific War, Homma was named commander of the 43,110 troops of the Japanese 14th Army and tasked with the invasion of the Philippines. He ordered his troops to treat the Filipinos not as enemies but as friends, and respect their customs and religion.

A Superior Officer Disliked Homma

This liberal approach towards Filipino civilians earned him the enmity of his superior, General Count Hisaichi Terauchi, commander of the Southern Army, who sent adverse reports about Homma to Tokyo from his headquarters in Saigon.

There was also a growing subversion within Homma's command by a small group of insubordinates, under the influence of Colonel Tsuji Masanobu. In Homma's name, they sent out secret orders against his policies, including ordering the execution of Filipino Chief Justice Jose Abad Santos and attempted execution of former Speaker of the House of Representatives Manuel Roxas, which Homma found out about in time, and managed to stop.

Homma failed to give consideration to the possibility that a retreat into Bataan Peninsula by Filipino-American forces might succeed in upsetting the Japanese timetable of a full-scale invasion. By the time he recognized his mistake, his best infantry division had been replaced by a poorly-trained reserve brigade, greatly weakening his assault force.

Rather than loose his men in furious frontal assaults, he tried to outmaneuver the American forces. This brought much criticism from his superiors who believed he had become "contaminated" by Western ideas about conserving the lives of his fellow soldiers and they believed a frontal attack was the only option.

2.61 Americans Surrender On Corregidor Island

The photograph above was taken on Corregidor on the 6th May 1942 when 11,500 American and Filipinos commanded by Lt. General Jonathon Wainwright surrendered to the Imperial Japanese 14th Army, which was commanded by General Homma.[11]

Worried about the stalled offensive in Luzon, Emperor Hirohito pressured Army Chief of Staff Hajime Sugiyama twice on January 1942 to increase troop strength and launch a quick knockout on Bataan. Following these orders, Sugiyama put pressure on Homma to renew his attacks against the Allied forces.

The resulting Battle of Bataan commencing in January 1942 was one of the most intense in the campaign. However, the deteriorating relationship between Homma and Sugiyama led to the removal of Homma from his command shortly after the defeat of Corregidor and he became commander of the 14th Army in name only.

---

[11] This photographic image was published before December 31st 1956, or photographed before 1946 and not published for 10 years thereafter, under jurisdiction of the Government of Japan, considered to be **public domain** law of Japan. According to article 23 of old copyright law of Japan and article 2 of supplemental provision of copyright.

2.62 Corregidor Island

The General Imperial HQ regarded Homma as not aggressive enough in the conflict, which resulted in the high cost of Japanese life and long delays in securing the American and Filipino forces to surrender, and also being far too lenient with the Filipino people in peace time. He was subsequently forced into retirement in August 1943.

After the surrender of Japan, the American authorities occupying Japan arrested Homma, and he was extradited to the Philippines at the express order of General D. MacArthur so that he could be tried by an American military tribunal rather than the International War Crimes Court tasked with prosecuting Japanese wartime leaders for war crimes connected with starting the war.

The noted historian Philip Piccigallo stated that Homma was convicted by the actions of his men during the death march, rather than having a direct hand in the actions themselves.

The Imperial Treasure mark for a treasure site on Corregidor dated 1945.

2.63   <u>Homma: Bataan Death March</u>

The photograph shows the American and Filipino POWs carrying the sick on the Bataan Death March north towards Camp O'Donnell.[12]

It is not clear whether Homma ordered the atrocities that occurred during the Bataan Death March, but it is very clear that his lack of administrative expertise and inability to adequately delegate authority and control his men had led to these terrible atrocities.

After American-Filipino forces surrendered the Bataan Peninsula, Homma gave the responsibility of logistics of transporting an estimated 25,000 prisoners to Major General Yoshitake Kawane. Homma publicly stated that the POWs would be treated fairly. A plan was formulated to transport and march the majority of prisoners to Camp O'Donnell, of which General Homma approved.

However, the plan was severely flawed, as the American and Filipino POWs were starving, weak with malaria, and numbered not 25,000 but a staggering 75,000 men, far more than any Japanese occupation plan had anticipated or indeed catered for.

---

[12] This photographic image was published before December 31st 1956, or photographed before 1946 and not published for 10 years thereafter, under jurisdiction of the Government of Japan, considered to be **public domain** law of Japan. According to article 23 of old copyright law of Japan and article 2 of supplemental provision of copyright.

Additionally, the Japanese thought that the surrender would occur some three weeks later than anticipated, a point at which food and medical supplies would have arrived from Singapore and Japan to feed and look after the captured prisoners of war.

On the Bataan death march, approximately 54,000 of the 75,000 prisoners reached their destination. The death toll of the march is difficult to assess as thousands of captives were able to escape from their guards. All told, approximately 5,000-10,000 Filipino and 600-650 American prisoners of war died before they could reach Camp O'Donnell in northern Luzon.

In his defense at his trial, General Homma also claimed that he was so preoccupied with the plans for the Corregidor assault that he had forgotten about the prisoners' treatment, believing that his officers were properly handling the matter. He claimed that he did not learn of the atrocities carried out by his men until after the war was completely over.

2.64 **Homma's Trial And Conviction**

Even so, General Masaharu Homma was convicted by the United States military tribunal for war crimes in the Philippines, including the Bataan death march, and the Japanese atrocities carried out at O'Donnell and Cabanatuan POW camps on starving and sick prisoners which followed. General Homma's chief defense counsel, John H. Skeen Jr., stated that in his opinion it was a *"highly irregular trial, it had been conducted in an atmosphere that left no doubt as to what the ultimate outcome would be."* Associate Justice Frank Murphy of the United States Supreme Court protested the verdict, and stated: *"Either we conduct such a trial as this in the noble spirit and atmosphere of our constitution or we abandon all pretenses to justice, let the ages slip away and descend to the level of revengeful blood purges."*

The statement was correct, in that someone had to pay with their life, even though the evidence against Homma was **non-existent.** Like Yamashita, he was made yet another *scapegoat* and was found guilty of crimes he did *not* commit, in effect he was murdered *illegally* by the American military. General Homma's wife appealed to General MacArthur to spare his life; her pleas were denied.

The ever-revengeful MacArthur ordered Homma shot, rather than sent to the gallows, the latter being considered the greater dishonour amongst military men. Homma was executed by firing squad, shot by Filipino and American forces on the 3rd of April 1946 outside Manila.

"Golden Lily" Activities

Was General Homma killed because he too knew about the Imperial treasure sites on Corregidor and Bataan? Was this the real reason MacArthur ordered him shot?

According to the late *Robert Curtis, Corregidor had a number of "Golden Lily" treasure vaults.
President Marcos failed to find and recover a massive "555" site hidden in the Malinta tunnels situated on the Island.

Other gold deposits were reported to be located very close to the old movie theatre and inside the old shell storage bunker situated close to the Crockett Battery field gun emplacement; the latter was visited by Prince Chichibu as a possible Imperial burial site when the storage facility was hit by an American aerial bomb, and subsequently rebuilt by the Japanese military to store tons of gold bullion.

For further information regarding Corregidor, *The Treasure Island of WWII* by Edward Michaud, relating stories of buried gold and how millions of silver pesos dumped into San Jose Bay were recovered by U.S. divers for the Japanese invaders and recovered, please see: www.corregidor.org/chs_trident/trident_02.htm

Corregidor Treasure Recovery Operations 1945-1988 ,see: www.corregidor.org/chs_trident/trident_03.htm

Battery Morrison: The Two Large Lockers Full Of Gold see: www.corregidor.org/chs_trident/trident_05.htm

The Grave-Gold Story, see: www.corregidor.org/chs_trident/trident_08.htm

The North Dock Gold-Hole Story, see: www.corregidor.org/chs_trident/trident_10.htm

The Golden Patrol OF U.S.S. Trout SS-202 Submarine Uses Gold Bars as Ballast, see: http://corregidor.org/chs_trident/uss_trout.htm

Up to date visit to Mariveles: http://corregidor.proboards.com/index.cgi?board=threads&action=display&thread=925

Robert (Bob) Curtis: Mining and metal expert asked to help Marcos re-melt gold and help in recovery of gold from "Golden Lily" sites. He photographed 173 of the 175 original "Golden Lily" maps, and was swindled out of his share of recovered gold by President Marcos during the mid 1970s.

On the next three pages I have included General Homma's treasure code book and, like General Yamashita, General Homma was tasked to take Corregidor and Bataan.

He, like Yamashita, was not in the Philippines to supervise Imperial treasures sites. He may have been asked by Prince Takeda and Prince Chichibu to oversee the closure of some sites around Bataan and on Corregidor during the Japanese occupation, his "Golden Lily" involvement was therefore very limited.

Homma's code book, like Yamashita's, was written for the burial of small war booty and not for vast amounts of gold bullion, as the number of symbols for gold and treasure help testify in section 2.67, page 3 of his code book.

2.65 General Homma Treasure Symbols Page 1

	IMPERIAL JAPANESE 14TH ARMY TREASURE SYMBOLS		
	GENERAL MASAHARU HOMMA		
	LOCATION: NORTHERN LUZON & CORREGIDOR ISLAND		
	DURATION: 1942-43	CODE:BLUE:LENGTH,NO.'S	
		CODE:RED: DANGER	
一	ONE	ᛌ	5 YARDS
二	TWO	ブ	20 YARDS
三	THREE	十尺	TEN FEET DEEP
丶	FOUR	正厉R之又	GAS
ム	FIVE	乙TH土	LOOK OUT!
六	SIX	土±=ナ✓	LIE DOWN
七	SEVEN	空=エ✓	TAKE CARE
八	EIGHT	応丁	DANGER
九	NINE	一○	DANGER
十	TEN	正厉R之又	BOOBY TRAP
┝ろ	ONE HUNDRED	乙TH土	LOOK OUT!

2.66 General Homma Treasure Symbols Page 2

IMPERIAL JAPANESE 14TH ARMY TREASURE SYMBOLS

GENERAL MASAHARU HOMMA
LOCATION: NORTHERN LUZON & CORREGIDOR ISLAND

CODE:GREEN:DIRECTIONS CODE:BLUE:LENGTH,NO.'S
DURATION: 1942-43 CODE:RED: DANGER

Symbol	Meaning	Symbol	Meaning
千	ONE THOUSAND	左R	LEFT TURN
岗	TEN THOUSAND	?	SURE DEPOSIT
亻光	ONE HUNDRED MILLION	~室	BELOW GROUND
低厌天	CENTIMETER	川	RIVER
十	HALF A DOZEN	尸ヨ	GATE OR DOOR
乭	DIG	早=	JANUARY
瓜	CARVE	=早	FEBUARY
~瓦	PASSAGE UNDER	三口	MARCH
⌒	OPPOSITE DIRECTION	I三A	APRIL
左ıR	TURN LEFT	ヌ耳	MAY
OOOOO	TRAVEL SIGN	⟶	INVERTED

2.67 General Homma Treasure Symbols Page 3

IMPERIAL JAPANESE 14TH ARMY TREASURE SYMBOLS

GENERAL MASAHARU HOMMA
LOCATION: NORTHERN LUZON & CORREGIDOR ISLAND

CODE:BLUE:LENGTH,NO'S   CODE:YELLOW: TREASURE
DURATION: 1942-43   CODE:RED: DANGER

Symbol	Meaning	Symbol	Meaning
	CASH		JEWELS
	SILVER		JEWELRIES
	WEALTH UNDER ROCK		GOLD DEPOSIT
	GOLD UNDER TREE		GOLD OPPOSITE SIDE
	TEN THOUSAND		TAKE CARE
	ONE HUNDRED MILLION		DANGER
	CENTIMETER		DANGER
	HALF A DOZEN		BOOBY TRAP

2.68 "Golden Lily": Roles Other People Played

A brief explanation is given here of other people's roles directly and indirectly involved with "Golden Lily":

Japanese:
General Doihara: Japanese Secret Agent: masterminded the looting of Manchuria and China for Operation "Golden Lily".
Yoshio Kodama: Japanese gangster helped "Golden Lily" by looting China's underworld.
Nobosuke Kishi: Japanese Prime Minister headed the looting of Manchuria.

The roles these Japanese people played in Operation "Golden Lily" was simple: Prince Chichibu oversaw the overall construction of the 175 Imperial Sites, where Prince Takeda ran the day-to-day operations of each site and its construction with the aid of Prince Asaska, and Prince Misaka visited the Philippines as and when they could play their part in surveying potential.

Prince Takeda supervised and gave orders to tunnel engineers, who designed and had to draw detailed construction maps of each site and supervise excavations.

Prince Takeda had his own valet boy, treasure sites and the day-to-day logistical decisions and actions a Filipino called Ben Valmores, who at the end of the war was given copies of only 172 of the 175 Imperial treasure maps for safe keeping stored inside an attaché case.

Many years later Valmores would meet another Filipino treasure hunter called *Roger Roxas who became friends with Ben Valmores who gave one of the Imperial maps to him showing a large deposit buried behind a military hospital in Bagiou. It was here that Roxas recovered the famous Golden Buddha, which was later taken by force from him by President Marcos's soldiers.

*Yamashita's Treasure-Roxas Buddha #1
See: http://www.youtube.com/watch?v=0Xpj0orZR0Y&feature=related

*Yamashita's Treasure-Roxas Buddha #2
See: http://www.youtube.com/watch?v=ZJV_59aRsBg

While working on the burial sites for Operation "Golden Lily", Prince Takeda had many senior officers helping survey and construct vast treasure vaults in tunnels and natural cave systems throughout the Philippines. They organised the transportation of treasure via ship from Singapore to Manila, arranged storage, and rail and road transportation to the sites across the Philippine archipelago.

Each Imperial site would have its own architect, chief engineer, a chief mining engineer, Japanese ceramic experts for making and moulding "natural-looking rocks, and hiding secret tunnel or cave entrances, demolition experts to booby-trap tunnels, and chemists for seeding each site with poison and killer gas capsules.

These key men included Brigadier General Kawabata, Col. Adachi, Col. Kaburagi, Col. Kasabuchi, and from the Imperial Japanese Navy: Captain Honda and Captain Takahashi.

Prince Takeda's code name was: **Kimsu Murakusi** and was guarded by three platoons of Imperial guards who were heavily-armed. They guarded him as he travelled around the Philippine islands visiting all of the Imperial excavation sites. He made sure that the sites were finished on time and to the high design standards expected to hold such vast wealth for the Imperial Family.

Each land site had to withstand earthquakes and allied aerial bombing, flooding and the ravages of time, therefore reinforced concrete walls and chambers were used in many of the underground treasure vault sites, many of which were disguised as military bunkers.

3.00   Japanese Military Involvement

The Japanese military were involved in potential site surveying, excavation and transportation of treasure from naval dockyards to remote locations using river barges, trucks, aircraft, and using the existing railway network system. In this section we explore the Japanese Engineering Battalion who was given the task of treasure tunnel construction and burial.

3.10 The Japanese Engineering Battalion

The Japanese Imperial Guard had a special Engineering Battalion attached to the Imperial Guard which protected the Imperial Family. Such an attachment would have been used in the Philippines under the direct orders of Prince Chichibu and Prince Takeda. These were called the 12th and later became the 18th Engineering Battalion.

Colonel Yugura was one of the officers given the task to construct tunnels and treasure chambers for the two Imperial princes. This man was professor of finance at the University of Japan before the war, and was now supervising tunnel construction.

In the case of treasure symbols, it is hard to distinguish which of these two groups above were responsible for writing this treasure code book. According to the Japanese Archive in Tokyo, they were written by a code writer on behalf of the ***Japanese Engineering Battalion.***

Therefore, we must assume that this is indeed correct. This Battalion would have been expected to rebuild roads, bridges, airfields, and to help in the construction of military reinforced concrete bunkers and underground concrete vaults for operation "Golden Lily".

We must also assume that these symbols belonging to this military group could be found anywhere in the Philippine archipelago, and will not be restricted to one island or location.

The Japanese Engineering Regiment (*Kohei Rentai*)

The Japanese engineering regiment consisted of approximately 900-1000 men, who were split into three engineering companies of about 250 men, in four 50 man platoons, plus 50 men assigned to the "material section", which included trucks and powered engineering equipment such as generators, lights, jackhammer, tools, and basic building materials attached to the Japanese infantry regiment, to provide basic light road repairs, obstacle clearing, and road bridge construction.

3.20 The Japanese Engineering Battalion Treasure Symbols Page 1

JAPANESE 12th & 18th ENGINEERING BATTALION
JAPANESE ENGINEERING REGIMENT (*Kohei Rentai*)

DURATION: 1941-44   CODE: GREEN: DIRECTIONS
CODE: RED: DANGER   CODE: YELLOW: TREASURE

Symbol	Meaning	Symbol	Meaning
⬍	GOLD	( )(8	TREASURE IN THE TUNNEL
Ð	BOOBY TRAP	(dog)	DOG: BOOBY TRAP
H	DANGER	(flower)	FLOWER: BIG BOMB!
⊕	BOOBY TRAP	≡	POISON
♡	POISON AT 7,10,13,17 FEET BOMB AT 12, 35, 45 FEET	⊐	POISON, ANY KIND OF MINERALS
☆	BOOBY TRAP	≈≈	POISON, DEATH
△ ▷	NEAR LOCATION 15 FEET DEEP	>	15 FEET DEEP
8	ALONG THE CREEK	⌒	DEPOSIT OR SITE
F→→	BURIED TREASURE TO BE FOLLOWED	I D Y	IN THE CREEK
ㄩ	ROLLING ROCKS OR BOULDERS	(face)	EYES POINT TO SPOT OF TREASURE WITHIN
⤳	POINTING TO OBJECT 2 METRES DEEP	×⊙/	AT THE END OF THE CUT-WAY

3.30 The Japanese Engineering Battalion Treasure Symbols Page 2

JAPANESE 12th & 18th ENGINEERING BATTALION
JAPANESE ENGINEERING REGIMENT (*Kohei Rentai*)

DURATION: 1941-44   CODE: YELLOW: TREASURE

Symbol	Meaning	Symbol	Meaning
K	TREASURE DOWN BELOW	(symbol)	GOLD IN LOCATION
X o D	GOLD DEPOSIT IN THE SPRING	HCT2	GOLD 45 FEET DEEP
Kn	COINS AT 3 FEET DEEP	7K	BOXES OF GOLD
A	GOLD OBJECT	(symbol)	TREASURE IN BOX
(symbol)	TREASURE ON THE SPOT AT 10 FEET	HENZ	GOLD
ICH	COINS	7KD	DEPOSIT UNDER BIG STONE
4K	INSIDE OR SIDE	7K	TREASURE UNDER THE SQUARE
(symbol)	TREASURE INSIDE THE CAVE	X	TREASURE UNDER THE SQUARE
(symbol)	GOLD BARS	(symbol)	BARS OF GOLD
7M	TREASURE UNDER THE WATER	(symbol)	TREASURE ON BOTH ENDS OF THE BRIDGE
(symbol)	TREASURE UNDER	(symbol)	JEWELS

3.40 Japanese Engineering Battalion Treasure Symbols Page3

JAPANESE 12th & 18th ENGINEERING BATTALION
JAPANESE ENGINEERING REGIMENT (*Kohei Rentai*)

DURATION: 1941-44

CODE: YELLOW: TREASURE
CODE: RED: DANGER

Symbol	Meaning	Symbol	Meaning
⬭	TREASURE	✕	DEPOSIT LEFT OR TO RIGHT
⛰	HOT UNDER 4 FEET DEEP	⌐★	BURIED GOLD
🗿	BUDDAH	DT	TREASURE UNDER TREE
G G	GOLD BARS	▭	TREASURE BOXES OF BARS
>o|	SILVER DEPOSIT	★★★	YAMASHITA TREASURE
🦅	SUMATRA BUDDHA	▤	TREASURE IN CHEST
∧·	TREASURE IN CAVE	∧	UNCUT PRECIOUS STONE
⁂	SEPARATED TREASURE	▱	ONE PART OR THE DIVISION OF TREASURE
→◎←	CENTRE TREASURE IN STAGNANT LAKE OR CURRENT	∼∼	TREASURE ON THE OPPOSITE SIDE
🐍	SNAKE POINTS TOWARDS TREASURE	▷ ㅁ	TREASURE UNDER THE CHURCH
🐟	GOLD	( )⑧	TREASURE IN THE TUNNEL

3.50   The Tanaka Detachment (2,000 men)

The Tanaka Detachment led by Colonel Tanaka Toru consisted of the 2nd Formosa Infantry, the 7th Tank Company, the 48th FA Battalion, the 1st and the 8th Independent Heavy Artillery.[13]

This detachment saw action on the night of 10th December 1941, when the Tanaka Detachment landed at Aparri in Northern Luzon. Due to light resistance on the 12th of December, the Tanaka Detachment linked up with Kanno Detachment and moved south towards Lingayen Gulf following the west coastline through Laoag, Vigan Bangar, Bacnotan, to San Fernando.

On the 23rd of December 1941, the Tanaka Detachment linked up with the 48th Division, and drove the U.S. and Filipino forces down the Pampanga river valley south to Manila, which was declared an "Open City" on the 27th December 1941.

The Tanaka Detachment were relieved on the 30th of December by the Imai Detachment, when they had failed to stop the American and Philippine forces reaching the Bataan defences north of Mariveles.

Colonel Tanaka may have had this treasure code book made up for the burial of any spoils of war he came across while fighting the campaign in Luzon, which started to subside in January 1942, giving him time to bury his treasure hoard taken from churches, banks and historical places, once he and his men were settled in a military camp somewhere in the Sierra Madre region in North East Luzon. It is rumoured that his body is indeed buried in this region, and a treasure site near to this grave would be a distinct possibility, to honour a fallen Japanese Officer of the Japanese Imperial Army.

---

[13] This photographic image was published before December 31st 1956, or photographed before 1946 and not published for 10 years thereafter, under jurisdiction of the Government of Japan, considered to be **public domain** law of Japan. According to article 23 of old copyright law of Japan and article 2 of supplemental provision of copyright.

3.60 Colonel Tanaka Toru Treasure Symbols Page 1

IMPERIAL JAPANESE 14TH ARMY TREASURE SYMBOLS
TANAKA DETACHMENT
COLONEL TANAKA TORU

LOCATIONS: APARRI, TAGUEGARAO, STA.CRUZ, BANGAR, LUNA, BACNOTAN, SAN FERNANDO, ROSALES, SISON, TARLAC, AND SIERRA MADRE, N.LUZON.

DURATION: 1941-43

CODE: GREEN: DIRECTIONS
CODE: YELLOW: TREASURE

Symbol	Meaning	Symbol	Meaning
⊕	GOLD VOLUMES	☼	GLITTERING DIAMONDS
⌒	JEWELRIES	↙×	SILVER
▭	TREASURE IN BOX	△	GOLD BARS
Mo	TREASURE ON THE OPPOSITE SIDE	∘△∘	SEPARATED TREASURE IN ROCK TRIANGLE
▫B	BOXES OF GOLD BARS WEIGHING 6.3KG EACH	⊙	TREASURE UNDER
⇉	TREASURE UNDER	⌒•	TREASURE UNDER
ㄩK	INSIDE	7	OBJECT UNDER OR TUNNEL
4	TUNNEL	Zhc	DEPOSIT UNDER
∪A	TREASURE UNDER	4	TREASURE IN ONE SIDE OF TREE / ROCK
⌒	TUNNEL	T	TUNNEL CLOSE
V	STRAIGHT TUNNEL	□\	HOLE

3.70 Colonel Tanaka Toru Treasure Symbols Page 2

IMPERIAL JAPANESE 14TH ARMY TREASURE SYMBOLS
TANAKA DETACHMENT
COLONEL TANAKA TORU

LOCATIONS: APARRI, TAGUEGARAO, STA.CRUZ, BANGAR, LUNA, BACNOTAN, SAN FERNANDO, ROSALES, SISON, TARLAC, AND SIERRA MADRE, N.LUZON.
DURATION: 1941-43   CODE: YELLOW: TREASURE

Symbol	Meaning	Symbol	Meaning
☻	COINS IN BARREL	ЛGЯ	TREASURE OF NO DESCRIPTION
ΔȻ	GOLD VOLUMES	A	GOLD OBJECT
♡	RICH HOME	～×～	TREASURE UNDERNEATH
6	GOLD INSIDE OR AROUND SIGN	IOɦ	COINS
Ch	COINS	⟶	MILLION DEPOSIT
☆☆☆	YAMASHITA TREASURE	⋅∕	TREASURE UNDER
XP	GOLD DEPOSIT SPRING LIKE WIRE	Ko	DEPOSIT UNDER BIG STONE
⑥ DRO	TREASURE CLOSE	→↑	TREASURE SIGN
▭ ׀׀׀׀׀׀׀	TREASURE BOX OF GOLD	万	JEWELRIES
_†ȣ⟩	MONEY DEPOSIT	⊙	SEPERATED BURIED TREASURE
⍟	GOLD VOLUMES	☀	GLITTERING DIAMONDS

3.80 Colonel Tanaka Toru Treasure Symbols Page3

	IMPERIAL JAPANESE 14TH ARMY TREASURE SYMBOLS TANAKA DETACHMENT **COLONEL TANAKA TORU**		
	LOCATIONS: APARRI, TAGUEGARAO, STA.CRUZ, BANGAR, LUNA, BACNOTAN, SAN FERNANDO, ROSALES, SISON, TARLAC, AND SIERRA MADRE, N.LUZON. DURATION: 1941-43 CODE: YELLOW: TREASURE		
⌒	JEWELRIES	⊥✕	SILVER
▭	TREASURE IN BOX	△	GOLD BARS
⋔ o	TREASURE ON THE OPPOSITE SIDE	₀△₀	SEPARATED TREASURE IN ROCK TRIANGLE
▯₿	BOXES OF GOLD BARS WEIGHING 6.3KG EACH	⊙	TREASURE UNDER
⇾	TREASURE UNDER	⌒•	TREASURE UNDER

3.90 Advanced Japanese Landings in December 1941

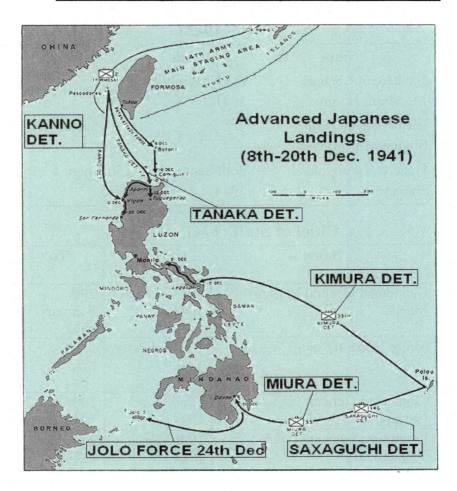

Later Japanese Invasions

The Kawamura Detachments invades Iloilo City on Panay on 16th April 1942, then carried on to attack Cagayan de Oro, Mindanao on the 3rd May 1942. The Kawaguchi Detachment invades Cebu City and Cotabato, Maguindanao Province, South East Mindanao.

Japanese Officers Commanding the Philippines (1941 - 1945)

	Name	From	To
1	Lieutenant General Masaharu Homma	6th November 1941	1st August 1942
2	Lieutenant General Shigenori Kuroda	1st August 1942	26th September 1944
3	General Tomoyuki Yamashita	26th September 1944	15th August 1945

Chief of Staff (1941 – 1945)

	Name	From	To
1	Lieutenant General Masami Maeda	6th November 1941	20th February 1942
2	Major General Takaji Wachi	20th February 1942	22nd March 1944
3	Lieutenant General Haruki Isayama	22nd March 1944	19th June 1944
4	Lieutenant General Tsuchio Yamaguchi	19th June 1944	28th July 1944
5	Major General Ryozo Sakuma	28th July 1944	5th October 1944
6	Lieutenant General Akira Mutō	5th October 1944	15th August 1945

4.00 Japanese Military Numbers On The 30th September 1944

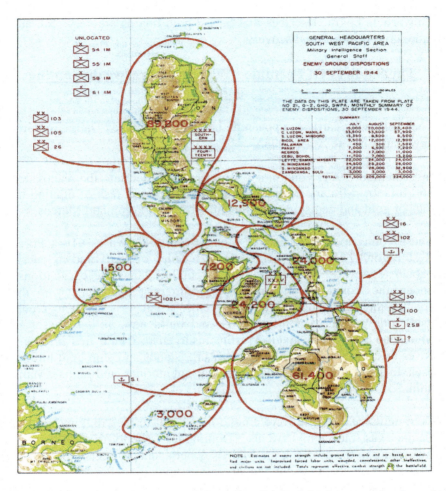

By September 1944, the Japanese Imperial forces numbered 224,000 men Source: U.S. Military Intelligence.

4.10 Are Imperial Japanese Treasure Sites In The Philippines Real?

This article below describes that buried gold hoards are very real, and more gold is awaiting discovery.

The Soldiers Of Fortune: "We were there, we dug up the gold!"

The following article appeared in the Philippine Daily Inquirer newspaper in late April 2008:

In September 1972, young men were first recruited into the reactivated 16th Infantry Military Battalion and given the secret task of digging up tons of gold and gemstones for the late President Ferdinand Marcos.

These young men were part of a larger group known as "Task Force Restoration" headed by Armed Forces Chief of Staff and *General Fabian Ver whose main task was to conduct "massive excavations" under the cover of fighting the communist insurgency in the countryside during the martial law years. (History is about to repeat itself today as the US military try and build new military bases in Mindanao in order to quell Muslim insurgency. Could this just be a cover to excavate one of the last treasure islands and ship gold bullion back to the United States using Naval submarines and ships? Many think so).

Dominguez and Caoile were among those sent to the "digging fields". Caoile was then only twenty, Dominguez: twenty-five years old. According to the soldiers, the Marcos generals and officers close to the late president knew about the operation, including President Ramos who was in the so-called "Rolex 12" circle and was chief of the Philippine Constabulary at this time.

General Fabian Ver's elite Presidential Guard Battalion watched and guarded the young soldiers with eagle-eyed attention while they conducted the digging operations at night. During the day, they slept or did their "standard" work of "restoration" or infrastructure development and other "field operations".

Throughout the thirteen years that the members of the Task Force Restoration did their work, only some thirty treasure sites out of 175 were dug up. The rest, as identified by Marcos and with the help of "some Japanese men" who had the maps, were untouched or may have been dug up by "those who knew where to look".

Their first digging operation was in early March 1973 near Lake Caliraya in Lumban, Laguna.

"In the early morning of the first week of March 1973, we soldiers were secretly tasked to provide manpower for digging operations and security to a huge part of the infamous and legendary Yamashita WWII treasures consisting of gold bars and gemstones buried by Imperial Japanese soldiers in the vicinity of Lake Caliraya Resort, in Cavinti, Laguna," they stated.

Their unit stayed in this area until the end of April 1973, but a platoon-sized detachment remained to "ward off New People's Army (NPA) elements operating there". They started the preliminary work, erecting steel sheet barriers around the area and constructing field barracks. We then dug the area as instructed by General Ver PGB and high-ranking officers inspected the construction of our field barracks and the "digging of long flat steel bars which served as perimeter fence before the actual treasure site could be excavated".

Dominguez, who was a member of the first group, recalled how they prepared to dig a hole in the ground 30 feet wide and 35 feet deep, as instructed by their superior officers. Their short stay of several months was later extended to a whole calendar year.

The soldiers were even told to make offerings – pigs or chickens, which were killed at the site to appease "enkantos" who were supposedly guarding the treasures. Otherwise, they could encounter severe difficulty at the digging site.

(Author's Note: "Enkantos" are believed to be supernatural spirits that guard the treasure site, and must be recognised as guardians of the gold, and appeased before anyone starts to dig over the protected area in question. If these entities or spirit divas have been formed using negative or greedy thoughts by the Japanese soldiers, then I would advise that the area is blessed with love and light,

burying pieces of rose quartz in the ground would be suggested before worked commenced.
A full cleansing of the area with incense sticks or white sage and prayers to the great spirit of creation would also be well advised.

The killing of animals only adds to the negative energy already there. The one who will succeed in retrieval of the gold MUST have compassion and love for those who were killed on the site, and ask for the angels to come and take lost spirits away with them by asking the souls of the dead to seek the light. A vision of golden light shining into the ground must be visualised in order to rid the site of Enkantos. Spiritual music, laughter and singing greatly help in the healing of the land and the people who live near to the site).

The soldiers claimed that the ground would mysteriously swell with water or some of their belongings would become mysteriously lost. Even the soldiers themselves were told to have no "dark intentions" and to be "pure in heart" so they could accomplish their objective, stated Dominguez.

President Marcos himself came to visit them at the site whenever there was a glimpse of success. He also made "numerous visits", arriving by military helicopter during the digging operations, they stated.

"During these operations, members of our unit saw four Japanese nationals together with President Ferdinand E. Marcos, Generals Fabian Ver and Ramon Cannu, Lt. Colonels Lachica and Javier D. Carbonnel, and Capt. Renato Jamora and some members of the elite Presidential Guard Battalion," the soldiers said.

But it was only on the evening of April 27th, 1973, at around 11 p.m., that the "treasure-digging activity finally reached its strategic conclusion". The soldiers had been using two bulldozers, two Kato type backhoes and a heavy-duty crane when they struck something very hard under the ground, the first of the group's findings.

"Several steel cylindrical drums measuring approximately 3 feet long and 1.5 feet in diameter, and an undetermined number of rectangular copper boxes (3 feet long, 1 foot wide and 2 feet high) entombed in several thick concrete vaults were unearthed at an estimated depth of 35-40 feet," they said.

One of the concrete vaults was accidentally hit by the Kato backhoe digger while the vaults were being dug up. Until this period of time, the soldiers didn't know what they were sent down there to excavate!

Because of repeated strikes, the teeth of the backhoe broke the body of the vault, hitting a steel drum inside it. The soldiers saw "heavy yellow metal gold which gleamed amidst the floodlights that were shining on the big digging area". One of the bars which they saw was a foot long, 3 inches wide and almost 2 inches thick.

Within forty minutes, three large helicopters landed near to the excavation site. Two Huey military-type helicopters came escorting the presidential chopper ferrying Marcos, General Ver, Cannu, Felix and some PGB close-in security personnel. They had come to inspect the treasure find and Marcos could not contain his excitement, the soldiers said.

The concrete vaults (*approximately 6 feet long, 5 feet wide and 5 feet high*) were lifted one by one by using a heavy-lift crane and were placed aboard three six by six military trucks which were on a twenty-four-hour standby near the battalion headquarter's command post situated near to the area of excavation.

"Before Marcos and his party left the place, we overheard him instructing General Ver apparently on where to transport and hide the gold bars which (task) was carried out by PGB elements," the soldiers claimed.

"Sometime in the fourth week of April 1973, we were pulled away from this area, but a platoon-sized detachment was left and stayed there for almost a year after the site was further improved as a new tourist spot into what is called now as a 'Japanese Shrine Sunken Garden,'" they stated.

After the digging at Lake Caliraya in Laguna, the other military elements of the reactivated 16th Infantry Battalion were utilized to provide the same security detail services and conduct treasure digging operations separately in the areas of Montalban, Antipolo, Baras and Teresa all in Rizal province from 1974 to 1981. This led to the activation of the "Task Force Restoration" under Lt. Col. Porferio Gemoto sometime between the years of 1977 and 1978.

"Task Force Restoration" had then extended its operations to the Intramuros-Manila Cathedral area near where the *Palacio del Gobernador* was built.

In 1972, before the diggings happened, Marcos's men discovered a vast tunnel network "within the Pasig River" along what is now the Napindan flood control project, underground tunnels from the Fort Bonifacio military reservation up to Villamor Air Base and Bicutan-Taguig via Fort Bonifacio Army General Hospital.

These secret tunnels preceded all the other treasure hunting and digging operations. The soldiers said the gold discoveries made by Marcos, as well as their operations, were the real reasons why he started his strongman rule "in the guise of a threatening rebellion by the alleged newly-revitalized CPP/NPA (Communist Party of the Philippines, and the New People's Army) and Muslim secessionism in Mindanao".

In fact, President Marcos allegedly had to create the conditions for this "threat" to justify martial law and allow the secret diggings to be done by newly-recruited soldiers sent to the countryside allegedly for "military field training exercises".

Marcos Gold (Philippine Gold): See:
http://www.youtube.com/watch?v=NSVb_JA97kg&feature=related

There were three groups: one group who dug, another group in charge of transporting the boxes containing the treasures, and another group who took care of securing the recovered loot before it was transported outside the country. The trucks which transported the crates of gold bars and other treasures were large six by six trucks heavily covered and boarded up. Some of the WWII gold bars were coated in **_black hardened tar and asphalt_** to "discourage innocent finders during these treasure hunting operations," Caoile stated.

The gold bars dug by the soldiers were stored in the vaults of the old Central Bank in Intramuros. Later, in the mid-1970s, Marcos "ordered the construction of a new and modern coin and gold minting and refining plant of the Central Bank along East Avenue in Diliman, Quezon City". (Gold Buying Station: ***Security Plant Complex, Bangko Sentral ng Pilipinas,. East Ave.*** Diliman *Quezon City*,
Tel. No. 929-7071 loc. 337; 925-7179).

According to the soldiers, this was to "further accommodate a massive bulk of gold bars and bullion for re-melting" to change their original forms and markings, which included the countries where the gold had *originally* came from.

There were strict orders from Marcos to erase the marks from the gold bars which the soldiers had dug up, Caoile said. This was to prevent the government of the countries which the Japanese had looted from rediscovering them and demanding their repatriation at a later date.

The different gold bars that the soldiers dug up had inscriptions such as "Cambodia" with five star markings; "Sumatra" with four stars; "Burma" with three stars; and other marks identical to the countries of their origin. The Cambodia gold bars weighed 6.3 kilograms each; the Sumatra gold bars weighed 6.2 kg each; and the Burma bars weighed around 6 kg each.

Upon orders from Marcos, the original size and weight of the gold bars were modified to make it appear that these did not come from the Japanese treasure loot; thus, the need to re-melt these at the Philippine **Central Bank**, the soldiers claimed.

The soldiers said "crates by crates" of gold bars were shipped out of the country via the Manila International Airport (now known as the **Ninoy Aquino International Airport**) using a C-130 Hercules military type aircraft after martial law was proclaimed. This was witnessed by perimeter security personnel working at the airport.

The soldiers said even before martial rule in 1972, Marcos had already successfully excavated gold bullions and gemstones at the *Manila Railroad Company* (MRRCO, now called the PNR) yard complex at Tutuban terminal. This was at the start of his first term as president from 1965 to 1969. He started treasure digging when elected president in 1965 but could not finish it in four years; thus the need to employ many soldiers to continue the work under **Task Force Restoration** when he was re-elected.

The soldiers claimed that in all, they excavated and retrieved more than ***600,000 metric tons*** of gold bars, bullions, and other precious metals such as palladium, platinum, chrome, nickel, zinc and little babbit bars. There were precious gems such as diamonds, both cut and uncut.

Among the "major" treasure sites which the soldiers had dug up were in Caliraya in Cavinti-Lumban, Laguna; Baras and Teresa in Rizal province; Montalban caves in Montalban, Rizal; Montalban Mascat; Sitio Mayagay, Sampaloc in Tanay, Rizal; Fort Bonifacio Tunnel; Fort Bonifacio hospital; the area of the Manpower and Youth building; Bastion de San Lorenzo in Fort Santiago; Muñoz in Nueva Ecija; Balok bridge, also in Nueva Ecija; site of the Central Luzon State University statue in Muñoz; Sta. Fe in Nueva Vizcaya; Campo 4 in San Jose, Nueva Vizcaya; and San Mateo in Rizal province.

According to them, the Japanese army units had ***subdivided*** the treasures they brought into the country and buried it in places classified as *major* and *minor* treasure sites. The Japanese allegedly used the Manila Railroad Co. to transport the treasures in question.

Major or minor treasure sites depended on the "suitability, concealment, permanency and location of man-made, built-up areas, mountainous and, or rolling hills, terrain with creeks, rivers, dams, big acacia, mango, camachile or duhat trees that serve as references for future retrieval of said treasure deposits," the soldiers said.

This excludes the four, six, eight or more pieces of gold bars usually found underneath big acacia or mango trees where they had been stashed by low-ranking Japanese soldiers while their superior officers were not looking.

In some of the major treasure sites, the soldiers even found skeletons still wearing their tattered uniforms and helmets, and with their swords beside them, and prisoners of war still wearing military dog tags indicating that they were once Korean, Chinese, American, British, Australian and Filipino troops.

In Fort Santiago alone there were more than one-hundred boxes of treasures which the soldiers found buried under the old torture chamber, Bastion de San Lorenzo, which is situated by the Pasig River.

(Charles C Mc Dougald in his book **Asian Loot,** *chapter one and twelve, writes about his and Robert Curtis's unsuccessful attempt to recover this treasure funded by the Leber group and the subsequent death of one of their diggers inside the excavated tunnel system situated deep under the Bastion). This treasure was taken by the Japanese from the Philippine Central bank and other banks in and around Intramuros in early 1942.*

Six vaults were constructed 30 meters below the ground. Each vault had 450 gold bars weighing 50kg each. (135,000 kg of gold bars from Sumatra, and Burma).

Caoile said Marcos's and other government officials including President Ramos would "never talk about the gold. Instead, they will deny and torture the minds and beliefs of the people by telling them that the

'Marcos gold' is nothing but a mere hoax, a fiction, or fantasies of a fertile and speculative mind," they said. "They do not want to expose the truth about the Marcos gold because they were expecting to benefit out of it in collaboration with foreign conspirators both here and abroad," they added.

General Fabian Ver was head of **Presidential Security Command** Director of the NISA **(National Intelligence and Security Authority)** (Born: January 20th, 1920. Died: November 21st, 1998).

Charles C McDougald's *Asian Loot* mentions colossal amounts of gold bullion, found and transacted after WWII. These quantities range from *20 to 52,589 tons*, the combined weight of 4,207,138 12.5 kg bars, worth in 1983 over *$800 Billion*.

Charles also states that General Ver was involved in gold bullion recoveries in 1971 and in 1972.
The first one was at Paco train station near Manila where 80 tons of gold was recovered, and the second one was at a church site at Agoo, La Union where 100 tons was excavated. These "finds" however cannot be verified (Page 34 of his book).

In the book *Gold Warriors*, written by Sterling and Peggy Seagrave, they have for sale three CDs packed with 1500 megabytes of documentation, photographs of actual gold recoveries made by President Marcos and the hundreds of transactions carried out between individuals, world banks, secret organisations and corporations between the years 1945 to 2001. The compact disc collection can be bought and viewed by those who are still sceptical by contacting: **www.versobooks.com.**

The photograph above was taken on the 2nd of April 1982, by Camera Operator: PH2 BALLARD U.S.N.
*(This file is a work of a sailor or employee of the U.S. Navy, taken or made during the course of the person's official duties. As a work of the U.S. federal government, the image is in the **public domain**).*

No one can deny that this treasure *"does not exist"*. My task here is to shed a little light on the treasure symbols that were used to bury the treasure in the first place and to explain what they mean to you, a current treasure hunter, and future treasure hunters that come after you. My book has been written in order to help understand the thought processes of the Japanese military machine that buried vast wealth in the Philippines during the Second World War.

American forces examining gold bars and other precious items taken from Japanese Imperial forces in the Philippines during WWII.[14]

On the 10th of February 1945, the GIs of the 33rd Infantry Division waded ashore at San Fabian, on the Philippine island of Luzon. As some of the GIs reached Rosario, Pangasinan, they were very surprised to find a vast amount of coins dumped inside a ditch by the main road as they marched towards the town.

The Japanese military had no time to flee with such a heavy cargo or even bury this large amount of stolen coins as the 33rd overran the Japanese garrison. This "find" would suggest that in this area other valuable treasures may be awaiting recovery.

---

[14] These photographic images were published before December 31st 1956, or photographed before 1946 and not published for 10 years thereafter, under jurisdiction of the Government of the USA, considered to be **public domain**.

4.20 Marcos: Does He Have The Largest Treasure Recovery In History?

Much has been said about the late President Ferdinand Marcos being the world's richest man. While this title was not officially designated to Marcos, the late dictator, however, was known as the man who stole the largest loot in history. This vast wealth reportedly consists of billions of dollars and many tons of gold bullions deposited in several banks in Switzerland.

Government lawyers claimed that Marcos had used dummy foundations to hoard this vast stolen hoard. Among such foundations that the Presidential Commission on Good Government (PCGG) had identified foundations called: Rayby, Sandy, Wintrop, and Xandy; others may still exist to this day.

Former Senate President Jovito Salonga, who served as the first PCGG chairman under the Aquino administration, stated that the agency had identified 51 Marcos bank accounts in Switzerland, 23 of which are in Credit Suisse; 3 at Swiss Bank Corporation in Fribourg; 15 in Swiss Bank Corporation in Geneva; 6 at Banque Paribas in Geneva; 3 bank accounts at Hoffman in Zurich; and one each at Lombard Odeii and at the Trade Development Bank in Geneva.

According to former Solicitor General Francisco Chavez, the Marcos family still keeps some **$13.4** billion **USD** in deposits at the Union Bank of Switzerland under the account of *Irene Marcos-Araneta*, on top of a hoard of 1.241 tons of gold at an underground bunker at Kloten Airport in Zurich. Chavez also disclosed that Imelda Marcos has ***800,000 ounces of gold*** in ***unfrozen*** accounts in Switzerland.

Before this, an Australian private investigator, Mr Reiner Jacobi, who served as a PCGG consultant in 1989, had unraveled the so-called Irene Araneta deposit account and even went to the extent of claiming that the Marcos family members had a **$250 billion USD** gold hoard held in Switzerland.

In October 1999, Filipino businessman Enriquez Zobel, a known close associate of the late president, told a senate committee that the Marcos wealth could have swollen to **$100 billion USD** in gold and dollar deposits, the bulk of which is deposited with the U.S. Treasury. In his sworn testimony, Mr Zobel said the Marcos wealth is distributed into gold deposits, dollar accounts, and real estate properties located in various parts of the world.

Why **successive Presidents** past and present have not tried to claim these riches for the Philippine people is still unclear when the evidence of such massive wealth and overwhelming evidence still exists today in 2012.

Mr Zobel also stated that the Marcos gold deposits may have reached a staggering **$35 billion USD**. Zobel had also mentioned the **$13.4 billion USD** Irene Marcos Araneta account at the Union Bank of Switzerland.

The gold bars are allegedly kept in various banks in Portugal, Vatican City, Switzerland, Spain, Germany, the Solomon Islands, and even in the United States itself. Zobel said Marcos obtained the gold bars after WWII Liberation (1946) from the *Yamashita treasure* and from soldiers who sold their gold bars for only $20 per bar, the latter being very hard to believe today.

In early February 2001, the Philippine Daily Inquirer newspaper disclosed the alleged attempt of Irene Marcos Araneta to launder billions of dollars in deposits under the 885931 accounts from Union Bank of Switzerland to Deutsche Banks in Dusseldorf, Germany. Aside from the Marcos family and the Philippine government, the 9,539 victims of human rights under the Marcos regime have interest in this amassed Marcos wealth.

The conclusion that one must take from these findings is that this "Marcos wealth" is very real and still in the hands of the Marcos family. No serious attempt has been made to repatriate this massive wealth back into the control of the present Philippine government in order to help build new hospitals, roads, and schools and to help millions of starving Filipinos who deserve a better life while the minority in power become richer and fatter as their people they are supposed to represent and should help remain the poorest on this planet.

The Central bank of the Philippines reported that the Philippine foreign debt in 2010 was **$60 billion USD** and the countries gross global reserves were only **$62.4 billion USD.** At this rate the country will soon become bankrupt.

The solution to solve this debt is so obvious: Marcos's wealth must be used to pay off debts that go back to the early 1980s when he was in power and plunged the country into massive debt.

Maybe the new President, Mr. Benigno Simeon Cojuangco Aquino III, also known as Noynoy Aquino or PNoy, the 15th President of the Philippines since June 2010, will change the status quo. He was voted into power by the people on the promises he made to his electorate to tackle greed and corruption in the government.

Time will tell as he starts his first six years as the new president. How this can be achieved when members of the Marcos family are still in seats of power and serve as senators in PNoy's "new anti-corrupt government" is beyond my understanding for decency and professional democracy for the Philippine people who voted for him and now cry out for real change.

Even today poor Filipinos try and recover riches under the ground with very little funds, tools and food, simply because they dream of a better life for themselves and family. If they had a better lifestyle and a better income they would not have to risk their lives digging deep excavations in the hope that some day they will be free of hunger, debt and poverty.

Here are just a few of the many requests I see every year from treasure hunters asking for help with their small- and large-scale treasure sites. Some Filipinos want metal detection equipment, others want funding for digging equipment, and some just want advice. Treasure hunting is <u>NOT</u> dead in the Philippines; it is very much alive and will continue to be so for many, many years to come.

16th of July 2012

Ricardo Says:

Hi Aquila, I would like to know if you have any information of treasures sites in Nasipit Agusan del Norte. I have a positive site pinpointed by a former Japanese soldier named Seiji before he migrated to Davao. He also revealed to me some minor treasure sites but were already taken cared of by *JICA. I just need a copy of Japanese treasure signs for my reference. Do you really believe that there are still buried treasures in the different islands in the Philippines? Do you know of some people who have successfully retrieved treasures? Have you tried operating a site before? What are the common hazards that you normally encounter?

6th of September 2010

Joshua Asks:

We have a site in Bicol region, Philippines we have detected with a positive result to have a gold mine. We need a guy who is willing to finance the project (digging and excavation with 3d scanner). Before the operation starts interested financier will bring scanner for us to prove that the area is positive with gold. If the financier is satisfied with the scanning results, we will sit down and plan on how to operate.
We will give 40% share to the financier.
    Thank you.
    Joshua

2nd of July 2010

Russell Says:

We have an on-going project here in Tigaon, Camarines Sur, Bicol, can anyone interpret the stones that we've found at 25ft, heart shape, yellow color,1" thick, 10"x10" size and at 35 feet we've found a bayonet covered by asphalt and a 3 inch by 1 foot concrete asphalt box covered in red paint. If you have any idea about this item we've found please contact me on my number.

* Japan International Co-Operation Agency:
See link: http://www.jica.go.jp/english

Many Filipino treasure hunters believe that this organisation carries out secret treasure recoveries throughout the Philippines by disguising gold-hunting excavations by building official new water storage facilities, bridges, and roads in areas where locals know there was either Japanese military occupation or where eyewitnesses have seen gold boxes being buried during WWII; these accusations cannot be proved in fact and are therefore unfounded. Mr Akihiko TANAKA, President of JICA, stated: "As the country's major development agency, it is important to emphasize that JICA's activities should reflect both the Japanese people's will and opinions".

4.30 Japanese Imperial Treasure Site Markings For The Philippines (Dated 1943-45)

JAPANESE IMPERIAL TREASURE MARKINGS

プリン―/ヤニ
フミクパン   BULACAN 1943

ねシミ↑リケ゛   INFANTA, QUEZON 1944-45

コリナシ'A 耕ラン   GUMACA, QUEZON 1944

まカ・テ   MAKATI, MANILA 1944-45

イ川氵ギ"ナ大   BAGUIO, NORTHERN LUZON 1943-44

ベ゛ワ―ノヌヤ
フ   BATAAN, SOUTHERN LUZON 1943-44

ナミトんパッフカ   PANDI, BULACAN 1945

丿カ゛ナ
カ川ノ   RAGAY 1944-45

フたメ   MAKATI, MANILA 1944-45

YCDdE+3l   JAPANESE IMPERIAL TREASURE SIGN 1945

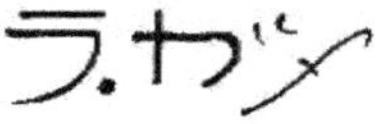

JAPANESE IMPERIAL TREASURE MARKINGS

ラ.カツ゛ン　　　RAGAY 1944-45

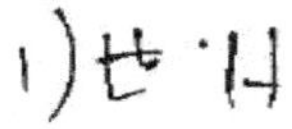

リセ・H　　　RIZAL 1943-44

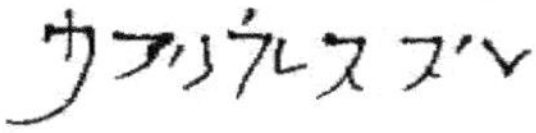

ウフ゛リフレス フ゛ン　　　CAMARINES SUR 1944-45

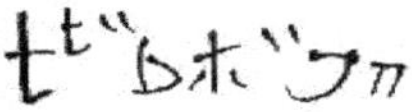

セ゛ヒ゛ホ゛フπ　　　ZAMBOANGA 1944-45

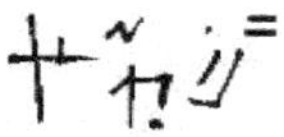

十゛カ゛ツ゛=　　　DIADI 1945-45

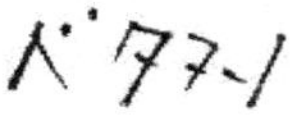

ハ゛タフーノ　　　BATAAN 1944-45

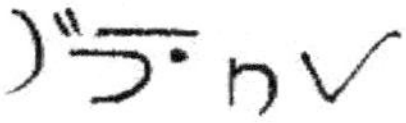

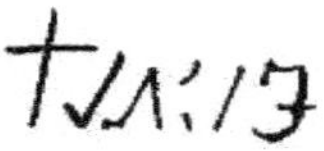

ハ゛ラ・nV　　　BULACAN 1943-44

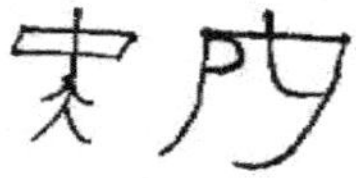

末内　　　CORRIGADOR 1945

†ノハ゛iフ　　　ANONTA 1944-45

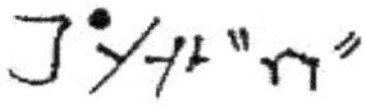

コ゛ン力゛ヿ゛　　　GONGAGA 1944-45

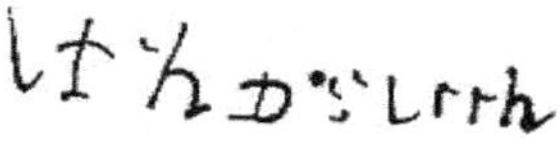

しナカカ゛しrrh　　　PANGASINAN 1944-45

Twenty-one Imperial treasure codes for various island locations are shown above.

The script style of writing vary in shape and size, it seems to be a mixture of many symbols and letters taken from **China, Japan, Korea and the English** alphabet.

4.40 Partial List of Known Japanese Imperial Treasure -Burial Sites On The Philippine Islands

Here I have included a partial list of the 175 Imperial sites compiled from many historical sources. Each site mentioned here are land-based sites. There were 34 water sites; these included ships, submarines, underwater caves and deposits hidden inside coral reefs. Some locations are mentioned more than once suggesting multiple treasure sites in the same location.

Alabang: 1943-44	Anonta: 1944-45	Aritao: 1943-44
Bulacan: 1943	Bataan: 1943-45	Bataan: 1943-44
Bamban Cemetry: 1944	Camarines Sur: 1944-45	Camp Eldridge, Los Banos
Christ T.King Church: 1943	Corregidor: Hospl Site: 1945	Corregidor: Crockett Bttry
Diadi: 1945	Dulao: Nueva Viscaya Tnl 8	Dulao: Nueva Viscaya Tnl 9
Gongaga: 1944-45	Gumaca: 1944	Infanta: 1944-45
Lubang: 1943-44	Makati: 1944-45	Makati: 1944-45
Manila Cathedral: 1944	Mount Makiling: 1945	Pandi: 1945
Pangasinan: 1944-45	Ragay: 1944-45	Ragay: 1944-45
Rizal: Teresa 1: 1943-44	Rizal: Teresa 2: 1943-44	San Pabloin: Laguna: 1945
San Fernando: Tunnel 8	San Fernando: Tunnel 9	San Augustin Church: 1944
Three Jars Site: 1944-45	Zambonga: 1944-45	

Note: these are **NOT** the burial GPS locations of Imperial treasure sites below, but only the location of where the town's cities and provinces are located for your reference only.

Areas of Known Treasure Locations	GPS Locations Of Cities And Provinces
Baguio City, Northern Luzon:	Lat: 16°24'59.73"N: Long: 120°36'0.01"E
Bataan Natural Park Area:	Lat: 14°39'59.58"N: Long: 120°25'0.95"E
Camarines Sur Province:	Lat: 13°31'29.83"N: Long: 123°20'54.56"E
Corrigador Island, Bataan:	Lat: 14°23'11.96"N: Long: 120°34'36.62"E
Diadi, Northern Luzon:	Lat: 16°37'59.56"N: Long: 121°21'0.16"E
Gonzaga, Northern Luzon:	Lat: 18°15'59.85"N: Long: 121°59'59.95"E
Gumaca, Quezon:	Lat: 13°55'11.02"N: Long: 122° 6'1.57"E
Infanta, Quezon:	Lat: 14°44'32.62"N: Long: 121°38'57.63"E
Makati City, Luzon:	Lat: 14°32'59.82"N: Long: 121° 1'59.98"E
Pandi, Bulacan:	Lat: 14°52'32.48"N: Long: 120°57'33.46"E
Pangasinan Province, Luzon:	Lat: 15°56'38.17"N: Long: 120°26'8.21"E
Ragay, Camarines Sur:	Lat: 13°48'59.71"N: Long: 122°46'60.00"E
Zamboanga City, Mindanao:	Lat: 6°54'43.37"N: Long: 122° 4'54.36"E

President F.C. Marcos Recovered Gold from "Major" Treasure Sites From These Locations:

1) Caliraya in Cavinti-Lumban	2) Laguna: Varas and Teresa in Rizal Province
3) Montalban Caves in Montalban	4) Rizal: Montalban Mascat: Sitio Mayagay
5) Sampaloc in Tanay	6) Rizal: Fort Bonifacio Tunnel
7) Fort Bonifacio Hospital:(Manpower&Youth Building)	8) Bastion de San Lorenzo in Fort Santiago
9) Muñoz in Nueva Ecija: Balok Bridge	10) Campo 4 in San Jose: Nueva Vizcaya
11) San Mateo in Rizal Province	12) University statue in Muñoz:Sta. Fe in Nueva Vizcaya

As previously mentioned, *Task Force Restoration* recovered treasure from thirty treasure sites. And we know that the Americans recovered another ten+ treasure sites during the late 1940s. No detailed evidence, however, is available to show how many of these were official Imperial treasure sites and how many were unofficial smaller treasure deposits, of which there are at least 500+ in number.

The remaining sites, as identified by Marcos and with the help of "some Japanese men" who had the original Imperial maps, may have been dug up by "those who knew where to look". No one knows for sure how many of these original Imperial sites remain untouched today. Many are still guarded by Japanese Yakuza for unknown pay masters who wait for a time in the future when they can buy the land and recover these vast riches at their leisure. Treasure hunting activity and past WWII history is very much alive in the Filipinas even today, and should make any red-blooded treasure hunter excited at the number of untouched treasure sites still awaiting discovery.

**Recovered Gold Bullion (Marcos) = 600,000 Metric Tons
** (Source: In Search of Gold book: Appendix 1: Email to Tomas Cyran from Bob Curtis who helped Marcos with many treasure recoveries in the 1970s).

4.50 The Famous Marcos Head Statue

The pictures are of the carved head statue of the late President Ferninad C. Marcos located very near to the coastal road that runs between Agoo and Bagiuo off the Marcos Highway Bagiuo City in Northern Luzon.
According to Tomas Cyran, an Australian adventurer, Marcos had so much gold he had to re-bury it in the old gold Benguet gold mines situated outside Baguio City in Northern Luzon.

President Marcos had a statue of his head carved high into the clifftop. It is said that this head overlooks several burial sites containing thousands of metric tons of gold bullion and historical artifacts looted from other Asian countries by the Imperial Japanese military forces.

In 1987 Marcos told a close friend that he had $500 million in bank accounts in Switzerland and $14 Billion in gold buried in *several secret locations* in the Philippines. Many of these treasure sites are still guarded by ex *RAM members and new recruits, there mission to keep these hiding places secret.

A very strong earthquake measuring 7.8 destroyed most of Baguio on the 16th of July1990. A significant number of buildings and infrastructure were damaged, major highways were temporarily severed, and a number of houses were leveled or severely shaken with a significant loss of life.

Because of these earthquakes, the entrances to old tunnels leading to these gold deposits usually collapse, burying the gold under thousands of tons of rock and mud, making future recoveries virtually impossible now. Some of the fallen buildings were built on or near fault lines. Baguio City was rebuilt, with the aid from the national government and various international donors like Japan, Singapore and other countries.

*Academy class of 1971 formed the Reform the Armed Forces Movement (RAM).

4.60   Japanese Imperial Treasure Maps

According to the late Robert Curtis, there were only three cartographers that were used by Prince Chichibu and Prince Takeda to draw the maps; the reason was obvious: security! In this section we will examine the maps that were used to document these vast hidden treasures.

Each Imperial site would have three maps drawn by a dedicated cartographer. The blue set would be used as the original engineering planning drawings, showing the layout of the site, a working "draft copy" that would not be used for future retrieval as this copy would be changed as and when needed, a "working copy" that would include every change to depth, water levels, changes in tunnel direction, concrete thickness, type of rock, main entrances, amounts of treasure and the placement of booby traps. "White copies" were rumoured to have been made; no one is sure whether these maps were exact copies of the red maps, an example of which is shown below.

Original "Red" Waxed Imperial Treasure Map

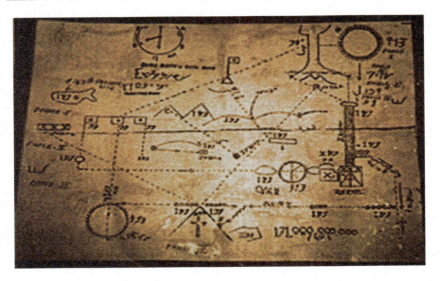

This red map is the recovery map that would have been used by the Imperial Japanese family to recover the buried treasure hoard underground. All of the necessary geographical features, such as old trees, hills, mountains are clearly shown together with clock angles, compass bearings and distances from each buried deposit. In section 5.8 I will explain in detail how this type of map should be viewed and read.

4.70   What Is The Key To Unlock The Map?

Each map had a key to unlock its secret, the key to unlock the precise location of where the treasure was buried was coded on a "clock face". Some clocks had four or three hands, two hands, one hand or no hands at all. The position of the hands referred to the "clocking recovery angles", the compass bearings and distances from the central shaft, to the entrances of the tunnels that were connected underground to the central shaft.

The map shows many measurements taken between each geographical feature around the central shaft and entrance tunnels. All of the angles in compass degrees and distances are carefully noted by the cartographer. I believe that the centre of the clock dial represented the central air shaft directly above the treasure chamber; the hand positions give the clocking recovery angles from the geographical features to the central shaft location.

The depth of each shaft and the distance between the central shaft and the tunnel's entrances were calculated by the mining engineer beforehand.

The entrances to the tunnels were very near or below the geographical reference points and many compass bearings were taken and noted and placed on the map in a form of circles and dotted lines.

Identifying key geographical features around the treasure site such as trees, mountains, rivers, hills, churches, historic buildings, etc would aid the Japanese to identify the main tunnel entrances at a later recovery date, and ultimately the main airshaft directly over the deposit, which would have been covered with large boulders, fast-growing trees and vegetation.

The other interesting feature of each map was the Japanese flag pole displaying the Japanese flag. If the flag was flying on the right, then the map itself was reversed. If this was the case, then the map was to be viewed in a mirror to find the exact location of the hidden gold and riches.

The numbers shown on the right-hand side of the map would represent the appropriate value of gold in Yen at the site, based on 1940's gold price of approximately $34 USD per ounce. In some cases the Yen price would be preceded by a "*" star instead of the "Y".

This meant that the weight of the gold was shown in grams. For example, 500,000,000 would represent a buried deposit of 500 million grams. This value in Yen was only for the gold content of each site. The value of jewels, coins, currency and other precious artifacts were not taken into consideration.

4.80   What was a 555 or a 777 site?

This was an Imperial treasure site where the total amount of gold was either *555,000,000,000* Yen or *777,000,000,000* Yen, the estimated market value in the 1940s ($34.50 troy oz). An example of a 777 site is shown on the next page.

4.90 A Basic Treasure Map: (Origin Not Known)

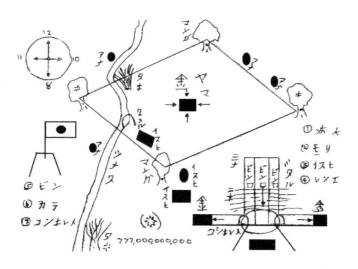

This map is interesting; it shows how the various deposits were laid out. The four trees and the river are used as geographical reference points.

See how the larger deposits shown as black rectangles were accessed via three vertical shafts, each separated from each other. All three shafts were serviced by a separate elevator which would have been used to transport workers and treasure down into the tunnels (see bottom right of the map).

This was the case on many larger sites. Prince Takeda used elevators, installed shafts to travel deep into the earth to inspect finished underground chambers, prior to sealing them when they were full of stolen plunder. In the map above, on the bottom right side, we can see the horizontal lines represent the water level; the three horizontal shafts are under the water table. The water could be used as a water trap if needed.

On the authentic "Golden Lily" maps, bombs were depicted by a turtle, water traps by wavy lines, and sand and rock falls ////// for left and \\\\\ for right

The clock face shows that we have four hands, one for each tree. The central airshaft is situated in the middle of them all, represented by a black square.

The 777,000,000,000 at the bottom of the map represents 777 billion Yen. 777 or 555 figures were both lucky numbers to the Japanese. There were 175 red series maps produced by Prince Takeda's team of three cartographers. 34 of which are of major importance, with 138 of these a lesser degree.

In the late seventies, eight sites were worth in excess of $5 billion dollars each. Today it has been estimated that only one third of the 175 sites have now been recovered, leaving 116.

But the ones that are not even mentioned are the smaller treasure deposits left by renegade officers and soldiers. The estimated numbers are between 700-1200 deposits. The figure is more likely to be in the region of 1500 deposits, ranging from one small tola bar to a 200-ton deposit.

5.00 How Did The Japanese Engineers Excavate The Tunnels?

The mining engineer would be told of the type of construction that Prince Takeda would require. This may have been making existing cave or gold mines suitable to be converted into treasure vaults, or in the case of a new excavation, the planning of a central shaft would be required, and at the bottom treasure vaults would be constructed.

The treasure map would be drawn and produced using the central shaft as the "Fulcrum Point" and all measurements taken from the central point outwards. Others have stated that geographical features such as a tree or a man-made object could have been used as a reference point to which the "fulcrum point" could have been found using a basic compass and a long tape measure. (See section 5.80.)

Each clock face shown on the map indicates the exact location of this central shaft; this would require a "Start Point" as a reference point. This start point would be coded with a "start here" treasure symbol such as the number "5".
The numbers around the clock face represent the number of meters from the Reference to the central shaft.

The excavation would be carried out by three or four separate teams, which would comprise of up to thirty diggers, and experienced miners, supervised by two Japanese engineers.

The men would either be "Makipilis" Filipino collaborators, or a team of Koreans, Taiwanese, Chinese, English or American prisoners of war. Each team was kept physically separate on treasure sites for security purposes. If two teams did work together, it was made sure that both teams could not communicate with each other simply because of forced separation or basic language barriers were used to aid secrecy.

The excavation of tunnels and shafts would be dug in stages. For example the first 10 meters would be dug by team "one" over a twelve hour period, then they would leave and team "two" would carry on with the next 10 meters, and so on until all of the tunnels and shafts were finished. Each team may only visit the treasure site once, and then be moved to another site many miles away to help excavate another tunnel or shaft elsewhere.

The maximum depth of an Imperial site excavation was 315 feet; others were shallower.

Once the digging was complete, the diggers would leave the site and a Japanese civilian construction crew employed by Matagumi Kaisha would be instructed to build the concrete tunnel network underground to exact engineering construction plans, supplied by Prince Chichibu and his military engineering team.

This civilian crew would then leave the site once the tunnels were completed and before any treasure was deposited inside. This team of tunnel constructors would then move to another site and start this process all over again.

In the case of the "Makipilis", they were known to have re-visited the same sites at different stages of construction. At the final stages of completion, when all of the gold, gems and religious artifacts were stored safely in cemented vaults deep underground, all who had been involved in the construction were asked to go into these treasure vaults for various reasons.

This included the Japanese Engineers, Japanese soldiers, and the prisoners of war. Usually the total would be between 200-260 men. The order would be given by Prince Takeda to dynamite the entrances shut, murdering all inside.

The layout of the treasure site would have depended upon the contours of the land, and its topography, geographic features such as hills, mountains, natural cave systems, limestone, chalk, rivers, ancient monuments, churches, trees, natural large rocks, military bases, road, and railway transport to and from the site were all taken into consideration.

The treasure site needed to have at least two major landmarks that could be used for reference purposes once the tunnel system was finished and filled with treasure.

5.10   Imperial Treasure Vault Construction

Once the treasure vault was completed, the tunnels would be backfilled using a combination of clay and very fine sand. In many cases cyanide glass capsules would be mixed with the backfill, and poison powder sprinkled on the gold bars. If the tunnels were later excavated, the backfill would cause the tunnel to collapse as the fine sand dried out and leaked out between the heavier clay.

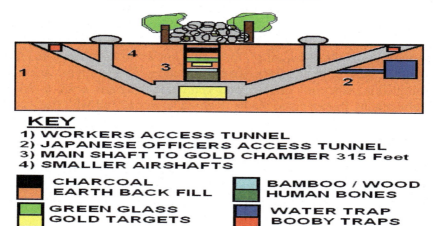

This is exactly what happened at Fort Bonifacio when Robert Curtis and Charles C. McDougald and Filipino diggers tried to excavate backfilled rooms inside the Bastion to recover gold.

The tunnel was dug through thick layers of viscous clay, which had been sandwiched with brown sand about twenty-five centimeters thick. Once this sand dried out it would trickle down the walls onto the floor, making cavities between the thick layers of clay.

The sheer weight of the clay on top of the tunnel would be *displaced* and result in a tunnel collapse. This is exactly what happened, crushing a young Filipino digger.

(Ref: Asian Loot by Charles C. McDougald: Page 198).

Backfill From The Bottom Up

The main airshaft was 312 feet deep (96 meters) and was also backfilled in quite a different way to that of the tunnels that were connected to it. The Japanese would use this shaft to access the gold in the future; it would have been backfilled in a completely different way to tunnels 1 & 2 shown in the diagram. **Note:** Robert Curtis stated that there were only two Imperial land sites where the depth of the main chamber would be found at 312 feet. All of the Imperial sites had treasure hoards buried at varying depths less than this depth.

The bottom of the shaft, the "roof of the chamber", would either be constructed of reinforced concrete, which had an access hole which was made of heavy wooden railway sleepers, or completely made of railway sleepers supported by reinforced concrete pillars standing on a concrete floor some 10-14 inches thick.

On the top of this "roof" were human bones to deter the faint-hearted. The next layer would be bamboo or a hard wood layer; the next level would include a small giveaway consisting of say 10-20 gold bars.

The idea being that the treasure hunter would find this small deposit and walk away, not realizing that the main treasure lay some 89 meters below. Above this would be a treasure marker indicating "treasure below"; a mark on a small stone or a pyramid-shaped stone.

Above this, broken green glass or blue broken ceramic pottery backfill to keep the treasure hunter on the right track and then near the top a layer of charcoal, and then on top of this more soil or clay backfill again.

The sequence in which these layers were placed seemed to differ from site to site. Some main airshafts would be blocked with a large boulder at 7 meters down, making life for the recovery diggers even harder.

5.20 Why Were The Imperial Sites Dug In This Manner?

A central shaft leaves no impression in the ground a tell-tale sign that something had been buried.

It is only when after say thirty+ years, when the earth has settled, that a sink hole or a depression appears in the ground, helping you, the treasure hunter, reveal where the central shaft is located. These sites had to be secretly excavated in such a way so that the many tons of soil extracted by the diggers had to be used to landscape the surrounding area, where Papaya or mango trees could be planted to disguise the fact that a Japanese Imperial treasure vault lay deep under the ground close by.

Once hostilities ended, and when the political situation was safe for subsequent recovery, then the retrieval of treasure would have begun, aided by the "red series" of Imperial maps, as seen in section 4.60.

How To Find The Approximate Distance To The Service Shafts Leading To The Central Treasure Vault

As previously described in section 5.10, we will assume that you have found the central shaft AC.

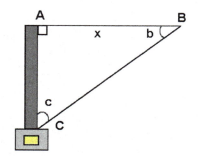

Now we need to find the location of the service tunnels that are situated at a distance AB in line with the treasure vault below on angle B shown in the diagram opposite.

NOTE: B will be the entrance to the tunnel itself.

Assumptions Made

We must assume that the gradient angle B will be very small to allow people to transport earth out of the sites and carry equipment and gold down to the vault. A steep angle would make excavations very difficult.

For this example we will assume that the values of angle B are:

i) 10 ii) 12 iii) 15 degrees.

And assume the depth of the central shaft AC is either:

iv) 150 feet or v) 312 feet.

Note:
In a right-angled triangle we know that all angles must add up to 180 degrees.

Using basic trigonometry to find the length AB (x) = Tangent of angle C = Opposite / Adjacent

For Example 1: B = 10 degrees, AC = 150 feet and C = 80 degrees

Therefore: Tan C = AB/ 150 = Tan 80 = AB/ 150.

Therefore AB (x) = Tan 80 x 150

So: AB(x) = 5.6712 x 150 = **850. 69 feet**

(So 850.69 feet is the distance from the central shaft to the entrance of the service tunnel at point B)

Table A

AC (value in feet)	Angle B (degrees)	Angle C (degrees)	Calculated AB(x)
150	10	80	**850.69 feet**
150	12	78	**705.69 feet**
150	15	75	**559.80 feet**
312	10	80	**1769.43 feet**
312	12	78	**1467.84 feet**
312	15	75	**1164.39 feet**

Now you measure this distance from the main central shaft in compass directions North, South, East, & West. If nothing is found try directions NE, SE, SW, & NW until you find a depression in the soil or a pile of boulders or large old tree marking the location(s) of the tunnel entrance B.

The distances to these tunnel entrances leading to the central shaft will vary as the angle of B increases as the angle of C decreases.

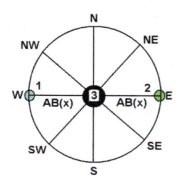

Left is shown the directions in which the entrances to the main treasure vault will be located. The outer circle represents the calculated AB(x) radius value shown in Table A above.

Key

1 Possible location of service tunnel leading to the treasure vault
2 Possible location of Officers tunnel leading to the treasure vault
3 Main vertical shaft leading directly to the treasure vault

5.30   Teresa 2: Imperial Site # 5

One of these Imperial treasure sites is situated southeast of Manila in a small town called Teresa, Rizal at GPS location: 14° 34′01.08" North and 121° 12′00.37" East. In 1942-3, very near to a Japanese army camp, Imperial treasure site number 4 and 5 would be constructed. These sites would be known as Teresa 1 and Teresa 2. (See below: the increase in open cast mining activity recently in this area can clearly be seen in the photograph below. Ask yourself: why would this be?)

According to a *Mikaplis* called Pol who worked on the construction of Teresa 2, Prince Chichibu ordered that a giant hole be excavated measuring two football pitches in length and width. This massive rectangular hole was dug by slave labour to a depth of 50 meters, the base of which would have a concrete base 2 meters in depth. Once this was completed by the 250 American, Filipino and Australian POWs, work began on constructing the massive tunnels using reinforced concrete and supervised by Japanese military mining engineers. Teresa 2 was going to look like a giant stick man with no head under the ground.

The main tunnel would be 300 meters long and each end had antlers branching off and each end measured 100 meters long, and the tunnels were to be 12 meters in height.

The treasure map that was drawn for this site states that the values of the gold bullion, gold Buddhas was 777,000,000,000 Yen in 1940's gold bullion value of approximately $34.50 a troy ounce.

In 1943 a convoy of six trucks arrived at Teresa 2 full of several hundreds of small boxes presumably packed with gold bars of unknown size and weight. These were carried down into the finished tunnel system by the forced labour consisting of POWs, together with jars of gems, barrels of diamonds, three very large golden Buddhas and last but not least trucks loaded with larger-sized gold bullion. This site was protected by at least two 1000lb Ariel bombs set with pressure switches primed to go off if the top of the main vent shaft concrete seal was broken or if the trucks laden with gold were moved out of the treasure vault into one of the exit tunnels.

Teresa 2 Excavation

After many months of digging, on the 6th of July 1974, Robert Curtis and many soldiers digging under the orders of General Ver managed to open up part of this site by finding one of three air shafts that fed fresh air into the main tunnel system, and the two tunnel branches that fed off at either end. This enabled Curtis to locate some of the gold-laden trucks for the late President Marcos.

5.40 Teresa 2: Imperial Treasure Site Map # 5 (1943)

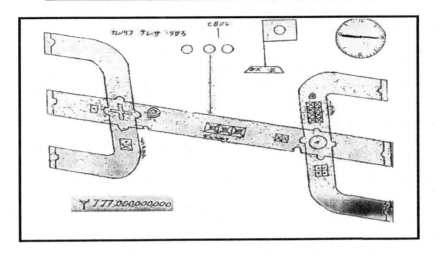

I have redrawn this old treasure map to explain more clearly what treasures were buried inside Teresa 2 during 1942, known as one of many 777 Imperial sites.

5.50   Teresa 2: The Buried Hoard Explained

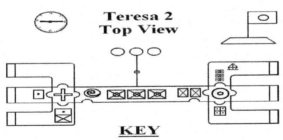

KEY

- ⊡ **Boxes of gold bullion**   ⊠ **Solid gold Buddha**
- ▨ **Gold and diamonds**   ⊠ **Jars of gems**
- ◉ **Spiral staircase**   ○ **Main air vents**
- ⊞ **Trucks full of gold bars**
- ▦ **Drums of diamonds**   ◉ **Millstone**

5.60 Teresa 2: Top And Side View Detail

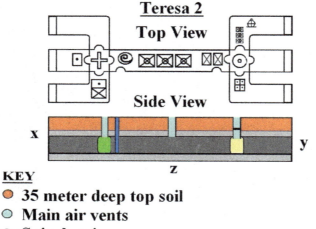

KEY
- 35 meter deep top soil
- Main air vents
- Spiral staircase
- 2+ meter thick wall
- Main tunnel
- Side tunnel "A"
- Side tunnel "B"

Dimensions
x: 50 meters deep
y: 12 meters high
z: 300 meters long

Above we can see the top and side view of the tunnel layouts and the extraordinary effort it must have taken to construct using basic hand tools and forced labour over many months between 1942-3. It seems that only the left side of this drawing was excavated by Curtis, and the jars of gems, solid gold Buddha's, drums of diamonds are still awaiting discovery.

If the right side was excavated by finding the main ventilation shaft, then logically access to the left side of this site can be achieved by finding the left main ventilation shaft that was used to supply fresh air to this part of the tunnel system. This would be quite a challenge today to a modern treasure hunter, but not an impossible task.

Remember it took an army of men to place the treasure hoard inside this massive concrete vault in the 1940s, and will take an army using modern excavation equipment today to get it safely out.

5.70 Teresa 2: How The Site Was Excavated In 1973

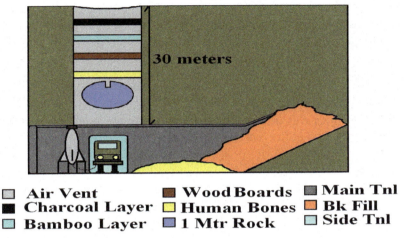

Teresa 2 Main Air Shaft (Side View)

☐ Air Vent   ■ Wood Boards   ■ Main Tnl
■ Charcoal Layer   ☐ Human Bones   ■ Bk Fill
☐ Bamboo Layer   ☐ 1 Mtr Rock   ☐ Side Tnl

As previously mentioned, Robert Curtis managed to gain access into the main tunnel system via one of three main air ventilation shafts that fed air into the tunnels for the POWs to breathe as they worked underground.

At 3 meters the diggers in 1973 encountered a layer of charcoal, at 6 meters a layer of bamboo, at 9 meters a layer of wooden planks that crisscrossed the air shaft.

When they had reached 12 meters they found a layer of human bones. Two more layers were found of varying material types like broken crockery, until at 25 meters the diggers found the 1 meter round rock (mill stone) with an 8cm hole drilled in the top.

This was the most positive sign yet that they were getting close to the buried treasure beneath. They continued to dig another 5 meters below this rock, when at last they reached the top of the tunnel roof.

On the 8th of June after months of digging the Curtis and Marco's team broke through the ceiling of the main tunnel. Within seconds a terrible smell escaped into the air shaft making the diggers sick; some came out with horrible boils over their bodies. The methane and stench from the poor POW's rotting bodies murdered by the Japanese military in 1943 was now threatening to kill the digging team inside the excavated air shaft.

Many were hospitalized for days afterwards. Work had to stop so that the gases could escape naturally into the air for many days afterwards. When digging resumed a large pile of human remains was discovered.

On the 6th of July 1974, diggers found a metal cable and a long metal object. On later inspection Curtis confirmed that the metal cable was connected to one of the 1000lb Ariel bombs protecting the site, and the long metal object was in fact the fender to one of the trucks storing gold bars on its flat bed at the rear of one of the side tunnels.

According to Charles C. McDougald in his book *Asian Loot*, President Marcos only managed to recover a small amount of gold bullion from Teresa 2. This gold would have been taken from the Japanese Isuzu Type 94 six-wheeled transport trucks stored in one of the side tunnels leading off the main tunnel, as shown in my diagram above. Each vehicle had the carrying capacity of 1.5 tons of gold. In section 19 I have included a photograph of this type of vehicle.

It is also noted that Robert Curtis did not manage to excavate Teresa 1 simply because of depth and its engineering complexity. The **GOLD** is still there but for how long?

Could this be why there is so much quarry excavation activity around Teresa in 2011? See section 5.30: the GPS photograph clearly shows four quarries being excavated in this area. Quarrying is a good *"cover story"* to hide behind secret treasure hunting activities and have been used many times in the past by groups to hide illegal digging and retrieval of gold bullion. These quarries may be genuine, but it is very odd to have four large pits situated in an area where there are **_known_** to be two large Imperial treasure sites situated close to these actual quarry sites.

5.80 A Basic Japanese Treasure Map Explained

The clock face was used by the map cartographer to record the exact positions of buried treasure, as previously mentioned. In this particular case we have four separate hoards buried at four different compass locations from a centralized reference point.

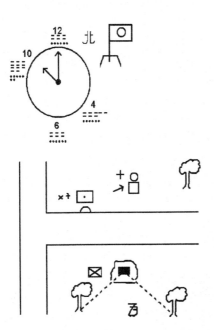

The reference point on this map above is shown as a black rectangle, making the tip of a triangle between two trees, as shown in the diagram above. This is our starting position from where we will take all our compass bearings and distances from. The centre of the clock face shown as a black dot must be placed in the centre of the reference point in order to track the exact locations of our treasure. This central point on the clock face is sometimes referred to as the "fulcrum point". In some cases, larger Imperial treasure maps show the black rectangle as the main central shaft leading down to the treasure vaults far below. In our example, the black rectangle is our reference point and matches with the centre of the clock face, the "fulcrum point". The Japanese flag is flying to the right of picture, meaning that this map must be read as it is. If, however, the flag was flying in the opposite direction, then the map must be read using a mirror in order to create a mirror image and read in this manner. In our case the clock face is showing the exact locations of where the treasure has been buried as shown on our treasure map.

Let us look at the clock diagram itself; we can see that the big hand is pointing to the 12 o'clock position, indicating "north". The reason I say north is that we have the Japanese sign of a two "T"s, the standard

Japanese sign for "north". In this case we will assume that this is compass north and not magnetic north.

The small hand is pointing to the 10 o'clock position, indicating that the compass readings distances and depths should start at 10 o'clock and be read in an anticlockwise direction to that of a conventional clock. If, however, the smaller hand was pointing to the 3 o'clock position, then the clock would be read in the conventional way: clockwise.

The clock is telling us that there are four separate treasure deposits buried at the 10 o'clock, 6 o'clock, 4 o'clock and 12 o'clock positions.

What Does This Mean?

These numbers will now correspond to standard compass bearings shown in degrees.
Each compass is made up of 360 degrees, and if we superimpose our clock face onto the compass we will see that each clock position is 30 degrees, therefore 1 o'clock is equivalent to 30 degrees, 3 o'clock is 90 degrees and so on.
In this case we will use a photograph of an old Japanese WWII compass to explain the following points:

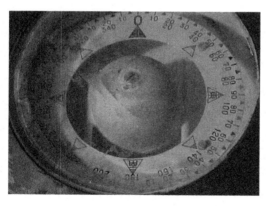

We can see now that the clock positions relate to the following clock numbers, namely:

12 o'clock is 0 degrees or 360 degrees, 10 o'clock is 270 degrees, 6 o'clock is 180 degrees and 4 o'clock is 120 degrees.
North is shown at 0 degrees, East at 90 degrees, South at 180 degrees and West at 270 degrees. The scaling on this particular Japanese Naval compass is a little confusing, but is to be used for illustration purposes in order to show that the Imperial forces used compasses very similar to allied forces at this time.

5.90 The Clock Face Reveals Its Secret

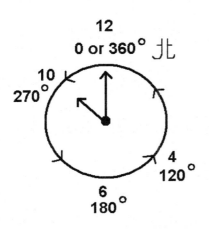

The positioning of the clock hands is very important in determining the way the burial locations have been laid out on our "treasure site". The small hand is to the left of the big hand, signifying that the compass directions must be read in an anticlockwise direction.

If the small hand was shown on the right of the big hand, then the compass directions must be read in a clockwise direction.

The first compass location will be at 10 o'clock not at 12 o'clock. Why? Because the *anticlockwise rule* stated previously applies.

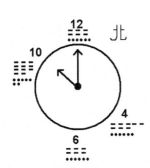

≡≡≡ Each Dash = 1 Meter Distance
••••• Each Dot = 1 Meter Deep

Here we see that the clock positions 12, 10, 6, and 4 have a series of dashes and dots by the side of them. These relate to the distances each treasure deposit is located from each other, and the depth in which the hoard will be found. We know that during the 1940s that the Japanese used the metric measurements when it came to map reading as this following passage explains, taken from the U.S. military archives from the time:

6.00 Treasure And Compass Map Layout Explained

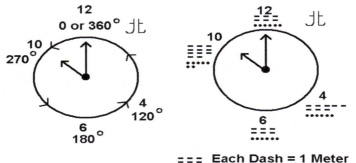

≡≡≡ Each Dash = 1 Meter
∙∙∙∙∙∙ Each Dot = 1 Meter Deep

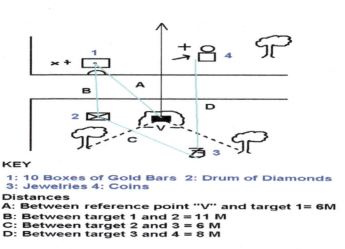

KEY
1: 10 Boxes of Gold Bars 2: Drum of Diamonds
3: Jewelries 4: Coins
Distances
A: Between reference point "V" and target 1= 6M
B: Between target 1 and 2 = 11 M
C: Between target 2 and 3 = 6 M
D: Between target 3 and 4 = 8 M

The light blue line signifies the compass directions. Target 1 is buried at a depth of 6 meters. (Data is taken from the 12 o'clock position and **not** the 10 o'clock position.) This is same for distance as shown in the diagram above. This was to confuse the enemy.

At target 1: The depth of the ten boxes of buried gold bars will be found at a depth of 6 meters.
At target 2: The depth of the drum of diamonds will be found at a depth of 7 meters.
At target 3: The depth of a box of jewels will be found at a depth of 6 meters.

At target 4: The depth of a barrel of coins will be found at a depth of 6 meters.

It is interesting to note that target one can also be reached by a tunnel system shown on the map as a half a semi-circle. Small treasure deposits were buried at depths of between 1-15 meters. The larger the deposit, the deeper the target would have been buried and protected by a series of booby traps.

Note: Reference point "V" is a large rock and further measurements have been taken and recorded between the two large trees shown on each side of the rock. Each dash represents 1 meter measured distance.

The reference point would be a structure or a geographical feature that would not be able to be moved or relocated over a period of time or destroyed by a counter-attack by Allied forces. These reference points would include prominent buildings such as cathedrals, churches, schools, road, and railway bridges.

Geographical reference point features like large rivers, large trees, waterfalls, main cross roads, railway intersections, large rocks, small and large mountain tops or unusual features that stick out on the skyline and are easy to find at a later date. Large trees would have been used if deemed that they were not susceptible to earthquake damage in future times, thus aiding subsequent recovery.

Major or minor treasure sites depended on the suitability, concealment, permanency and location of man-made, built-up areas, as I have previously stated. Mountainous and or rolling hills, terrain with creeks, rivers, dams, big acacia, mango, camachile or duhat trees were used as reference points for future retrieval of said treasure deposits.

6.10   **Clock Face Examples**

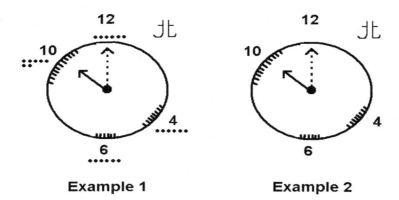

      Example 1   **Example 2**

Example 1: Shows the large hand is shown with six dashes where six dashes represent 6 meters as in our previous treasure map. The remaining distances are shown as dashes around the inner face of the clock.

Example 2: Is the same layout as Example 1, but without the depths being shown at each treasure location.

Note: These examples are not a definitive list of all the various clock faces used by the map cartographers, but they give you, the reader, an idea of how the clock face was laid out and how to go about reading its hidden secrets.

6.20   Lucky Japanese Symbols

In this part of the book we will explore Japanese symbolism in order to understand how the Japanese thought process worked, both militarily and spiritually, at this period of history. These symbols are found to some degree on Imperial treasure maps and convey marker directions and the importance of the buried treasure site.

Therefore it is important to understand why certain symbols were used and by whom, and the message they convey to you, the treasure hunter. In this section we are looking at Japanese symbols that are considered "lucky" to the Japanese people and their ancient culture.

The Japanese have lucky symbols that are maybe found in places where you would not expect any treasure to be hidden; it is therefore important to recognise these symbols and always be aware that they could have been used as pointers or markers before a known treasure symbol or target is found and recovered.

Lucky Japanese Symbols

BAMBOO

In eastern Asia it is thought to bring good luck, and was planted by the Japanese forces to be used for Nipa huts and defensive bunker buildings, and water irrigation; hollow bamboo makes an excellent water pipe and in some cases as a food source. The soldiers ate the edible bamboo shoots, which were sliced and boiled in coconut milk.

Treasure has been found underneath Bamboo trees; Golden Bamboo has links with Buddhism, and in Toa-ism the plants growth rings represent individual steps of spiritual development. Therefore, Buddhas are usually found buried between the trees or very near to them.

The Japanese buried many items under bamboo; the roots of the bamboo act as a cage, sealing around the treasure making it harder to recover, and the female Black Cobra makes her nest in the fallen leaves and her offspring wait for the unwary treasure hunter. The babies will bite and inject all of their poison into you so be aware under bamboo leaves, especially when the cobra are rearing their young.

Bamboo is the fastest-growing plant on Earth; it has been measured surging skyward as fast as 121 cm or (47.6 inches) in a twenty-four-hour period.

THE CHRYSANTHEMUM

In Japan and in China, the Chrysanthemum is a symbol of happiness and long life; this is because of the "ray-shaped petal arrangement" is also a symbol of the sun. This symbol can be found near to large Imperial burial sites, and the Chrysanthemum is the emblem of the Japanese Imperial House.

CHERRY BLOSSOM (*SAKURA*)

A symbol of purity, beauty and of "good fortune" in Japanese culture, a cherry blossom carried away by the wind is a symbol of an ideal death, since cherry blossoms bloom for a short while and quickly fade away, like humanity. The cherry blossom was used as a symbol by the Samurai, who were always ready to die for their lords and masters.

Note: The pink colour of the cherry blossom was used to identify treasure targets; this light pink or cherry pink colour is mixed with cement and moulded into heart-shaped rocks hiding gold bars either inside or close by. The pink colour is a very good treasure sign. Please see Heart Symbols and examples of pink cement photos on a later page of this book.

THE DRAGON

In China and in Japan the dragon is revered as something that brings good luck and wards off evil spirits and demons. Also, the dragon is closely associated with water powers and the *YIN* principle.

THE FROG

The frog is closely associated with rain and water. In Japan, the frog was thought by many to be an auger of good luck. The rock shaped liked a frog will be found near water, either a spring, a man-made lake, pond, river or stream. These rock shapes and symbols are usually markers and pointers to the deposit; the nose of the frog points towards to treasure.

Rocks that are shaped like the backs of frogs, and have indentations similar to that shown in the photograph below, must be viewed as a good treasure sign. Usually three holes are drilled in the frogs back shown in the shape of a triangle meaning: the treasure is buried in water, or near a triangle of rocks or trees. Another code states: "On the spring or near to a creek".

6.30   **SAKURA MUSIC AND WORDS**

The Words

Sakura Sakura - Cherry Blossom Song:

Sakura ...... sakura .... noyamamo satomo

Miwatasu kagiri

Kasumi-ka kumo-ka .... asahi-ni niou

Sakura .... Sakura..... Hanazakari

English translation of the Cherry Blossom Song:

Cherry blossoms, cherry blossoms. On mountains, in villages.

As far as you can see.

They look like fog or clouds. They are fragrant in the morning sun.

Cherry blossoms, cherry blossoms. In full bloom.

It is said that Prince Takeda was always humming this song to himself as he visited the many Imperial treasure sites throughout the Philippines during the Second World War.

6.40 Japanese Writing Explained

Kung Who?

Before I start this section I want to make it very clear that there is no such thing as *"KUNG"* symbols or script! This term was made up by the late Robert Curtis to convince other treasure hunters he worked with, into believing that only he knew what the treasures symbols meant on the Imperial maps in his possession.

He claimed wrongly that Kung was a script that was over two thousand years old and only known by certain Japanese Shinto priests during the Second World War.

I spent months researching for such an ancient language simply because of this man's false statement. Kung symbols have never been used as treasure codes or indeed exist as a secret language either on Imperial treasure maps written by the Japanese code writers, or used in any of the treasure codes researched in this book.

The oldest written Japanese language dates back to 712 A.D. and includes Chinese characters, and modern Japanese writing stems from the Meiji (1868-1912) a period spanning only 44 years, when the Japanese had formed a uniform standard language to follow, as stated by Charles C. Mc Dougald in his book "Asian Loot" (see page 186).

Charles knew Robert Curtis very well and worked with Curtis on imperial treasure sites at Fort Santiago, and smaller sites on Corregidor such as the old theatre site.

6.50 Japanese Writing: A Brief History

In order to identify which symbol shape belongs to which nation, I have included in this section a brief history about Japanese writing symbols in order for the treasure hunter to be able to identify and understand what Japanese writing looks like, and to have a basic understanding of how Japanese words are created. In this way, the treasure hunter will be able to identify:

1) *Hiragana*: *"The Phonetic Alphabetic"*   2) *Katakana*: Script
3) *Kanji*: Symbols

HISTORY

Chinese symbols first came to Japan on products imported from mainland, China; an early instance of such an import was a gold seal given by the emperor of the Eastern Han Dynasty in 57 AD. It is not clear when Japanese people started to gain a command of by themselves, but the first Japanese documents were probably written by Chinese immigrants.

It is known that the diplomatic correspondence from King Bu of Wa to Emperor Shun of the Liu Song Dynasty in 478 has been praised for its skillful use of allusion. Later, groups of people called *fuhito* were organized under the monarch to read and write Classical Chinese. From the 6th century onwards, Chinese documents written in Japan tended to show interference from Japanese, suggesting the wide acceptance of Chinese characters in Japan.

The Japanese language itself had no written form at the time kanji was introduced; originally texts were written in the Chinese language and would have been read as such. Over time, however, a system known as *kanbun* emerged, which involved using Chinese text with diacritical marks to allow Japanese speakers to restructure and read Chinese sentences by changing the word order and by adding particles and verb endings in accordance with the rules of Japanese structured grammar.

Chinese characters also came to be used to write Japanese words, resulting in the modern *kana* syllabaries. A writing system called *man'yōgana* (used in the ancient poetry anthology *Man'yōshū*) evolved that used a limited set of Chinese characters for their sound, rather than for their meaning. Man'yōgana written in a *cursive style* became *hiragana*, a writing system that was accessible to women (who were denied higher education at the time).

Major works of *Heian era literature* by women were written in hiragana. *Katakana* emerged via a parallel path, when monastery monks simplified *man'yōgana* to a single constituent element. Therefore over time the two writing script systems *hiragana* and *katakana*, referred to collectively as *kana*, are actually descended from ancient *kanji*.

6.60   Hiragana Script

The main Japanese symbols that interest us are the two Japanese phonetic writing symbols that are cursive in shape called *hiragana*, and the angular shaped symbols called *katakana*. *Hiragana* is used for prefixes and suffixes to be added to the Chinese characters called *kanji* and used for purely Japanese words and sentences. *Katakana* is used for words of foreign origin and will be found on official Japanese documents.

Here is a chart of 46 *Hiragana* symbols; *Hiragana* is "*The Phonetic Alphabetic*", which means each *Hiragana* character is a sound character, and each character shown is separated into 46 different sounds. The chart starts with the normal vowel sounds we all recognize: a, i, u, e, o and ends with Wa, Wo, and N.

6.70 **Hiragana Script Symbols**

あ	い	う	え	お
A	I	U	E	O
か	き	く	け	こ
KA	KI	KU	KE	KO
さ	し	す	せ	そ
SA	SHI	SU	SE	SO
た	ち	つ	て	と
TA	CHI	TU	TE	TO
な	に	ぬ	ね	の
NA	NI	NU	NE	NO
は	ひ	ふ	へ	ほ
HA	HI	FU	HE	HO
ま	み	む	め	も
MA	MI	MU	ME	MO
や		ゆ		よ
YA		YU		YO
ら	り	る	れ	ろ
RA	RI	RU	RE	RO
わ		を		ん
WA		WO		N

6.80 Katakana Script Symbols

There are basically 45 *Katakana* characters. Not 46. Unlike *Hiragana* script, there is no WO character with the *Katakana* scripts.

ア	イ	ウ	エ	オ
a	i	u	e	o
カ	キ	ク	ケ	コ
ka	ki	ku	ke	ok
サ	シ	ス	セ	ソ
sa	shi	su	se	so
タ	チ	ツ	テ	ト
ta	chi	tsu	te	to
ナ	ニ	ヌ	ネ	ノ
na	ni	nu	ne	no
ハ	ヒ	フ	ヘ	ホ
ha	hi	fu	he	ho
マ	ミ	ム	メ	モ
ma	mi	mu	me	mo
ヤ		ユ		ヨ
ya		yu		yo
ラ	リ	ル	レ	ロ
ra	ri	ru	re	ro
ワ				ン
wa				n

Hiranga And Katakana Word Examples

Examples of both Hiranaga and Katakana writings:

The word "Sakura", meaning cherry blossom is shown below using *hiranaga* symbols in Example 1. And *katakana* symbols in Example 2.

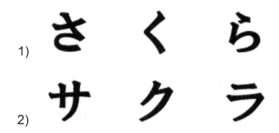

1)
2)

Here the Japanese word for treasure, "Takara", is shown below using *hiranaga,* and *katakana* script.

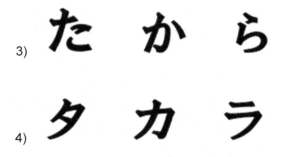

3)
4)

Kanji Treasure Symbols

Kanji symbol for "Treasure"
"Takara"

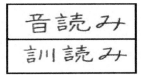

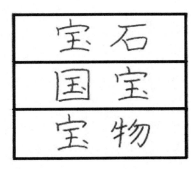

"Houseki"- Gem or Jewel

"Kokuhou"- National Treasure

"Takaramono"- Treasure

Now we look to see if there is an equivalent for the *kanji* treasure symbols shown on the previous page, using both *hiragana* and *katakana* script by breaking down each Japanese word.

The first word is Houseki, which will be broken down as: "ho", then the vowel "u", two letters "se", and finally "ki", as shown, the first is *hiragana*, the second using *katakana* script shown below:

"Ho" "u" "se" "ki"

Using the same technique "Kokuhou" and "Takaramono" written using *hiragana* script, will look like this;

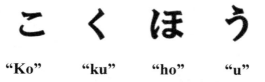

"Ko" "ku" "ho" "u"

Note: There is no *katakana* script for the Japanese word "kokuhou" (national treasure).

Below we have *hiragana* and *katagana* script for the Japanese word for treasure.

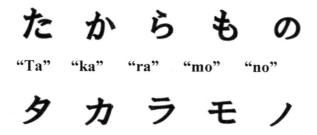

"Ta" "ka" "ra" "mo" "no"

Now the treasure hunter should be able to identify hiragana, katagana, and kanji writing when found on potential treasure sites and treasure maps.

6.90 The Japanese Calendar Used During WWII.

The Japanese have had three Imperial reigns, these are:

The Meiji Era (1868-1912)
The Taisho Era (1912-1926)
The Showa Era (1926-1989)

The war years we are interested in includes the periods between: 3rd September 1939 to the 14th August 1945, during the time Hirohito was the Emperor; "The Showa Era", the so called "Enlightened Peace".

The Japanese monthly calendar, like the western version, starts in January as the 1st month and ends in December on the 12th month.

Hirohito's reign, "The Showa Era", started when Hirohito ascended to the *Imperial Chrysanthemum Throne* in the year 1926.

Therefore, in order to know the "Showa" year, we *add one* onto the year 1925, therefore:

1926=1 1927=2 1928=3 1929=4 1930=5 1931=6 1932=7 1933=8 1934=9 1935=10 1936=11 1937=12 1938=13 **1939=14 1940=15 1941=16 1942=17 1943=18 1944=19 1945=20**

Therefore the date 27th December 1941 will be 27/12/41 in English or 12/27/41 in the U.S. or in Japanese it would appear on official Japanese documents as: **16/12/27**.
Completely different to what we in the west would expect.

This could be very helpful when we as treasure hunters find old Japanese maps with dates that are hard to decipher, but now knowing the above information we can verify that the map or documents are indeed genuine and were possibly written during the Japanese "Showa Era" years 14-20 (1939-1945).

7.00 Basic Japanese Numbers

Kanji	Number	Reading	Alt. reading
〇	0	zero, maru	
一	1	ichi	hitotsu
二	2	ni	futatsu
三	3	san	mittsu
四	4	shi, yon	yottsu
五	5	go	itsutsu
六	6	roku	muttsu
七	7	shichi	nanatsu
八	8	hachi	yattsu
九	9	kyuu	kokonotsu
十	10	juu	too
百	100	hyaku	
千	1,000	sen	
万	10,000	man	
億	100,000,000	oku	

Examples:

四十九	49	(yonjuukyuu)
一百十二	112	(ippyakujuuni)
千三百八十六	1,386	(sensanbyakuhachijuuroku)

Japanese numbers can be written in the usual English way of counting 0-9, which is more often used when writing horizontally. Or using Kanji 0-9, which is more often used when writing numbers vertically.

When using kanji to write down numbers, a positional system is employed. For example, 25 is written "two ten five", 1246 is "thousand two hundred four ten six". Note that there is a character and word for 10,000 (man), but not for a million. To say a million, you have to say "one hundred ten-thousand".

7.10 The Lucky Seven Gods Of Japanese Mythology

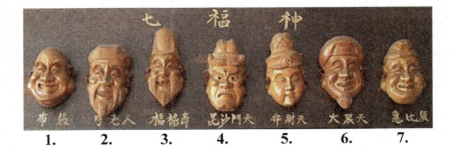

1.　　2.　　3.　　4.　　5.　　6.　　7.

七福神 *Shichi Fukujin* refer to the seven gods of good fortune in Japanese mythology and folklore. They are often the subject of netsuke carvings and other Japanese representations.

Each God has the following traditional attributes:

Hotei: The fat and happy god of abundance and good health.

Jurōjin: The god of longevity.

Fukurokuju: The god of happiness, wealth and longevity.

Bishamonten: The god of warriors.

Benzaiten: (Benten-sama) The goddess of knowledge, art, music and beauty.

Daikokuten: (Daikoku) The god of wealth, commerce and trade.
Ebisu: The god of fishers or merchants, often depicted carrying a sea bream.

Many figures in Japanese myth were transferred from Chinese origins (some having entered China from India), including all of the Seven Lucky Gods, except **Ebisu**. Another god, **Kichijōten**, goddess of happiness, is sometimes found depicted along with the seven traditional gods, replacing **Jurōjin**, the reasoning being that **Jurōjin** and **Fukurokuju** were originally manifestations of the same *Taoist* deity, the Southern Star. However, as is often the case in folklore, Japanese gods sometimes represent different things in different places.

The seven gods are often depicted on their ship, the *Takarabune* (宝船), or **"Treasure Ship".** The tradition holds that the seven gods will arrive in town in the New Year and distribute fantastic gifts to worthy people. Children often receive red envelopes emblazoned with the Takarabune, which contain gifts of money. The *Takarabune* and its passengers are often depicted in art in varied locations, from the walls of museums and art galleries.

Q: Why Are These Seven Gods Important To Treasure Hunting Activities?

The Seven gods are important in understanding references to the lucky number "7" and to references of good fortune and wealth.

Note that the gods: ***Hotei, Fukurokuju, Daikokuten*** (Daikoku), are recognized as gods of ***abundance, wealth, and happiness.***

All of which could have been used in name or in Kanji symbol form to convey references to buried wealth by code writers that Japanese people would instantly recognize as a special treasure hunting code or secret reference to buried treasure. This code could be applied to very large and small amounts of hidden loot buried by the Imperial Japanese Army and also by renegade soldiers during WWII.

The seven gods are often depicted on their ship, the Takarabune (宝船), or **"Treasure Ship".** Again important reference to a treasure ship, the Kanji Symbols for the Takarabune (宝船) could have been used to mark the location of sunken treasure ships around the Philippine Islands on Imperial Japanese water site treasure maps. As *treasure hunters* we must have open minds and assume that these lucky gods and the Takarabune may have been used in a *symbolic way* to point the way to hidden treasure deposits both on land and under the water.

As we will see on the following page, the number "7" has been used by Japanese code writers to convey buried gold on land and water and to also make us aware of dangerous poisonous chemicals.

7.20   ## The No. 7 Treasure Symbols

7✗ Deposit Down

7̄3 Treasure Poisonous Chemical Elements

733 No Of Boxes Poisonous Chemicals

7✵ Buried Gold

7̄0 In Slope or Cave

7M Treasure Under Water

7K Boxes of Gold

7.30 Korean Writing

한글자모 / 조선글

Some treasure hunters say that the writing they have found is a code written using Korean writing. We will look briefly at the shapes of each character and how it differs to that of Japanese hiragana, katakana and kanji writings.

A Brief History

Chinese writing has been known in Korea for over 2,000 years. It was used widely during the Chinese occupation of northern Korea from 108 BC to 313 AD. By the 5th century AD, the Koreans were starting to write in Classical Chinese – the earliest known example of this dated from 414 AD. Three different systems were devised for writing Korean with Chinese characters: **Hyangchal, Gukyeol** and *Idu*. These systems were similar to those developed in Japan.

The *Idu* system used a combination of Chinese characters together with special symbols to indicate Korean verb endings and other grammatical markers, and was used in official and private documents, similar to that of using **Katakana** in the Japanese writing system. The *Hyangchal* system used Chinese characters to represent all the sounds of Korean and was used mainly to write poetry.

The official Korean alphabet was invented in 1444 and promulgated in 1446 during the reign of King Sejong (1418-1450), the fourth king of the Joseon Dynasty. The alphabet was originally called **Hunmin jeongeum**, or "The correct sounds for the instruction of the people", but has also been known as *Eonmeun* (vulgar script) and **Gukmeun** (national writing). The modern name for the alphabet, *Hangeul*, was coined by a Korean linguist called Ju Si-gyeong (1876-1914). In North Korea the alphabet is known as *josoen guel*.

The Koreans borrowed a huge number of Chinese words, gave Korean readings and meanings to some of the Chinese characters and also invented about 150 new characters, most of which are rare or used mainly for personal or place names.

The shapes of the consonants are based on the shape the mouth made when the corresponding sound is made, and the traditional direction of writing (vertically from right to left) most likely came from Chinese, as did the practice of writing syllables in blocks.

Even after the invention of the Korean alphabet, most Koreans who could write continued to write either in Classical Chinese or in Korean using the *Gukyeol* or *Idu* systems. The Korean alphabet was associated with people of low status, i.e. women, children and the uneducated.

During the 19th and 20th centuries, a mixed writing system combining Chinese characters (***Hanja***) and ***Hangeul*** became increasingly popular. Since 1945, however, the importance of Chinese characters in Korean writing has diminished significantly. Since 1949, *hanja* has not been used at all in any North Korean publications.

7.40 The Hangeul Alphabet

The Hangeul Alphabet is shown below. I have not yet come across any Korean symbols using the Hangeul alphabet. There is only one treasure code book written by a Korean code writer who was stationed in the area of Davao in Mindanao Province, where **99%** of the symbols used are geometric in nature, but this does not mean that a special "Korean Hangeul" treasure code does not exist and was used elsewhere in the Philippines, or indeed in Southeast Asia. Therefore this section may be useful to the treasure group who may discover such a code book in the future.

The Hangeul Alphabet

ㄱ	ㄲ	ㄴ	ㄷ	ㄸ	ㄹ	ㅁ	ㅂ	ㅃ
기역	쌍 기역	니은	디귿	쌍 디귿	리을	미음	비읍	쌍 비읍
giyeok	ssang giyeok	nieun	digeut	ssang digeut	rieul	mieum	bieup	ssang bieup
g, k	kk	n	d, t	tt	l	m	b, p	pp
k, g	kk	n	t, d	tt	l, r	m	p, b	pp
[k/g]	[k*]	[n]	[t/d]	[t*]	[l/r]	[m]	[p/b]	[p*]

ㅅ	ㅆ	ㅇ	ㅈ	ㅉ	ㅊ	ㅋ	ㅌ	ㅍ	ㅎ
시옷	쌍 시옷	이응	지읒	쌍 지읒	치읓	키읔	티읕	피읖	히읗
shiot	ssang shiot	ieung	jieut	ssang jieut	chieut	kiuek	tieut	pieup	hieut
s	ss	ng	j	jj	ch	k	t	p	h
s	ss	-ng	ch, j	tch	ch'	k'	t'	p'	h
[s]	[s*]	[Ø/-ŋ]	[ʧ/ʤ]	[ʧ*]	[ʧʰ]	[kʰ]	[tʰ]	[pʰ]	[h]

The double consonants marked with * are pronounced "*fortis*". There are fourteen basic consonants and ten basic vowels.

Vowels (모음/母音)

ㅏ	ㅐ	ㅑ	ㅒ	ㅓ	ㅔ	ㅕ	ㅖ	ㅗ	ㅘ	ㅙ
a	ae	ya	yae	eo	e	yeo	ye	o	wa	wae
a	ae	ya	yae	ŏ	e	yŏ	ye	o	wa	wae
[a]	[æ]	[ja]	[jæ]	[ʌ]	[e]	[jʌ]	[je]	[o]	[wa]	[wæ]

ㅚ	ㅛ	ㅜ	ㅝ	ㅞ	ㅟ	ㅠ	ㅡ	ㅢ	ㅣ
oe	yo	u	wo	we	wi	yu	eu	ui	i
oe	yo	u	wŏ	we	wi	yu	ŭ	ŭi	i
[we]	[jo]	[u]	[wʌ]	[we]	[wi]	[ju]	[ɨ]	[ɨj]	[i]

The vowels shapes are completely different to that of Japanese *katakana* and *hiragana*; they are very angular in shape, and easily recognisable as Korean writing.

Korean is a language spoken by approximately 65 million people living in South Korea, North Korea, China, Japan, Uzbekistan, Kazakhstan and Russia. The relationship between Korean and other languages is not clear, though some linguists believe it to be a member of the Altaic family of languages. Grammatically, Korean is very similar to the Japanese language, but 70% of its vocabulary comes from the Chinese influence over many centuries.

In 1938, Japan lifted its ban on foreigners serving in a "combatant" capacity, and began the ***Army Special Volunteers Act.*** This act allowed the residents of Japan's overseas territories and colonies to serve in its army, and was first enacted in ***Korea*** in 1938. The first few recruitment drives were limited in scale, with only a few hundred openings available to a relatively large number of applicants.

The scale gradually expanded in order to replenish the loss of manpower on the battlefield. In 1943 a special ***Navy Special Volunteers Program*** was established, when ***Korean nationals*** were allowed to serve in the Japanese Navy. This was in direct response to the United States entering the war on the Allies side in 1942. Korean servicemen served alongside Japanese servicemen in the Philippines. This would explain the Korean nationals' healthy interest in treasure hunting activity on the islands even today.

7.50 A Basic Tick List To Go Treasure Hunting In The Philippines

Now we come to some basic equipment that all treasure hunters need, namely:
Maps, drawings of the treasure site, live pointers and witness statements of persons alive who saw the activities of the Japanese soldiers.

1) A gridded map showing the area to be searched.
2) Philippine treasure laws and how they apply to the treasure hunter.
3) Weather window for safe recovery.
4) A valid Treasure Permit and a search and recovery agreement, signed by the landowner and yourself.
5) Basic equipment: water bottle, compass, boots, hard hat, gloves, raincoat, first aid kit, string, wellingtons.
6) Shovels and other mining tools.
7) Metal detectors and dowsing equipment.
8) Heavy machinery, such as a backhoe or an excavator.

Before you set out, you will need to have a basic search and recovery agreement with the landowner before you can do anything. Please make sure that the landowner owns the land and has a land deed showing he is named as he landowner and NOT the tenant.

If he is the tenant, then at least 75% of what is found will belong to the absent landowner, like the Philippine government, or some other department like the military.

Digging on military land is prohibited, so please do not do so for your own safety.
If you are a Filipino treasure hunter a Treasure Hunting Permit should not be a problem in acquiring from the regional Barrangay Captain or the local mayor's office.

Ensuring digger's safety is paramount and public liability and life insurance should be paid up for your team members before you start any excavations. Diggers die; it's part of the dangers of treasure hunting. Insurance helps pay for funeral costs and looking after the family that will be left without a future income.

7.60 Some Of The Relevant Treasure Hunting Laws Regarding The Philippines

Now I have your attention regarding the wealth that is **still** buried in the Philippines, the next question that has to be asked is**:**

How Do I Get Permission To Recover Buried War Booty?

The treasure hunter must have a valid Treasure Hunting Permit from the local government official, and be a Filipino by birth, and have public liability insurances covering the site excavation and injury insurances for the diggers. Also a search and recovery agreement in place with either the registered landowner **OR** the government agency that owns the site stating the terms and conditions regarding the recovery and percentage split between landowner and treasure locator **BEFORE** any excavation can begin. These laws below apply to Filipinos and all treasure hunters that are **NOT** native to the Philippines. Failure to do so will lead to arrest, large fines and confiscation of all digging equipment.

Presidential Decree No. 1726-A

To understand Philippine treasure hunting law, begin with Presidential Decree No. 1726-A, entitled **Providing Guidelines on Treasure Hunting**, signed on October 1st, 1980 by former President Ferdinand Marcos.
This decree applies to treasure hunting on **government property** and basically states that a treasure hunter must first obtain a permit, that the government will oversee the digging and take possession of all items recovered and sell them, that deductions for government expenses will be made, and that the remaining value will be divided equally between the government and the permit-holder. If the treasures consist of war spoils of booty or anything of value buried by Imperial Japanese Forces during World War II, the split will be 75/25 toward the government's favour.

Again, this decree is relevant to treasure hunting on government property only and specifically states in Section 7 that "treasures found in private properties shall be governed by the Civil Code".

The Civil Code of the Philippines
Republic Act No. 386:

Approved on June 18, 1949, known as the *Civil Code of the Philippines*, consists of 2270 articles.

Only a handful of the articles mention hidden treasure, the most significant of which being Article 438, which clearly states that "hidden treasure belongs to the owner of the land, building, or other property on which it is found". This means that the legal landowner is 100% owner of all treasure located on or under his property.

Article 438 also affirms that, assuming a treasure hunter is not trespassing (*e.g.* holding a contract to excavate), he is entitled to 50% of the find on another's property.

It should be noted that these laws pertaining to treasure found on *private* property have been in place since 1949 and that no effort has since been made to change, repeal, or modify them.

National Caves and Cave Resources Management and Protection Act

Republic Act No. 9072, dated April 8, 2001, is known as the National Caves and Cave Resources Management and Protection Act. The act is mainly concerned with the protection of animals living within natural caves and the defacing of natural mineral formations such as stalactites and stalagmites.

Section 14 states that "Presidential Decree No. 1726-A

Is hereby "modified and that treasure hunting in caves shall be governed by the provisions of this Act."

The term "cave" is defined in Section 3(a) as "any naturally-occurring void, cavity, recess or system of interconnected passages beneath the surface of the earth or within a cliff or ledge and which is large enough to permit an individual to enter", therefore **man-made** caves and tunnels are not covered by the Act. However, all **natural caves**, whether on public or private property, are covered.

Cautionary Note: All water sites, and there were 34 Imperial Sites still deemed by the Philippine government to be on "Federal Land", which means that 75% of the recovered treasure must be shared as stated previously, as a 75/25 split. Please check current regulations.

7.70 DENR Relevant Treasure Hunting Laws

December 21ˢᵗ 2007: Partial Article From The Manila Times:

The Department of Environment and Natural Resources (DENR) now require treasure hunters to secure a permit from the DENR before they can proceed with their activities.

Very recently, a new edict by the DENR Environment Secretary Lito Atienza will place all treasure hunting activities under the watchful eyes of government regulation to protect the nation's natural and cultural heritage, and natural wealth as well. Mr Atienza stated that *only Filipinos citizens will be allowed to conduct treasure hunts*, and will be required to pay for a one-year permit from the Department of Natural Environment and Resources and post a surety bond, regardless if the hunt takes place on public or private lands.

The directive also banned treasure hunting from sites with cultural value, including ancestral domains and significant caves. The government will have ownership of all finds found to have historical value, and a committee will determine what to pay the finders for the treasure.

DENR Administrative Order No. 2007-34

"Stipulates the guidelines in conducting *treasure hunting* activities in caves in order to protect the country's natural wealth and heritage and to preserve the country's cultural properties," Mr Atienza said. Under these guidelines, an individual or entity may apply for a treasure hunting permit upon payment of a non-refundable application fee of **10,000 PHP** payable to the Mines and Geosciences Bureau Regional Office. The guidelines further stipulate that the DENR permit has a maximum term of **one year**, and can be renewed only once for the exclusive use and benefit of the permit holder.

However, Atienza stated that the guidelines **do not cover** caves with cultural, paleontological and historical values, caves within ancestral domains, and other significant caves.

The sharing scheme as stipulated in the guideline provides that for treasures recovered within public land, 75 percent goes to the government and 25 percent to the permit holder, while for treasures recovered in caves within private lands, 30 percent goes to the government and 70 percent will be shared by the landowner and the permit holder.

The government will have **ownership** of all finds found to have historical value, and a committee will determine what to pay the finders for the treasure.

Only native Filipinos are allowed to apply for treasure hunting permits that are valid for *one year*. Foreigners have been banned from actively hunting for treasure in the Philippines, simply because of bad publicity and public outcry that the wealth, when found, is taken away from the Filipino people who desperately need this money to live and survive.

See link: http://www.denr.gov.ph/index.php/home.html

7.80 Weather Recovery Time Window

When Is The Best Time Of The Year To Start Excavating The Site?

The answer to this question is when you have finished your research into the history of the potential site, and you have concrete proof that the Japanese soldiers were there, and 100% confirmation you think may have something of value buried on your chosen site.

You have interviewed eye witnesses, studied war journals, old photographs, and read as much about the transport infrastructure of road, rail and shipping routes of the town, city or port. These routes would have been used to transport the very heavy treasure ultimately to this destination.

Old Manila Railway maps show stations and sidings that could be very useful in pinpointing possible treasure hot spots. All this study must be carried out between the months of July to December, and completed before the dry season for site surveying and excavations begin.

All necessary survey and detection equipment, digging equipment, diggers and valid treasure permits must be "on hand" in order to start on-site operations by January and conclude by the end of May before the wet season begins. This is more important in Northern Luzon than say Davao in Mindanao.

The Japanese dug tunnels and buried treasure one metre below the water table in the dry season, and usually two days after the new moon, when the water table would be at the lowest level. Knowing the phases of the moon would greatly aid recovery, especially when digging by rivers and sea shore treasure sites.

The climate in the Philippines is typically tropical – hot and humid year round. Although the actual weather pattern is fairly complex, it can roughly be divided into January to June (dry) and July to December (wet). January is usually the coolest month and May the hottest, but the temperature does not fluctuate far from 25°C (80°F) year round.

December to February is usually the *"cool dry"* months, while March to May is the *"hot and dry"* months. It rains nearly every day from July through September. In May, Manila usually has daytime temperatures of 35-40°C (65°-104°F), and at night the temperature does not drop much below 27°C (81°F).

The best time to travel is from December to May. In December and January, however, you must contend with the rains on the east coast. March through to May is officially the summer months. Normally, for large areas of the Philippines, the rainy season starts in June. However, over the past decade, the dry season has occasionally extended into the month of July.

7.90 Typhoon And Monsoon Season

Travel around the Philippines is not really affected by the occasional downpour, but more by the *unpredictable* typhoons that usually come with the wet, monsoon season from May to November. The southwest Visayas and Mindanao lie beneath the typhoon belt. In September 2011 Super Typhoon Nanmadol hit the Philippines, bringing heavy rains and wind gusts of up to 230km/h across northern parts of the main island of Luzon.

The term "super-typhoon" refers to any typhoon with winds of at least 185 km/h (115mph). Typhoon Mina (international name Nanmadol) is the strongest storm to hit the Philippines in 2011, killing at least twenty-nine people and leaving around eight missing. Over 61,000 people in the Philippines were forced to evacuate their homes as Nanmadol caused widespread landslides and flooding across several regions in Luzon.

The Pacific Ocean coastline, comprising Luzon, Samar, Leyte, and Mindanao, lies in the path of the northeast trade winds, ensuring a mild oceanic climate. The winter monsoons take place from December to May and bring rain to the Pacific coast, but primarily dry pleasant weather to the rest of the land.

The summer monsoon blows from June to December or January and brings heavy rains to the Manila area. The typhoons in the Pacific region are predominantly in the Marshall and Caroline Islands. They travel in a northwesterly direction towards the Chinese mainland between June and November, mainly in August/September.

8.00 The Search And Recovery Agreement (Sample)

Here is a basic example of a search and recovery agreement that needs to be completed and signed by all parties concerned before any excavations can begin. Each party must know in advance what is expected, and who is responsible for what at the beginning, during and after the agreement remains in force.

Many treasure hunters forget that finances must be put to one side to pay for filling in holes and landscaping, if nothing is found for example, and a logistical plan for transporting heavy gold bars to a secure location prior to selling must also be planned for well in advance before any excavations can begin.

This agreement which becomes effective on (**dd/mm/yy**) is made between:
Mr **(FULL NAME HERE)** hereinafter referred to as the **Locator/Financier**
AND Mr/Mrs (FULL NAME HERE) **Residing in:** (ADDRESS AND PROVINCE HERE) Who will hereinafter be referred to as the **Land Owner.**

WITNESSETH:

The Locator has the means to search for and recover valuable metal, precious stones, or other valuable items/commodities of any kind, and has entered into this Agreement under the following Terms and Conditions:

1. The Land Owner will allow the Locator and his Group access to and from the Property at any time the Locator wishes. Beginning from the date above, only the Locator can end the project.
2. Land Owner will not sign any other Agreement with any other Group or individual for the same purpose until this Agreement expires.
3. After government cost and percentage are deducted, any and all valuable items recovered within the Project will be split as follows: **75%** percent to Land Owner, and **25%** percent to the Locators.
4. Land Owner declares that he is the rightful landowner of the Property and has the Legal Right to enter into this Agreement.
5. If either Party to this Agreement passes away, this Agreement remains in force with the Estate of the deceased.
6. Land Owner will endeavour to ensure that all persons who have no right to be on the Property are barred from entry to it whilst this Agreement is in force.
7. The Land Owner will not sell the Property covered under the terms of this agreement or transfer the title for this Property to any other party whilst this agreement is in force. If the Land Owner wants to sell the Property during this time, then the Land Owner agrees to give first opportunity to purchase the Property to the Locators and to no other during this period.
8. Site Locations identified are: 1) xxxxxxxx 2) xxxxxxxx 3) xxxxxxxx
   (GPS Coordinates here:)

   Locator: **Mr xxxxxxxxxxxx Signature:** _____

   Land Owner: **Mr xxxxxxxxxxx Signature:** _____

NOTE: ALL PREVIOUS CONTRACTS AND AGREEMENTS ARE VOID & CANCELLED.

AS WITNESSED BELOW, THIS AGREEMENT IS EXECUTED ON
DAY OF _____ YEAR: _____

Signed: _____ Signed: _____

Now you have your treasure permit, and a signed and dated search and recovery agreement stating the terms and conditions of how the treasure or findings are going to be divided and what is expected of the landowner and the treasure hunter.

If you are the locator and funding the operation, then you may ask for a larger share of the treasure, say 40-45%. Of course the obvious question you should be asking yourself now is:

What *hard and solid evidence* do I have to believe that treasure is buried on the owner's property in the first place?

Please check that this agreement is a legally binding document with a qualified Philippine lawyer before it is signed by all parties concerned.

Major Treasure Sites

The definition of *solid evidence* must be in the form of military buildings, bunkers, tunnels, fortifications, accommodation for troops and POWs, HQ buildings, any historical documents backed up with old photographs showing where the military stayed, any old treasure maps, old drawings from live pointers who worked for the Japanese military during any burial operations.

Many of these workers were murdered once the treasure was buried, so always ask others about the site, and get as many stories as you can about its past history. All these things help build up a *picture* of the site, and should help identify potential hot spots that need to be investigated further.

The next step is to look for Japanese treasure markings or strange-shaped rocks on your property or the landowner's property; something that you can physically see or touch.

For example, artifacts that definitely shows that the area was once *occupied* by the Japanese military during the Second World War. For example, old Japanese beer bottles, broken china, military artifacts such as gas masks, uniforms or old military hardware. It would be very useful in giving you clues to Japanese occupation of the site you may think treasure may be buried.

If gold or jewelry had already been found near or on the land under investigation, the assumption you make is that there could be more to be excavated at the same spot, only deeper, or close by. If the assumption is close by, then you need to look for pointers and treasure markers showing exactly where to look.

Minor Treasure Sites

Have you found any man-made tunnels or natural cave systems on your site?

If the answer is *yes,* have you explored the area for chalk or limestone cliffs or hills where potential treasure or military supplies could have been hidden during the Japanese occupation?

Look again for symbols on rocks or markers pointing to closed tunnel entrances, and find out if anyone else has recovered any thing of value from your site or nearby before you take interest in it.

I am assuming now that you have already done all the basic homework and background study, and now know that you are not wasting your time on a wild goose chase. You are *100%* certain that there is something buried on your site; now you need some simple steps to locate where the treasure is buried.

8.10 **Finding Buried Treasure**

Here three procedures are suggested in order to locate quickly and identify whether your site is a veritable "gold mine" or just a place where the Japanese buried old junk. (Many old garbage dumps are mistaken for large treasure deposits too.)

This search technique assumes that you have lots of funds at your disposal that you could use to find potential gold burials. On subsequent pages of this section of the book I mention other less expensive ways of locating treasure by using dowsing rods, a digital watch, and an inexpensive metal detector.

Here I will explain one successful way to identify your buried hot spot and how to verify it is the real thing before you start digging. Here are three basic techniques that, if followed correctly, will make you a very successful treasure hunter. These techniques are:

A) Resistivity Ground Testing

B) Ground-Penetrating Radar Scanning

C) Spot Bore Drilling

A) Resistivity Ground Testing

The first resistivity ground test will prove two important things; for instance, whether a mass of metal exists underground that is worth further investigation. (Gold as a metal is very conductive, and will be found quite easily using this method of detection.)

This test will also highlight whether the mass of metal is stored inside a man-made tunnel or a natural cave system where the entrances have been blocked in the distant past.

Please note that this type of instrument will not tell you the precise depth of the object, only its location on your site.

According to Bob Fitzgerald, his Mother Load Locator ™ has found many a gold bar in the Philippines. This device will operate to a depth of 130 feet.

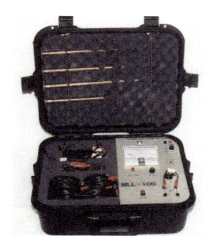

Please see http://treasurenow.com/html/MLL.html for a more detailed explanation about how this device operates.
All Trade Marks acknowledged.

B) Ground-Penetrating Radar Scanning

Ground-Penetrating radar scanning proves to you that the cave or tunnels exist underground, and that the original soil strata have been disturbed by previous digging operations by persons unknown. The scan will also show any unique objects buried below the ground either in or outside a void, and give you an indication of the actual depth of the target in question.

This device cannot tell you whether the target is indeed gold, silver or indeed made from concrete, but only where the object is situated under the ground and at what depth.

The type of GPR scanning system and whether the soil is highly mineralized will have an effect on results.
Two types of GPR are available: the first model uses a high frequency transducer, which means that the transmitted frequency will give less ground penetration and depth than the second model that uses a low frequency transducer, which will give more ground penetration but at a lower display resolution.

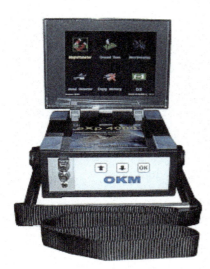

The OKM EXP4000™: Depth 25 meters; can detect voids and discriminate between different types of metal.

Note: Advances in metal detection are developing all of the time, and I therefore strongly suggest you investigate these new technologies before you spend thousands of dollars on equipment.

All Trade Marks acknowledged.

See: http://www.geofizz.co.uk/products/exp4000.htm

C) Spot Bore Drilling

Once you have identified that "yes" you have a target and you know its location and its depth, then the decision has to be made whether you are going to hand dig down to the target or whether you are going to save time and hire or buy in a drilling rig for the job.

There are many portable water drilling rigs available in the Philippines. These are used primarily for drilling water wells or for mining exploration.

These portable drilling rigs are usually transported to site on a trailer, and can be set for drilling within two hours. These rigs can be hired from the mining or water drilling companies, which usually charge by the meter drilled; the deeper the hole, the larger the cost.

See:http://www.drill2water.com/Water.html

All Trade Marks acknowledged.

8.20   Excavation Considerations

Water Wells
On many potential treasure sites, villagers have drilled bore holes into old tunnel systems, or are using the same old water well the Japanese constructed during WWII. This water is pumped to the surface for drinking and washing. As a treasure hunter, you come along and decide to pump their "water source" dry without realizing it; very soon all of the locals will be shouting "where did our water go?" Especially if you are digging in the dry season and water levels are already low. This recent article below illustrates my point about having the correct permits and being considerate to the local community:

Yamashita Treasure Hunt Stopped Quezon Inquirer
September 2011

The Department of Environment and Natural Resources (DENR) and local government officials have ordered a Manila-based treasure hunters' group to stop excavating a hilly part of Mauban town in Quezon facing Lamon Bay after worried residents staged a protest on Wednesday.

Carrying a letter from the National Museum, Mauban Mayor Mr Fernando Llamas and local environment chief Mr Alfredo Palencia were accompanied by local policemen when they destroyed the padlock of a bamboo gate of the treasure hunting site in Sitio (sub-village) Swa in Barangay (village) Daungan.

No Permits To Excavate

The mayor stated that the treasure hunters also failed to secure local government and barangay permits, as stipulated in the permits issued by the national government.

Inconsiderate Digging

The digging activity of the diggings even at night was really disturbing local people, who were losing sleep because of the noise. "We were also afraid that their continuous excavation could loosen the hill and cause a landslide during heavy rains," said Rosa Banagan, one of the residents. Llamas also stated that treasure hunters had also struck the water source that the neighborhood used for drinking water.

Neighbourhood Complaints

The digging had long been the subject of complaints by residents living in the neighbourhood. Local people gathered in front of the site and shouted with joy when the authorities forcibly entered the treasure site.
"We already stopped digging," said Mr Rolando Mendieta, the owner of the 90-square-meter lot. He told the officials that nine diggers had already left the excavation site two days previously.

They had already reached a depth of more than 50 feet and were starting to excavate horizontally to create tunnels into the base of the hill, Mr Mendieta stated to the police.

Mr Palencia said Mr Mendieta's admission of digging to a depth of 50 feet was enough to cancel the excavation permit immediately, simply because the diggers were only allowed to dig to a maximum depth of 40 ft deep, he said.

Mr Llamas stated: "With these admitted violations, the local government was justified in closing the site for the safety of the residents."

8.30 Basic Equipment For Treasure Hunting Activities

BASIC EQUIPMENT FOR TREASURE HUNTING ACTIVITIES

1. Heavy Duty Gloves
2. Weighing Scales
3. Torch/Flash Light
4. Poncho & Emergency Blanket
5. String For Marking Out
6. Gas Mask & Filters For Toxic Gases
7. Diving Mask
8. Water Bottle And Carry Pouch
9. Day Glow Orange Nylon Chord
10. Multi Tool
11. Compass
12. Safety Goggles
13. Walkie Talkies
14. 10 Litre Water Carrier
15. First Aid Bag
16. Methane Gas Detector

8.40   **Basic Detection Equipment**

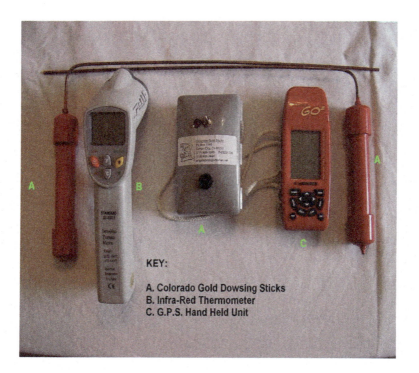

KEY:

A. Colorado Gold Dowsing Sticks
B. Infra-Red Thermometer
C. G.P.S. Hand Held Unit

In the photograph above, we have:

A: Colorado Gold Dowsing Rod System, where the unit in the centre is tuned into the resonant frequency of buried gold. The unit is placed around your neck and switched on; the sounder gives off a high pitch sound in front of the treasure hunter. The two dowsing rods are held in each hand; the theory is that when you approach buried gold the sound wave projected in front of you disturbs the ionic plume given off the gold when it has been buried in the ground for a long time.
The dowsing rods pick up this "ionic disturbance" and the rods will move towards each other and eventually make a cross, marking the centre of the gold deposit below.

B: This is a useful laser thermometer, which fires a laser beam at a surface and will read the surface temperature, in Fahrenheit or Centigrade. This will help locate "hot spots" under the ground, and secret tunnels.

A mass of gold buried under the ground tends to absorb heat. The Japanese knew this and covered the gold bars in bitumen to stop the heat radiating outward and being detected by other treasure hunters. A mass of gold stacked on top of each other can reach a core temperature of 35 degrees centigrade.

By scanning the walls and the floor of tunnels and caves, hot spots can easily be identified by the Infrared thermometer, saving valuable survey time for excavating the right spots.

C: Global Satellite Positioning System: For planning trips into unchartered mountains and logging the position of new sites and tunnels that need further investigation. This unit uses nine satellites to give location accuracy to a target of +/- 3 meters.

8.50   A Useful Digital Watch

My **Casio™ PRG-50** watch, made by Casio Computer Co. Ltd. Tokyo, Japan (shown left).

This watch can help you find treasure buried by the Japanese! I love that: using Japanese technology to locate buried Japanese treasure; what could be more exciting?

This is a Casio PRO TREK™ watch, which has various functions; one of which is "Digital Compass Mode". I found this watch to be an ideal instrument to detect large metallic objects under the ground, and have used it to verify various potential treasure sites in the Philippines, where heavy metal deposits are buried in either sand or soil.

The watch has a built-in magnetic bearing sensor that detects terrestrial magnetism; that is to say the watch detects magnetic north and not true polar north, as used on maps. Therefore, any strong sources of magnetism or blockages to the mother earth's electromagnetic field will cause the watch to give an error reading, and ultimately an alarm will sound inside the watch.

This watch will detect electromagnetic disturbances under the earth and will detect concrete reinforced structures under the ground; my theory is that large amounts of buried gold bars packed inside a concrete vault will block the watch sensor detecting any natural magnetic fields from mother earth. This means the magnetic bearing sensor has no reference point in which to display where magnetic north is located, and will start to alarm to indicate a "False" reading.

By walking over and over the site of interest in a grid type pattern, the wearer of the watch can gauge the size of the buried target as the watch continues to give off its built-in alarm sound as the buried gold blocks off the earth's natural magnetic field.

We put this theory into practice at four different locations, and I can tell you it does work in the field of exploring potential treasure sites. Further verification will be needed by using metal detectors or other devices, but for basic identification of large buried bunkers, metal or gold deposits, this is a "must have" watch to aid you in your treasure hunting activities.

I cannot guarantee that this watch will find a massive treasure hoard for you, but it helped me verify three sites where the electromagnet field had become cut due to a mass of metal that required further investigation using a deep search metal detector or a ground-penetrating radar unit to verify my assumption that I had indeed found a large deposit of gold bullion.

Other Casio watch models that have the same digital compass feature as the PRG-50 are listed below:

1) PRG-240-1ER   2) PRG-240T-7ER 3) PRG-240B-2ER
4) PRG-80-1VER 5) PRG-40B-2VUR   6) SPF-40-1VUR
7) PRW-2000-1ER

See link: http://www.watches2u.com/mens-casio-watches.html

All Trade Marks acknowledged.

8.60 The Casio Watch: How Does It Work?

I stated that the inbuilt compass sensor inside the watch detects the natural magnetic field that flows from the north to south. Once the watch sensor loses its sense of direction, the watch will give an audible alarm to say it has lost the magnetic reference from mother earth.

The compass cannot give a true reading of where "magnetic north" is located in relation to mother earth, and the magnetic north pointer starts to move backwards and forwards over the affected magnetic field area in question, sounding its built-in alarm.

By walking over the area in a grid pattern you can assess the size of the area affected by this magnetic distortion or lack of magnetic field strength. This technique worked very well when we used this Casio watch on "compass setting". We successfully identified four large treasure deposit sites all along the sea shore during our site survey trip to Mindanao.

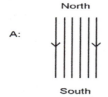

A: Conventional magnetic field flow from North to South through Mother earth.

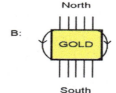

B: Magnetic field cut or disturbed flow through a mass of gold or metal.

Another Mindanao Treasure Site

The surrounding area around the treasure site will be affected by the concentration of magnetized rocks buried on top of the treasure deposit. This magnetized field will affect compasses and metal detector readings.

As the hole is opened to the air, the naturally-magnetized rocks will increase the magnetic field around the hole, and will give false detection readings when you are trying to locate the buried target underneath.

The center of the target could be as much as 1-2 meters to the left or right of the excavated shaft. Therefore, in order to achieve a precise reading, all magnetized rocks and stones must be removed from the area before a proper investigation can begin to locate the precise treasure location.

Key

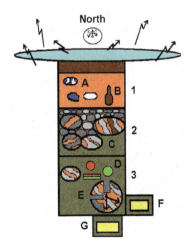

A = Blue & White Ceramic Plate.
B = Saki Bottle.
C = Small Stones & Magnetized Iron Pyrite Rocks.
D = Green & Red Balls or Coloured Wood Markers.
E = Large Boulder, with holes either on top or on the side indicating treasure deposit.
G & F = Treasure Deposit.
1= Depth 5-7 feet. 2 = Depth 7-15 feet.
3 = Depth 15-25 feet.

8.70   A Basic Metal Detector

I could write a whole book about metal detectors; the different types, how they operate, and what to buy. Many more detection devices are sold throughout the world and the price ranges from a few hundred dollars to many thousands of dollars.

If your budget is tight then please consider a detector that will operate in the highly-mineralized volcanic soil you will find in the Philippines. The electronic circuitry must be able to be tuned in such a way as to cancel out interference and false targets when the receiving sign bounces back from salts and silica that make up the soils constitution, and be rugged enough to give many months of trouble free detecting in humid weather conditions.

This particular detector featured below is a "hoard" treasure seeker which will detect a small metallic 4x4 feet box at a depth of 20 feet. The manufacture has also stated that it will detect tunnels and caves at the same depth. It is manufactured by "Discovery Electronics™" in the U.S.A.
Its rugged construction makes it an ideal search and recovery tool for smaller stashes of gold coins and small tola bars carried and buried by the ordinary Japanese soldier.

Treasure-Finder 900 Automatic (Below) Made by: Discovery Electronics™. Inc. U.S.A.

All Trade Marks acknowledged.

For large cache and treasure hunting, the **Treasure-Finder 900 Automatic** deep-seeking detector is unsurpassed in its depth capabilities while ignoring ground mineralization. **Used to locate large treasure caches**, gold or silver bullion, larger relics, old wells or tunnels, and large mineral deposits such as **gold-bearing black sand**. **Patented Ground Reject Circuitry** gives you the greatest detection depth possible for caches and large relics even in the toughest mineralized soils. **Factory set nulling** and auto-tune features make this the **easiest-to-operate two-box unit.**

Some Technical Features:

Dual Frequency operating modes: 12.5 kHz and 73.5 kHz . Built-in speaker and 1/4 inch headphone jack. **Automatic LED Battery Test Light. Handle-mounted push button** for easy "thumb-set" control. **Ground reject VLF** circuitry and ground reject control. **Sensitivity control. Factory preset** electronic null circuitry. Snap together all-aluminum construction. **Tone adjustment control. Two automatic tuning/pinpoint modes**. Durable baked-on powder coat finish. Single 9-volt 6 cell "AA" battery pack. **Twenty-forty-hour battery life**. Weighs only six pounds. **One year warranty.**

8.80 An Inexpensive Data Logger To Show You 3D Images Underground

Prior To Excavation

See link: http://www.lrlman.com/

The Arc-Geo Logger allows you to use a metal detector to log the sound output signal from the headphone jack out socket. Then the data can be downloaded to a PC and displayed in a grid fashion to show all target locations within the plotted area. The software ASLT is used for ground resistivity and shows the data from the logger similar to a ground resistivity grid. This is a first for a metal detector owner to log data and have a hard copy of a site for later reference.

The Arc-Geo Logger was designed around the **TF-900 detector** by Discovery and can be used with many detectors on the market today! Here is a list of detectors that has been tested so far with the Arc-Geo Logger: **Whites,** Garrett, Tesoro, Deepstar PI and almost any detector with a headphone connection! Since the detector is the sensor part of the unit depth, discrimination and other settings only add to the ability of the logger.

See link: http://www.lrlman.com/arc-geo%20logger.htm for images

All Trade Marks acknowledged.

8.90 Detector Used in The Philippines Whites TM 808™

The **Whites TM 808™** has been used in Mexico, the *Philippines*, Greece, the Dominican Republic, Germany, Holland and Italy. The TM 808™ is ideal for locating coin caches, treasure chests and hoards of gold or silver in either coin or bullion form. It features high detection sensitivity even through mineralized soil.

The TM 808™ can be used almost anywhere, regardless of interference or ground minerals. It's easier than ever to tune, plus it features a great combination of factory settings with operator adjustments for complete flexibility. There are preset settings on each control for hassle-free setup. The **TM 808™** recovers buried treasure at depths of 4-20 feet.

A 75 kg Bar found by Bob Fitzgerald's search and recovery team in the Philippines.

This was part of larger cache. (See appendix for contact details.)

All Trade Marks acknowledged.

9.00 The "ABC" of Generic Japanese Treasure Symbols And Relevant Documentation

Introduction

In this section, I have included many of the generic symbols that have been used by many of the treasure code writers that have similar meanings. Placed in alphabetic order, this part of the book is to be used as a quick reference guide when you find a "heart-shaped stone", or a large footprint carved on top of rock.

Many of the commonly-found symbols crop up time and time again throughout the treasure site regions that make up the Philippine archipelago. I have supplied many photographs, drawings and detailed explanations to help you understand the meanings of such signs and made specific observational notes of interest to help you, the treasure hunter.

Many photographs illustrate points to help you open your eyes to what is seen and unseen. I urge you to always look and look again, for many things are there to be seen and can to the naked eye *"appear hidden"*. By practice, and lots of patience, you will become a master at finding the treasure signs that await the "enlightened" one that seeks them. When you visit potential treasure sites, take as many photographs as you can; these images will give you so much information and incredible detail that you may have missed on your visit.

Therefore, I give you the ABC of generic Japanese treasure symbols and essential treasure hunting documentation, section number 9 – the largest section in this book.

9.01 Arrow Signs

Arrows are used to show the treasure hunter the direction in which to follow. The interpretation of each arrow differs from one code writer to another. It is therefore important to know as much as you can about the arrow symbol you have found before you run along the path to try and find the next marker stone or symbol.

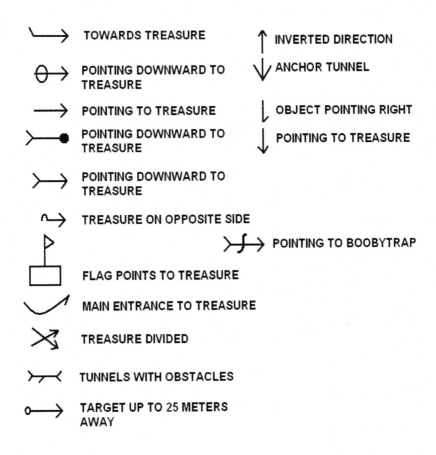

9.02   Bird Treasure Signs

Japanese Engineering Battalion Sign

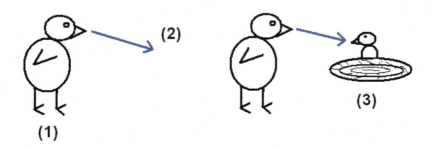

The bird symbols means "Nestling Wealth is here".

Key:

1) The bird's beak is pointing towards the place the treasure is buried.

2) The bird's beak is pointing to the baby chick.

3) The baby chick is nesting on top of the rich object or treasure deposit under the nest itself.

Other code writers have used the bird's head and beak to point to the location of where the Japanese had hidden a golden Buddha.

9.03 Box Treasure Signs

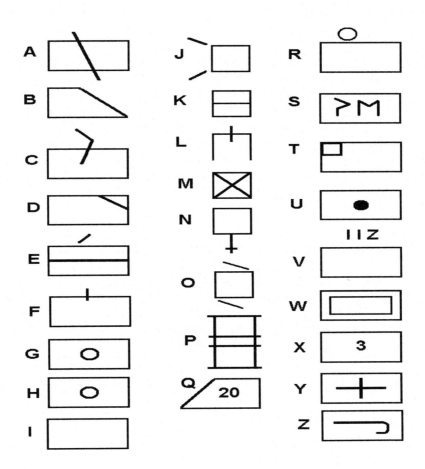

Key

A: Object Inside. B: Rock Enclosed Treasure. C: Inside. D: Treasure in Box. E: Gold Bars. F: Inside. G: Treasure On This Spot 10 Feet Down. H: Treasure On Spring. I: Treasure in a Box. J: Jewelries. K: Treasure Inside. L: Inside. M: Object Under Here. N: Artifacts in Trees. O: 130 Gold Bars Deposit Here. P: Stairs Going Down Shaft. Q: Treasure Here. R: Buddha. S: Deposit Underwater. T: Treasure. U: Scattered Around. V: Treasure Under Big Flat Stone. W: Treasure On The Spot 10 Feet Deep. X: Antique. Y: Grave With Cross Locating Treasure. Z: Cemented Treasure Inside.

9.04 The Secret Of The Cemented Box Revealed!

Inside a rectangular cement box you will find at the centre of it an iron rod.

This rod will have markings on it which match, in meters (unless otherwise stated on the rod itself), the precise location of where the treasure deposit is located.

If the rod has a point on one end then follow the direction in which it is pointing. If not then the directions in which to look for the treasure is shown in the diagram below. If the cemented box has been moved from its original location for any reason then the whereabouts of the treasure could be lost too!

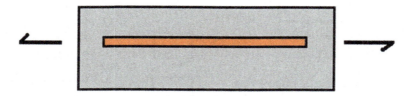

The cemented box may be coloured with a pink dye to make identification and future location easier to the returning treasure hunter like yourself.

9.05 **Buddha Treasure Signs**

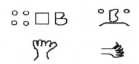 Any representation of hands means Buddha is near or present. Buddha statues would have been placed under bamboo trees and outside caves or possibly near running water so that the Japanese soldiers could pray. Many Buddha images were then hidden in holes, tunnels or natural caves for safety when attacks or fire fights took place against the American or Filipino forces attacking Japanese military strongholds.

Q: What Japanese and Korean Symbols Represent Buddha?

This Japanese Kanji sign can mean Buddha or Buddhism.

 This Kanji was actually a shorthand way to write Buddha in Chinese (popular around the 13th century). Somehow, this became the version of this Chinese character that was absorbed into the Japanese language, and thus became part of standard Kanji writing centuries later.

Below is also a rare Korean Hanja symbol for Buddha:

These two symbols can mean Buddhism or Buddha depending on how they are used in context; this word can be used to refer to the religion and lifestyle of Buddhism, or in some cases the Buddha himself.

Note the first character is also a rare form of Korean Hanja – though seldom used even when the Korean Hanja writing system was more common one-hundred years ago.

<u>Note:</u> Many Buddha's were made of solid gold to show to the Buddhist monks and worshipers that the image was spiritually pure. In many circumstances these images would be covered in a thick plaster and painted so that the image would be protected against thieves knowing the true monetary value of such statues.

The Japanese military, who were mostly Buddhist themselves at this time, knew about this deception and used to break open the plaster surrounding the Buddha to see if the statue was made from solid gold before stealing it from the country that they had invaded.

Some of the Buddha's where up to 14 feet high and would weigh up to 8 tons in weight. Many were re-melted for their gold content, but others were hidden in tunnels in various Philippine Imperial treasure vaults and smaller Buddha images would be re-used by Buddhist Japanese soldiers to pray to wherever they were stationed. These Buddha statues have been found buried in river banks, inside old military storage tunnels, inside old trenches, and under old bamboo trees – areas once occupied by the Imperial Japanese forces.

9.06   **Bridge Treasure Sign**

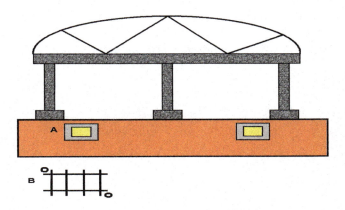

Key:

A: Gold bars inside a concrete vault buried near or under the foundation of the bridge.

B: Treasure Symbol: Treasure On Both Sides of the Bridge.

(From the Japanese Engineering Battalion Code Book).

In 1994, the Philippine Department of Public Works and Highways carried out a project entitled: "Rehabilitation and Maintenance of Bridges along the Arterial Roads".

They conducted a nationwide inventory of all main road bridges. One of the components of the project was the "Nationwide Bridge Inspection" study, which covers the investigation and assessment of 7,259 bridges located along the national road network. The final output of this study was the formulation of the Bridge Master Plan of the DPWH. In 1999, DPWH reviewed thoroughly and produced an updated report. It was found that 1,707 bridges throughout the Philippines were in a deteriorated condition. How many of the original military style road and railway bridges that could still hide treasure today are not known.

There must be some of these military style type bridges still standing in remote mountain areas that have survived the war, floods, typhoons and even earthquakes that could be hiding a secret hoard of treasure underneath the concrete foundations and steel support structure. Deposits have been found just under these types of bridges on either side, underneath where the bridge starts and the road ends.

One such example was located at GPS Location:
16°47'2.01"N and 121° 7'15.55"E.

9.07   Broken Ceramics & Glass Markers

As previously mentioned, pieces of broken pottery, like a jar, china plate or even glass are all good treasure signs, and should be investigated fully.

The age of broken bottles or china should give you a clue as to when they were discarded in the first place. The favourite colours are green or blue, but old saki bottles can be brown or clear in colour.

Look at broken beer bottles; you will see Japanese markings. Maybe the shape of the bottle will give you an indication of its age or origin. These treasure markers will be found on the surface of a site used as a marker, or buried at a pre-determined depth.

Broken pottery inside a known Japanese treasure cave and sea shells must be explored, especially when we can see cement with a slight pink colour, like on the left of the picture.

The shells are pointing upward, which means "Deposit Under", and lots of broken ceramics and glass is another good treasure sign. Whole bottles with the neck buried but the bottom sticking out of the ground means there is a tunnel below. The buried neck of the bottle is pointing the way.

9.08 **<u>Broken Ceramics & Glass Examples</u>**

At a depth of 28 feet we found old broken bottles and plates, all dating from the mid 1940s.
A sure sign that someone had dug this hole before. This was a small Japanese garrison quarters, and we knew we were getting close…

9.09 <u>The Carabao Secret</u>

The carabao, or swamp buffalo (*Latin:* ***bubalis carabanesis***) of the Philippines and Southeast Asia. Water buffalo have been domesticated for five-thousand years and have become economically-important animals. They provide more than 5% of the world's milk supply and 30% of the farm power in Southeast Asia. In the Philippines, these giant gentle creatures are used to plow rice fields and transport sugar cane and other heavy items on specially-built carabao carts.

(I took this photo while I visited Glan in Mindanao in 2006.)

<u>Why Are These Animals Important To Treasure Hunting?</u>

In rural areas where vehicle access is impossible, these creatures can help transport heavy items to an excavation site on carabao carts and also help transport treasure hoards out too! The carabao have a very sensitive nose, and have found small hoards of treasure through their great sense of smell, especially if there are human remains nearby, or a change in ground vegetation, or areas that have been disturbed by human activity.

Carabao have also stumbled into small holes or depressions in the soft ground and accidently found a small stash of gold and jewelry left by a Japanese soldier during WWII. One case in particular comes to mind.

The carabao love water, and on a recent trip to a treasure site in the Philippines I found that one particular animal liked to bathe in one part of the river. This part of the river had a secret underwater cave situated inside the river bank near Crow Valley in Northern Luzon. The water was flowing in and out of this cave that held a golden Buddha and 200 gold bars. Maybe the animal liked the spiritual Buddha energy of this place; who knows, but many old Filipinos have told me that the carabao can sense many things. These special "animal sixth senses" may be picking up the electromagnetic disturbances that precious metals emit when buried in the ground, causing a distortion in normal mother earth's electromagnetic field paths.

Please do not underestimate the secret assets of the humble carabao; he or she may just be the "*Sherlock Holmes*" of finding buried treasure in places such as rice fields, rivers, hill sites, muddy fields, and unknown battle sites where human remains are still left undiscovered. Always ask the carabao owner if his animal has found something of interest for you and ask him if the animal acts strangely when he walks near a particular structure or area that may conceal hidden tunnel entrances or deposits. You may be pleasantly surprised at what the humble carabao can do for your treasure site research. It may help validate other documentary evidence you have for a site requiring further investigation.

9.10 Cone-Shaped Mountain

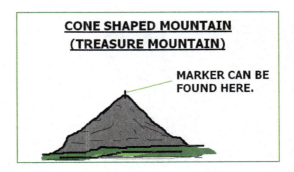

A coned-shaped mountain similar to Japan's Mount Fuji represents a treasure mountain.
This landmark does not have to be the size of Mount Fuji! It can be a small hill shaped this way. Some cone-shaped hills are now smaller than they once were, or have been removed by farmers levelling their land. Old photos taken during the Japanese occupation will show where these were situated as you view the surrounding landscape.

These cone shape mounds were used as reference points, gun emplacements or places to bury treasure. The tunnel systems or deposit will be found either at the base of such a mountain, or directly behind the marker on the other side, hidden from view, or half way up the mountain on the eastern side.

These were also used by the Japanese military as look out posts, and places where anti-aircraft guns were placed. Gold bars have been found under the old foundations of where these guns once stood.

9.11 Concrete Steps And Hidden Gold Bars

These steps here were found near Glan in Mindanao. The negative photograph shows that the cement colours are different (Example 1 & 2). The Japanese Nipa hut is long gone, but the Japanese knew that the concrete steps would remain. Sometimes a normal metal detector will give a positive reading through concrete therefore these steps will have to be broken up to see if there is a small gold deposit inside.

These old concrete steps are a good place to hide a few gold bars, especially when the middle section, highlighted in green shown on the photo above, was usually filled with rubble. Also under the steps themselves is a good hiding place. The Japanese military knew that even if the old Spanish-style house they were living in at the time was destroyed by the Americans as they counter-attacked, the concrete steps would remain. Retrieval of the gold bars would be easy after the war was over.

9.12 **Diamond Symbols**

On this page I have included a selection of symbols that represent uncut or finished diamond deposits.

⊠ = Box Of Diamonds

Three Jars Of Diamonds

Jewelries Or Diamonds

9.13 **Fall Rock In Cave**

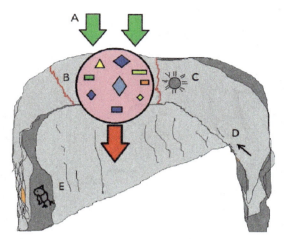

KEY:
A: SAFE ACCESS TO TREASURE DEPOSIT HERE
B: FALL ROCK BOULDER C: JEWELS TREASURE SYMBOL
D: ARROW POINTING TO DEPOSIT E: NESTING TREASURE SYMBOL POINTING UPWARD TO FALL ROCK BOULDER IN CEILING

When you enter a cave or tunnel system always look up and observe what could be hidden above your head. There may be a rock fall boulder full of gold and jewels high above, attached to the ceiling awaiting discovery. Look for treasure symbols pointers just inside the tunnel or cave similar to those shown above (D and E).

Are these symbols pointing to a particular spot on the ceiling? If so look closer you may come across a treasure symbol that will look the same as example "C" in the diagram above. The boulder itself will be man-made and could be pink in colour. Coloured shaped glass, crystals or stones will be embedded into the boulder itself, signifying gold bars and jewelry are located inside the rock itself.

Safe recovery must be attempted by accessing the boulder B from the top of the tunnel or cave labelled: "A" in the above diagram and not directly underneath for obvious safety reasons. The fall rock is intended to kill the treasure hunter who tries to access hidden riches inside the boulder from underneath so be warned.

9.14 **Footprints Explained**

My Left Foot

The footprint carved on a rock, what does it mean? Well there are a lot of footprint symbols that need explaining.

The Left foot on its own was used by the Japanese Engineering Battalion and it means: **"Dead End. Or The Treasure Trail Has Ended"**.

Sometimes either the small or the large toe is drawn in such a way as to point in the direction of where the treasure is buried.

The left foot is saying: Treasure trail has ended. If there are no toes pointing like above, then assume the treasure is directly underneath this symbol or just in front of it.

If one of the toes is pointing in a different direction than you expect, either on an angle or to the left or right, then follow it to the next symbol or to the buried deposit.

As we see on the next page, the right or left foot can be used as a treasure pointer, where one of the toes points towards the buried treasure. This depends upon who wrote the treasure code and its geographical location that the code was applied to. If the left or right foot toes point in "funny" looking directions, then follow my instructions on the next page that explains how to measure the exact distance to the target.

9.15 My Right Foot

The right foot on its own, according to the Korean treasure code for Davoa means:

"**Volume of Treasure**". In another code the right foot means: "**5 Yards to the Object**".

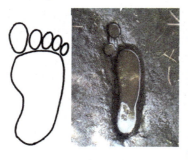

The photograph on the left is an unusual right foot of a soldier's shoe. Two circles are seen in the top left of the picture. These circles mean two treasure deposits are buried very close to this sign. In this case we would follow the directions of both circles to look for further signs that would indicate where the treasure is buried. In the case that two deposits will be very near. In the case of the left circle below the top one: 1-10 meters. and the top left circle: a little further 10-15 meters away.

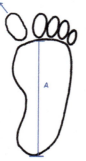

If you find a symbol like this one, whether it be a right or left foot, where one of the toes seems to be pointing in a different direction, then please take note.

The distance "**A**" shown in blue must be measured in centimeters and then converted to meters. This will give you the distance to the target.

In the case of Korean codes used in Davao, it would be sensible to measure "**A**" in inches, and convert the inches into yards.

For example "**A**" is measured in cm first: **A** is 10cm long: 10 meters away the treasure will be found.

I have the same treasure symbol in Davao (Korean Treasure Code). Therefore I measure "**A**" again, using inches this time: **A** is 10 inches long: 10 yards away is the treasure deposit.

Once you have the distance, just follow the direction that the big toe is pointing.

Note: It could be *any* of the toes that are pointing towards the treasure, therefore look very closely at the positioning of the toes in relation to the foot itself.

9.16   Two Feet

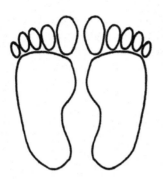

Two feet usually means the treasure trail has ended and the deposit is either under the feet, or in front or very close by.

9.17   Crossed Feet

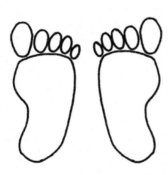

Crossed feet is a different way to tell the treasure hunter that "X marks the spot".
If you were to cross your feet in this way you make an "X" with your legs. Therefore, the treasure has been buried between the two crossed feet.

9.18 **Two Feet With Treasure Symbols**

In this case both symbols below are telling us that the treasure will be found directly under the feet. In the first example, however, the ***Tanaka Detachment*** code says that the circle with a cross (as shown) means: "Booby trap".

Therefore, know which code book may apply for the geographical region in which your site is situated. Always use caution when reading treasure symbols, simply because many have numerous meanings. Be aware of who wrote the symbol and apply the correct code book meaning to your site. If in doubt, leave the area alone just in case there is a bomb guarding the buried treasure.

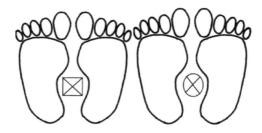

Another code shown on the right tells us that the box with a cross means: "**Rice Field Treasure**".

9.19   Gate Guard

The precious object or buried treasure inside a tunnel or a vertical shaft will be protected by a gate guard. This person could have been a Japanese POW victim or even a Japanese soldier. The body will be buried in such a way that it is surrounded in a layer of charcoal and ash.

Usually the top layer will be 2-4 feet thick. Once the digger disturbs this protective layer around the remains of the gate guard, the smell of rotting flesh and methane will be released into the confined space in which the digger is standing, thus killing the digger instantly or rendering him unable to carry on with his digging activity.

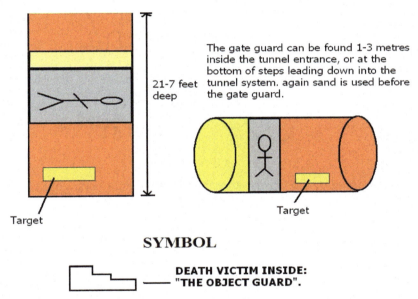

SYMBOL

**DEATH VICTIM INSIDE:
"THE OBJECT GUARD".**

If you come across a layer of charcoal while you are digging stop and think about how you will protect yourself and your diggers against methane gas poisoning before commencing. A methane gas detector will monitor the level of gas seepage inside tunnels and holes, and give an audible alarm signal to the diggers before the gas build-up becomes life threatening. Gas masks should also be supplied for additional protection, to diggers as an added safety measure. Always be prepared for the worst situation while excavating new sites.

9.20 **Gold Treasure Signs**

GOLD SIGNS

ORE

XP
XO
A
6
XcD
7K

Above are some of the generic treasure signs for gold bars, gold coins, gold bars in boxes, and the golden Buddha.

9.21 <u>Gold Bar Types</u>

Gold bars are manufactured in different units of weight to accommodate the needs and preferences of different countries and geographical regions. The Latin name for gold is "Aurum Utalium", which has been abbreviated to **"AU"**.

The Gram is recognised internationally, but ***"Troy Ounces"*** are used in Countries such as USA, UK, and Australia.
The ***"Tola"*** is found as a weight measurement in India, Pakistan, Middle East and in Singapore.
In Chinese speaking countries such as Taiwan, Hong Kong and mainland China, the unit of weight for gold is the ***"Teal"***.
Thailand is different in that they use the ***"Baht"***, and in Vietnam the ***"Chi"*** is used.

In Korea it changes again to the ***"Don"***.
It is important, therefore, to know how much a gold bar should weigh, and have an idea about its origin, and its value, before contacting a reputable gold buyer.

Before 1968, gold traded at a fixed price of only $35.00 per troy ounce under the "Gold Standard".
In 1970, the United States decided to abandon the "Gold Standard" and gold rose in value over the next twenty years peaking in 1980 at $850.00.

In recent years the gold price has fluctuated; now as I write this book the price is $1360.80 a troy ounce. A treasure hunter must be aware of the London Metal Exchange price for gold, which is "fixed" twice a day during a normal stock exchange trading five-day week. Please see: **http://www.goldprice.org/gold-price-per-gram.html** for gold prices shown in various currencies including U.S. Dollar ($), Philippine Peso (PHP) and British Pound (£) and the various international price charts for gold and other metals traded internationally.

Another site is: **http://www.metalmarkets.org.uk/metals/gold.html**.

Below is a useful weights conversion table for the different bars mentioned on the previous page.

GOLD WEIGHT CONVERSION TABLES		
TYPE	**GRAMMES**	**TROY OUNCES**
100 grammes	N/A	3.215107456 oz
1 Ounce (oz)	31.1035 g	N/A
10 Tola	116.638 g	3.750 oz
5 Teal	187.145 g	6.017 oz
10 Baht	152.440 g	4.901 oz
5 Chi	18.7500 g	0.603 oz
10 Don	37.5000 g	1.206 oz
KILOGRAMS	**GRAMMES**	**TROY OUNCES**
1.0 kg	1000 g	32.15074656 oz
6.5 kg	6500 g	208.9798526 oz
1000 kg (1 Metric Tonne)	1000000 g	32,150.74656 oz

Nitric Acid Test For Checking Gold

If you want to check to see if a gold bar is indeed the "real" deal, then use a few drops of nitric acid on a clean surface area of the metal to check to see if the metal you have is indeed real and not fake.

It may be a good idea to wash the gold or metal under test with warm soapy water and rinse with warm water.
This will make the surface of the metal clean and warm, meaning that if there is a chemical reaction between the acid and the metal it will be instantly recognizable as a fake.

When nitric acid comes into contact with real gold, platinium or silver, there will be no reaction on the surface of the metal when the acid drops are applied.

If, however, the nitric acid starts to boil and bubble and then suddenly turns a greenish colour then this metal is fake. In the case of a gold bar check the whole length of the bar.

Just in case the bar may be made up of different metal types; for example one end of the bar may be gold, the second half may be made from brass or another heavy metal such as lead. The whole length of the bar must be tested with a line of nitric acid. You decide if you want to test every side of a bar and its facets to make sure it is indeed the genuine article.

Note: Nitric acid is very corrosive to the skin and it is advisable that rubber gloves and safety glasses should be worn for safety reasons. This "acid test" must be carried out in a well-ventilated area and persons must be aware of the toxic fumes that will cause breathing or respiratory failure.

Any smoke or toxic fumes resulting from the metal chemical reaction with the acid must not be inhaled, as this will cause corrosive damage to your lungs and nasal passage.
A filter mask should be worn if this test is going to be carried out in a closed room for security reasons, or, even better still, inside a proper ventilated chemical fume cupboard that has built-in extraction fans that suck the harmful fumes away from the person carrying out the acid test.

Please also be aware that there are many gold bar buying scams and criminal groups ready to pounce on the gullible and unaware in the Philippines. Do not become another victim; look at the website link below where many scams are discussed in detail.

See: http://www.tseatc.com/goldscams.html

9.22 Calculations For Estimating The Weight Of A Gold Bar

Gold Fineness Table

Divide Karat % x 24.024

Karat %	Fineness
24	0.999
23	0.957
22	0.916
21	0.874
20	0.832
19	0.790
18	0.750
17	0.707
16	0.666
15	0.624

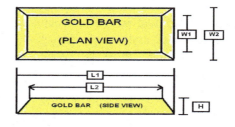

Step 1: Measure the bar length in centimetres: Note the widths, height and lengths as shown above, then firstly add the two lengths together (**L1 and L2**) and divide by two to get the exact length, and then the same for (**W1 and W2**) and divide by two to give the correct width.

Step 2: Multiply: Bar **LENGTH X WIDTH X HEIGHT to give you the cubic volume of the bar.**

Step 3: Multiply: Step 2's answer by **19.3** (The Specific Gravity of Gold). Answer: **xxxx kg.**

For Example: We have measured a bar, and the dimensions have been recorded below:

The Length (L1+L2/2) = 12.5 cm X (W1=W2/2) = 9 cm X H = 3 cm X **19.3 = 6.513 kg**

Gold price using the second fixed price from the London Bullion Market Association is $1519.70 per troy ounce as of 12-05-12 (1 kg = 32.15 troy ounces). We will say that this bar is a **24**-Karat Bar. Therefore, we have: $1519.70 X 32.15 X **0.999** (from **Gold Fineness Table** above) X 6.513 kg. This bar is worth: **$317,896.25** (minus the buyer's commission of 20-25%). See: **www.lbma.org.uk**

To give you a guide price in dollars for recovered weights of known gold bars at say **22**-Karat:

$1519.70 X 32.15 X **0.916** X 6.3 kg = **$281,951.79**
Let's say each bar below is **22**-Karat for this example, then:

Cambodia:	5 stars 6.3 kg:	**$281,951.79 USD**
Sumatra:	4 stars 6.2 kg:	**$277,476.36 USD**
Burma:	3 stars 6.0 kg:	**$268,525.51 USD**

The gold prices will fluctuate as the demand for gold increases (**goes up**) and decreases (**goes down**). Please be aware of what you have found, and what your recovered bar is actually worth **BEFORE** you talk to a registered reputable buyer. As I write this book, the price of gold is at an all time high, and may even top $2000 USD a troy ounce due to the increasing demand for precious metals from China and the weakness of the U.S. dollar against other foreign currencies worldwide.

China will soon issue a new international currency, and this will be backed by gold reserves held by the Chinese people. This currency will in time topple the dollar. The dollar is not backed by a recognised gold standard and will fail because of a greedy Federal banking system. As gold prices climb, so will the number of treasure hunters looking for buried gold around the world. The Philippines will attract its share of serious gold mining companies, corporations, governments and foreign gold hunters to many of the island's shores over the next twenty plus years. The Yamashita golden legend is very real and lives on. Will you be part of this legend and follow your dreams?

If you are not sure of the karat content of the gold, purchase an M24 Stock# TES-170.00. This device will assay gold ranging from 9-24-Karat. **See:** http://www.shorinternational.com/TestGold.htm.

9.23 Heart-Shaped Rocks And "Heart" Treasure Signs

There are many different heart-shaped signs which are used to signify that the treasure is either buried near, under, or slightly away from the "Heart" sign. A "Heart" sign means "Rich Home" to the Japanese soldier. The treasure is buried close by.

A heart-shaped rock must be inspected closely, and if found to be pink in colour may have treasure stored inside (see below). Other heart shapes may tell the treasure hunter of hidden booby traps, as shown later in this section, and extreme caution will be needed before continuing.

This heart-shaped coral rock was found in Mindanao by the author himself. You can see that the underneath has been hollowed out and re-filled with hard pink concrete.

Pink to the Japanese signified the "cherry blossom", a very special lucky symbol to the Japanese people. The rock has one or two gold bars inside, and was probably hidden by a soldier or an officer who never returned to claim it! I was not allowed to take this rock from this private beach I am sad to say.

9.24   **Heart-Shaped Rock Photograph**

I took this photograph of a large heart-shaped rock just up the coast from the first, sitting on the beach and weighing in at approximately twenty tonnes. (See the strange markings on the bottom of this rock.)
The Japanese had hollowed out a large coral rock and placed the treasure inside then filled it up with pink cement, which has set hard over a long period of time.

The owner of the land told us that Japanese soldiers were trying to break it open with hammers and chisels. When he asked them why they told him it was filled with gold bars and gold coins! He told them to get off his beach and land and never to come back! The rock, I believe, is still there, waiting to be opened.

This rock can be seen and would be used as a "marker" for returning Japanese after the war, so that the main treasure site could be found easily once this monster of a rock was located.

At the top of the track, leading up to a coconut plantation, we came across treasure markings on rocks. In a small valley, now planted with coconut trees, we found the main treasure site. The heart-shaped rock is the "Giveaway". The main cache of treasure is buried some 150 metres away further in land. In May 2012 a young Japanese national has visited this site claiming to have the original treasure map for this site. He has stated to my Filipino contact that it belonged to his late grandfather, a high-ranking Japanese officer stationed in Mindanao during the Second World War.
He plans to excavate this site; how he will succeed without proper planning, authorization and heavy equipment remains to be seen.

9.25 **_Heart Treasure Signs Example 1_**

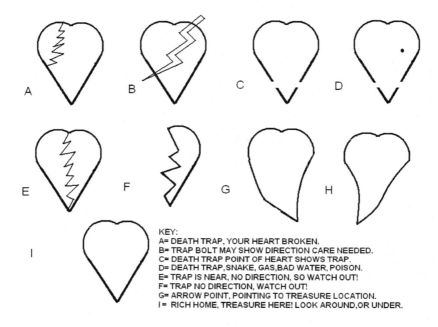

KEY:
A= DEATH TRAP, YOUR HEART BROKEN.
B= TRAP BOLT MAY SHOW DIRECTION CARE NEEDED.
C= DEATH TRAP POINT OF HEART SHOWS TRAP.
D= DEATH TRAP, SNAKE, GAS, BAD WATER, POISON.
E= TRAP IS NEAR, NO DIRECTION, SO WATCH OUT!
F= TRAP NO DIRECTION, WATCH OUT!
G= ARROW POINT, POINTING TO TREASURE LOCATION.
I = RICH HOME, TREASURE HERE! LOOK AROUND, OR UNDER.

Here are some of the heart symbols that are used to mark treasure deposits. There are many other heart symbols that use the heart shape as a central symbol surrounded by other symbols drawn by different treasure code writers during the Second World War. On the subsequent pages you will see many other examples.

9.26 <u>Heart Treasure Signs Example2</u>

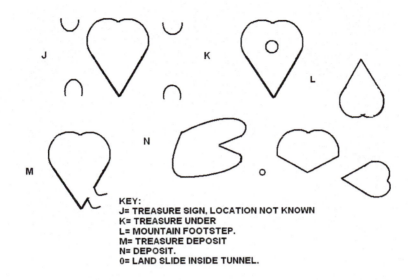

KEY:
J= TREASURE SIGN, LOCATION NOT KNOWN
K= TREASURE UNDER
L= MOUNTAIN FOOTSTEP.
M= TREASURE DEPOSIT
N= DEPOSIT.
O= LAND SLIDE INSIDE TUNNEL.

Photograph 1: Heart shape in concrete: Deposit under.

Photograph 2: Mountain footstep: follow point of heart shape and seek another marker along the trail.

9.27 Heart-Shaped Rock As Part Of A Treasure Site

This photograph shows a heart-shaped rock in the foreground, carved out of coral rock, pointing towards two deposits nearby. Above this picture was an old Japanese bunker that the treasure hunters thought would hold the treasure. They really should have concentrated their efforts in looking closely at this area of the WWII Japanese military camp before they spent eight weeks trying to break into the old reinforced bunker, in which they found nothing! This heart-shaped rock is part of a larger treasure site; it is a marker and a symbol stating "Hey it's here come and find me". The coral rock that the heart shape is made out of is easy to carve, and easy to hollow out. Always look underneath these "heart" rocks and on top of them to see if they have been re-filled with pink concrete, fine sand or small pebbles. A shadow face is looking into a small cave, another place to hide the hoard. (Ringed above in purple.)

Site Observations

Take as many digital photographs of the site as possible and compare them with old WWII images or maps of the area and see what physical changes have occurred over the passing years.

Always observe strange shaped rocks and geographical features and take as many pictures with your digital camera as you can. Allow yourself time to study them over a period of two to three days after you have left the site, and allow these photographs to tell you the story of the past, and always have an open mind about what they are telling you. Historical WWII documentation may not match up with the photographic evidence, simply because over time earthquakes, landscapes changing due to landslides floods, and tree cutting, have resulted in landscapes changing forever.

Always write down the thoughts that pop into your head when you are studying and observing strange geographic features or rock markings that your camera has captured and you have not observed using your naked eye. This lack of observation may have been caused by too many distractions while you visited the site. Photographic images allow you to take a more pragmatic "observer's approach" to treasure seeking.

Remember a well rested treasure hunter will be able to detect more visual information than a dirty sweaty tired one! Give yourself time to absorb the images and the vibrations of the subject area.

Confirm your theories about the site and adjust your future excavation plans after you have taken in the scenery.

Remember anyone can be a "busy fool"; you are different and want to be rich, therefore apply action based on clear observation and known facts. With practice you will become a master at spotting subtle treasure markers and signs that others will miss completely. This photographic example above proves my point.

This site was sold to another party that went on to recover riches here, simply because the original team ignored my advice regarding where to dig and failed to put my recommendations into action.

Sadly it was their loss and someone else's financial gain; in this case a rich American! As the old proverb states: **"You can lead a horse to water, but you cannot make it drink."** This is the sad fact, so remember if you want the job done correctly do it yourself! Don't rely on others to do the job for you.

9.28   Heart Treasure Signs On Rocks

A heart carved into a rock with another five-sided symbol meaning "Treasure" or Pentagon; five deposits near to each other. The heart is pointing down, therefore dig below the treasure heart symbol to recover what is buried here.

9.29   Korean "Heart" Treasure Sign

In the photograph (left) we can see a heart with a circle on top. This symbol was found in Davao, Mindanao and is different to any other symbols I have seen. If the circle was in the middle of the heart then this would mean: "Treasure Under". In this case the circle is outside of the heart, meaning that there is a deposit, but where?

The Solution:

Only by dowsing the rock and looking for a gold target did I manage to find a hot spot in the centre of the heart. Therefore, the deposit (a giveaway) is to be found inside the rock itself. I would also check under the rock to see if there was a larger deposit buried at a depth of approximately 5-9 feet.

Here is another heart-shaped rock I photographed on a known treasure site near Bamban Luzon, where eleven trucks packed with gold bullion are still buried inside a closed tunnel system.

This one site would make an excellent second book of how this treasure was excavated. Maybe one day…

9.30 Hollow Rock Treasure: A Photographic Example

In this section of my book I explain all about hollow rocks and how the Japanese camouflaged rocks to hide treasure inside them. The photograph below gives us so many clues as to where treasure is located; look out for pinkish marks in the rock itself; the angular shape of the rock is important as a marker; and the faded carved treasure symbols you will find anywhere on the rock itself.

In this case, as shown in the photograph below, the sheer size of the rock on the landscape means that it will be easily recognizable as a marker by a returning Japanese soldier who would want to recover his treasure when the war was over.

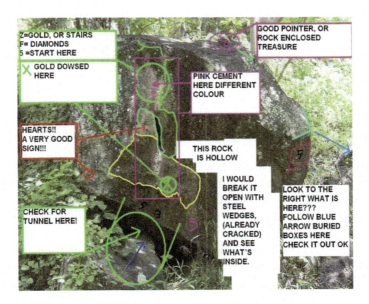

This huge rock has a hollow slit in the centre, which has been filled with pink concrete.

There are three deposits here: one inside the rock, another under the rock in a tunnel system, and a separate deposit to the right of this picture. (Follow the dark blue arrow). The type of hollow deposits can be found on the next page.

9.31 Hollow Rock Treasure: Diagrams And Symbols

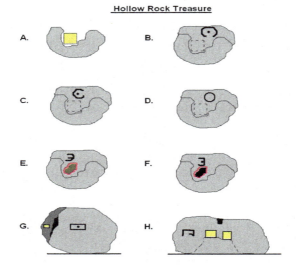

Hollow Rock Treasure

KEY:

A: Coral rock or soft sandstone is hollowed out, and the treasure placed inside.
B: The treasure and the hollow cavern is filled with crushed shells, coral and pink cement and the new top cemented into position. "Enclosed Treasure" symbol is added.
C: Another enclosed treasure with another symbol meaning the same as B.
D: This rock shows a circle meaning "Enclosed Treasure" inside.
E: A smaller rock cemented to block a hole in the hollow rock hides a small deposit inside.
F: The same as above.
G: Pink concrete added to the rock and hiding a small deposit. "Enclosed Treasure" symbol is used again to convey this message.
H: Hole drilled in the top of the rock means: "Deposit Inside **OR** Deposit Under". Also the "Enclosed Treasure" symbol can be seen on the left-hand side of the rock.

On the next two pages there are three more examples showing you what to look for and where.

9.32 Hollow Rock Treasure: Photographic Examples A & B

KEY

A: The rectangle left under coral rock when a certain American treasure hunter found a box containing one gold bar on a beach near to Glan in Mindanao. I took this photograph of his handiwork in 2006.

He ran off with the landowner chasing him. The same man had also broken many rocks along this coast line, found on private land, and had stolen gold bars found inside hollowed-out rocks from the poor inhabitants in this area.

B: This rock found on a larger treasure site has been refilled using cement and crushed rock. The pink lines show colour differences over time, and the triangle symbols means: "Rich object between rocks or trees". The gold bars **ARE** inside this rock behind the triangle, but the four guys in the picture did not know this…until now.

9.33 Hollow Rock Treasure: Photographic Example C

The above photograph is an example of E & F, as seen in section 9.31 previously.

A hollowed-out rock where the opening has been plugged with coloured concrete, which over time has shrunk and fallen away. The triangle symbol means that there is treasure between rocks or a concealed entrance to a deposit here or close by.

9.34   *Pink Concrete: How To Break It*

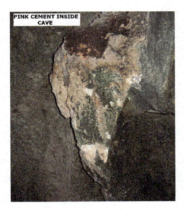

Pink concrete used by the Japanese military all over the Philippines to either hide treasure inside or cover a treasure site. The use of fine china clay and special mix of hard cement powder made a very hard concrete which still survives today in man-made shaped rocks, and for filling holes or entrances to tunnels. The pink colour represents the "cherry blossom" a lucky symbol to the Japanese and an easy treasure marker to recognise.

9.35 <u>Pink Concrete: Using Acid</u>

This concrete is still very hard, even after all of this time. American treasure hunters stated that ordinary cement can either be dissolved using using Hydro Chloric Acid (<u>HCl</u>) or Thermite, or a Jackhammer. This is not ordinary cement. The sand and mix of fine clay and special cement makes it as hard as marble rock; very hard to break. Its cohesive bonding strength is very strong, therefore some thought has to be given to how it can be broken up in a safe and easy manner.

<u>Disadvantages of Hydro Chloric Acid:</u>

This acid is very dangerous to transport, corrosive, and causes breathing problems in small confined areas. The acid will continue to react with the silica in the concrete, and will require a lot of water to neutralise the effects of the acid before the excavations can start up again.

<u>Concentrated Sulphuric Acid Experiment</u>

In December 2008 an experiment was carried out in a laboratory based in Liverpool, England with three samples of pink concrete taken from the large heart stone, as seen in section 9.22, taken from a beach site in Mindanao by the author of this book.

The cement samples were placed into a glass beaker, and concentrated sulphuric acid was poured over the samples until they were completely submerged. The exact time for these small pieces of pink concrete only weighing 3 grams each took thirty-six hours to completely dissolve into the acid solution.

Therefore, unless you have years to wait, this is not the way forward, and not the correct solution to dissolving hardened pink concrete.

9.36   **Pink Concrete: Use Thermite**

Thermite is a pyrotechnic composition of aluminium powder and a metal oxide which produces an aluminothermic reaction known as a thermite reaction. It is not explosive, but can create short bursts of extremely high temperatures focused on a very small target for a short period of time.

The aluminium reduces the oxide of another metal, most commonly iron oxide, because aluminium is highly combustible. The products are aluminium oxide, free elemental iron, and a large amount of heat. The reactants are commonly powdered and mixed with a binder to keep the material solid and prevent separation.

Thermite is very volatile when lit; I would not use it inside a cave simply because the lack of space and the fumes that are released at very white hot temperatures could ignite natural gas in the air and trap explosive gases below a concrete slab you are trying to destroy.

It is not a safe substance to transport by air, and if it gets wet it becomes useless. Ordinary thermite mixture is too slow to burn through pink cement or even hardened cement unless other chemicals are mixed with the aluminium oxide and iron oxide to make the reaction burn at an even higher temperature and for longer periods.

The late Robert Curtis, the famous American treasure hunter, increased the rate at which the mixture burnt by adding additional oxides; this higher temperature meant the cutting ability of the white hot flame cut down the time the thermite took to burn through re-enforced bunker concrete. He achieved this by carrying out many experiments in the U.S. There is no record to tell us whether he ever tried his new formulae on pink concrete. Sadly his thermite formulation was a closely-guarded secret, and died with him.

9.37   **Pink Concrete: "The Solution"**

Over the last three years, I have been researching the international market to find a chemical that is safe to transport either by road, air or sea, which is safe to handle and will break up pink cement in a controlled and safe manner for all concerned. Well I think I have found every treasure hunter's dream to this very old "pink" problem!

The chemical is powder based and is called "Dexpan".

What is Dexpan?

DEXPAN is a non-explosive, controlled demolition agent, which is used for demolition, rock breaking, concrete cutting, and quarrying.

It is packed in moisture-proof boxes, <u>Size</u>: (38cm x 28cm x 18cm), <u>Weight</u>: 20 kg, with every box containing four plastic bags each holding 5 kgs of Dexpan powder.

Once mixed with clean water, it is poured into holes pre-drilled in the material you are working with. It can be poured into the same holes where dangerous explosives are usually placed.

The treasure hunter can do more work safely, while providing controlled expansive cracking.

This material can also be used to achieve perfect slabs and blocks from limestone, marble, granite, sandstone or whatever material you are working with.

DEXPAN can be applied in the field where cracking by means of explosives is not suitable due to explosive gases or other dangers.

9.38 *Pink Concrete: Using Dexpan*

DEXPAN makes cleaning up on the job site safer, faster and easier to stay within environmental and local Health and Safety regulations.
Environmental implications are obvious: (i) Little to clean up, (ii) Dissolves in water after use, (iii) No chemical residue and (iv) No gaseous fumes. Ideal for treasure hunters!

DEXPAN is safe to use in close quarters, where large equipment cannot reach and dust contamination is totally out of the question.
This product helps to cut costs and increase safety. When explosives have to be used, it can be used to structurally weaken buildings in order to use fewer explosives and to help ensure an even safer collapse.

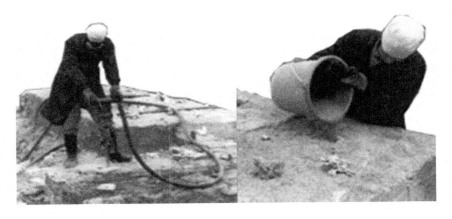

This product can be used to break: marble, granite, sandstone, limestone, onyx, reinforced concrete cutting, tunnel excavation, demolition under water.

Use an air drill to make the holes, then after cleaning the holes mix Dexpan powder with water; this is poured into the holes, then wait thirty-six hours. The results below speak for themselves:

 The photograph on the left shows how Dexpan has broken up this large concrete slab with ease.

If this was covering a treasure site, it would be easy to remove each broken section of concrete without disturbing the excavation or whatever was stored beneath. Any escaping methane or other toxic gases can vent freely into the air and be detected prior to diggers going back into the shaft to continue the excavation.

For further information please see the appendix at the rear of this book.

9.39 The Pulley Secret Explained

Some treasure hunters have said that they have wandered inside natural cave systems and man-made tunnels and found an old pulley wheel hanging down from the ceiling of the tunnel.

This pulley is usually found approximately 3-5 meters inside the tunnel or cave entrance itself and is only seen when a bright light is shone up onto the ceiling area.

Usually this object is very rusty and its brownish colour has over time blended in with surrounding colours of the rock which it is bolted securely into. Look closely for rusty brownish areas on the ceiling and high up on walls.

The physical size of the pulley will give you an idea of the weight it was expected to lift at the time it was installed.

A Large Pulley System

The positioning of the pulley is important in that it tells us the people who used such a device inside the tunnel or cave complex wanted to lift a heavy weight and then lower heavy objects either onto a cart or the bed of a truck (if the entrance was wide enough) to transport the object(s) out of its hiding place and to be taken away.

There is, however, another reason why the pulley could have been bolted onto the ceiling at this precise spot. The secret burial of objects that were so heavy and valuable only a large pulley system would enable their safe burial, being assured no damage would occur as the precious items were lowered into an already-dug deep hole or pit.

These items would have included such things as golden Buddhas, gold bars, barrels of gold coins, boxes of gold bonds, foreign currency, boxes of diamonds and fragile antiques.

9.40   Rock Tunnel Maps Explained

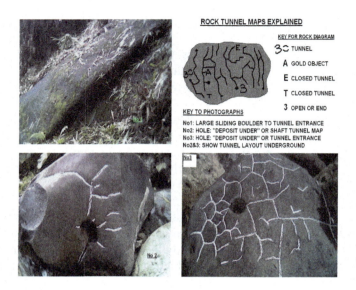

Here are some photographic examples of tunnel maps drawn on rocks showing the tunnel routes underground. Usually these rocks are turned upside down, hidden from view, and found by treasure hunters simply by chance. Tunnel map rocks have been found in the middle of rivers or stream beds, as well as on the sides of hills. Entrances to these tunnels can be found via hidden cave entrances, slits in the rocks, or shafts where entry could be behind sliding boulders that part like a pair of sliding doors, or under a flat stone as shown in the photograph No.1, top left. A top tip is to look at whether the area is made up of limestone or chalk – ideal places for tunneling and secret tunnel entrances waiting to be discovered.

Note: large flat rocks make excellent places to carve maps of tunnels or buried deposits. These flat stones would then be turned over to hide the map from preying eyes and left in a prominent position away from areas that may flood in the rainy season, but easy to locate when the time came to recover the hidden booty.

Note: Always be aware that snakes and other creatures hide under these rocks, so caution is needed when you go to turn the large flat stone over to see what it may be concealing; there may be a nasty surprise waiting to bite or nip you.

9.41   Rock Analysis By Water

A carved animal found very near to a Japanese man-made lake.
This marker is pointing and has a "5" symbol. The shapes could also represent the shape of the lake and where to look for the next symbol or deposit.

Man-made pools and lakes made by the Japanese military are ideal places to hide treasure. Who would check muddy water for boxes of gold bullion? These lakes are usually fed from a diverted spring or stream. Water is a very good barrier to deter the treasure hunter. Always check lakes and ponds made by the imperial forces, and ask: why did they make the lake in the first place? Could it possibly hide a secret flooded entrance to a treasure site or indeed a treasure deposit? Always check it out thoroughly.

9.42   Rice field Treasure Symbols
Ricefield Treasure

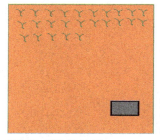

Note: A 4 feet x 4 feet concrete vault buried in the corner of the rice field 3- 6 feet down.

SYMBOLS

⊠ Lying on one side of rice field treasure below.
⊠ Deposit in rice field area 1-200 meters.

By probing the mud with a long piece of bamboo, this rice farmer found the cement vault at 3 feet down in the corner of his field. The measurements were: 4 feet x 4 feet x 1 foot. Waterlogged areas of a field could hide buried concrete structures underneath, especially if plants will not grow there due to the concrete vault submerged below, absorbing the water meant for the rice plant.

If, however, crops do grow over buried concrete structures, the soil depth will be a lot shallower and the root system of the plant growing on top will not receive the nutrients needed for good growth; therefore, the plants will be shorter in height than the surrounding crops. In the dry season, sometimes the outline of the structure below the ground can be seen through the dry earth on top, revealing hidden concrete bunkers buried just under the surface of the ground.

9.43   River And Waterfall Burial Locations

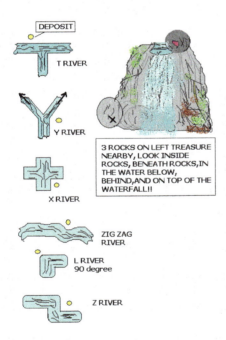

The Japanese military would bury smaller deposits inside the river banks, under the water, inside or under large rocks sitting in the river. Treasure deposits have been found in areas where Japanese soldiers used to communally bathe together in large natural pools, in rivers, or man-made pools. These sites are usually marked with stone turtles, frogs, or fish symbols, or stone shapes that represent these animals. All of these creations are pointing in the direction of where the deposit is hidden and will be found.

See section 9.47 for 34 water-based treasure symbols.

217

9.44 Waterfall Photograph: Spot The Treasure Clues

The photograph (left) of a waterfall looks very natural in all its splendour, but in actual fact it has been made by man, and hides treasure secrets. Can you spot the symbols and the treasure clues?

9.45 Waterfall Photograph: Symbols Revealed

The heart symbols on the bottom left and right of the picture are pointing to deposits under the water. The "5" and arrow are telling us "start here and follow the arrow" a short way to the face, which is looking into the water below. The rock that makes the eyes has been sliced in two and the eyes themselves are man-made using diamond chisels.

The interpretation of the symbols found on the head is very interesting. Above is a "5" for "start here". Below on the head: "Z" for "gold" or "stairs going down". I would take the head rock off to see what was inside. (See top yellow circle on right-hand side).

Always look and look again for any strange symbols around waterfall sites. Becoming a good observer of these places will reveal so many secrets that others have missed or cannot see. Become a "master of observation" and you will find what you seek!

9.46   River Burial Locations And Clues

In the diagram below, we can see that a concrete vault full of gold bars has been buried at a depth of 20+ feet. The water source has been piped to the shaft housing the concrete vault to create a water trap.

The water is held back using coconut matting, small stones and a glue-type jelly substance, which is held in place by the left side of the heavy cement vault pressing on the side of this man-made water plug. (See diagram below).

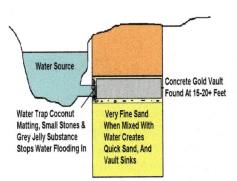

If the treasure hunter decides to break the vault inside the hole, then the cement vault will sink into the fine sand; with every sledge blow the vault will sink further, thus activating the water trap and flooding the shaft. The sand then becomes saturated with water and the heavy cement vault sinks into the deep shaft full of fine sand below, creating a "quick sand trap", drowning the treasure diggers as the concrete vault is sucked under the fine watery sand mix.

The solution is to make sure that the water source into the shaft is cut off prior to excavating the concrete vault itself. The safest way is to extract the concrete vault completely out of the shaft by using heavy lift ropes and pulleys before even trying to break the vault open.

Japanese Military Riverside Occupation "Photographical Evidence"

Photograph A: Japanese tunnel entrance in the river bank. Above the entrance a carved Japanese symbol.

Photograph B: A stone carved Japanese oven used by soldiers for cooking rice and making tea. The smoke of the fire would diffuse through tall grasses high above the river bank, concealing the soldiers.

9.47 River Digging And Water Treasure Symbols

A small treasure hoard was to be buried in the river bed or very close to the river bank.

The Japanese would make sure that the treasure was encased in either bitumen or covered by a concrete jacket prior to burial in order to protect the rich object against water and mechanical damage and to conceal its real identity. Gold does not corrode under fresh or salt water. The hole would be dug to a maximum depth of 10 feet in sand or to a depth when the water reached neck level of the digger. In the case of soil being present at the chosen treasure site, the depth of the hole would be 12 feet, or to a depth where the water again reached neck level.

These hoards would be buried during summer months, when the river levels would be at the lowest point, and possibly two days after the full moon, when water levels would be expected to be at their lowest.
Always look to see if a treasure hoard is also concealed inside the river bank, behind rocks or a dense covering of bushes and trees.

Water Treasure Symbols

In this part of the book I have included thirty-four symbols associated with buried targets in or near water, creeks, springs and rivers. I make no apology for duplicating some of these symbols found later in this book in section 21, entitled "Directions" colour coded in green. The reason for this duplication is a simple one: in this section these symbols can easily be recognisable under the "water section" of this book, giving you, the reader, the task of finding out what the symbol means when you are exploring water-based treasure sites a lot easier. Therefore, I give you water treasure signs and a brief explanation of each symbol's meaning.

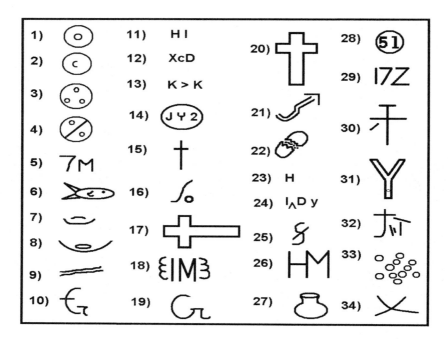

KEY

1) Gold on spring. 2) Spring gold. 3) Gold on spring. 4) Gold on spring. 5) Treasure under water. 6) Treasure by or gold under water. 7) Object under water or stream. 8) Tunnel under water. 9) Treasure near creek. 10) Deposit under water. 11) River or water. 12) Gold deposit in spring. 13) Object in water. 14) Deposit under water. 15) The long part of the cross points to treasure on water. 16) Below water. 17) Treasure in water. 18) Deposit under water. 19) Deposit under water. 20) Treasure buried in creek. 21) Object in side of creek. 22) Object under the water or bridge. 23) Pointing to tunnel in water. 24) Treasure under water. 25) Deposit under water. 26) Treasure under water. 27) Deposit under water. 28) Gold under water. 29) Deposit under water. 30) Under water five yards ahead. 31) Treasure on creek or Y tunnel. 32) Object in big river. 33) In water or in spring. 34) Object in water, treasure inside straight hole.

9.48 Sun And Spoke Treasure Symbols Explained

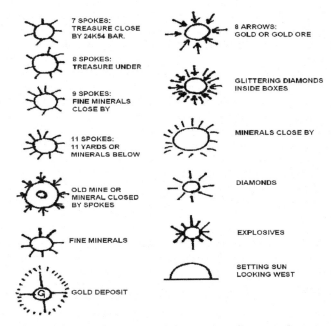

Sun symbols signify the burial of gold or fine precious stones that have been buried on the spot or nearby. The spoke system, or number of rays of light around the "sun" circle, signify what is buried and where. In some treasure codes *one spoke* represents **one yard or 39 inches.** Count the spokes to find the distance at which the treasure is buried.

If no other arrow symbol gives you a direction to follow, then you must assume that the treasure location will be inside the radius of the number of spokes; the location of the Sun and Spoke symbol is the center point. For example, eight spokes equals 8 yards; you draw a circle using the Sun and Spoke symbol as the centre, and measure from the centre a radius measurement 8 yards wide. Somewhere in this circle, where the diameter of the whole circle is now 16 yards wide, the treasure deposit will be found using a deep search metal detector.

9.49 Snake Symbols

 Golden Snake: Treasure Underneath

 Striking Position: Points Towards Treasure

 A Coiled Snake: The Treasure Is Buried Underneath This Symbol

 Small Snake: Points To Treasure Up The Tree

Wild Snake: Treasure Cache is Near

The snake symbol is used to show that it is the guardian of the treasure, and protects it with gas or poison capsules inside the earth that surrounds the treasure deposit. Real live snakes frequent old tunnels and caves. Many local native Filipinos believe that these creatures sleep on top of treasure buried in these places and will fight to protect these precious items.

9.50   Tree Markers And Treasure Signs

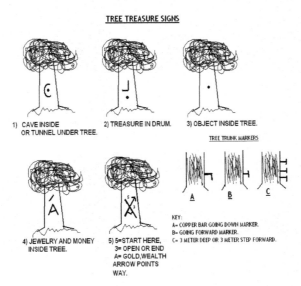

Tree signs are carved on many trees in the Philippines; the trees that the Japanese used were ones that stood out, so that they could be found easily when they returned at a later date to recover the treasure. The very large Acacia trees, the tall Coconut trees, old Mango trees, also the Duhat (Black Plum) tree, Pine tree and the Camachile trees were favourite places to bury or hide treasure.

Bamboo was also very popular, because it grew quickly, and the roots would protect the treasure from treasure hunters. The Bamboo was a very spiritual tree to the Japanese, and would be used to pray to Buddha when the weather was hot. Its long branches gave shade from the midday sun.

Where to Look

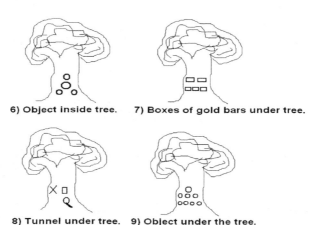

6) Object inside tree. 7) Boxes of gold bars under tree.

8) Tunnel under tree. 9) Object under the tree.

All of the markings on the trees are now to be found higher on the trunks of the trees, as they have grown over the last sixty-four plus years. The copper markers would also be higher up than when the Japanese first hammered them in.

Copper nails were a favourite to be used as markers, simply because they would last longer in the tropical heat, and would not rust away too quickly like steel type nails.

Ex. President Marcos knew the locations of many Imperial treasure sites, and ordered many symbol-signed trees to be cut down to protect the larger Imperial sites from other treasure hunters finding them before he could get around to excavating them himself.

There are many places in the Philippines where the Imperial Japanese soldier buried private stashes of gold finger bars; the favourite places seemed to be under the coconut or mango trees, especially when the Americans were counter-attacking their positions and the Japanese were taken by surprise.

These finds were not buried very deep, typically 1-8 feet down. Ammo boxes full of jewels were also buried under mango trees situated in Mango Groves, either on a hill side or near to a geographical feature such as a river or inside a natural limestone cave, again for ease of recognition after the war, and hopefully a peaceful recovery by the fleeing Imperial Japanese Soldier.

This photograph below shows a triangle, meaning "rich object", between rocks or trees and a symbol below indicating a tunnel, and a number "5" which means "start here". Or a tunnel is located behind this tree.

The markings have grown up the tree with age as seen above.

Some Tree Treasure Symbols:

Key

A) Under tree. B) Under tree here. C) Centre of tree or rock. D) Gold bars under tree and stones. E) Under tree or near here.

9.51 Trees With Eyes

The eye shown in the photo is pointing towards another treasure symbol carved on the tree shown in the next photograph.

9.52 Triangle, Dead and Bonsai Tree Markers

The triangle symbol here means "rich object" buried between the rocks or trees. The target is very close to this marker.

Note: One treasure hunter was told the Japanese military had buried four boxes of gold bars under a balite tree. The technique the Japanese used was to remove the main tap root and bury directly under the tree itself. Dead trees can also hide treasure underneath the root system or have tunnels running directly underneath the tree itself. If a tree is struck by lightning many times over many years, take a closer look at the tree! Many treasure hunters have found gold bars either inside or under the tree itself!

Dead Tree

On some sites trees that are dead have been found to have dry tunnels running directly underneath them. The roots have found their way into a dry tunnel system lacking both earth and water to keep the tree alive.

The Bonsai Tree Treasure Marker

The bonsai tree was planted as a treasure marker and the branches would have been trained to grow in a certain way so that they would form a double shaped cross.

These crosses signify that a treasure hoard has been buried either under the tree itself or very close to where the tree is positioned.

These trees will still be growing in places where known Japanese forces would have been living, either on military camps or in local communities.

Look closely at any old bonsai tree growing near to your suspected treasure site; it may be hiding a secret past that may lead you to a forgotten hidden treasure.

9.53 **Turtle Treasure Signs**

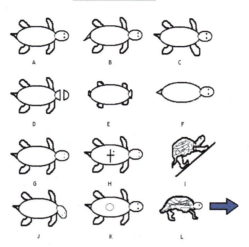

Turtle treasure signs have been used all over the world as pointers and markers; they are used to give the treasure hunter directions, depth of object, and distance to the target, or directions to next treasure marker. The above turtle signs show different signs and positions that can be found while treasure hunting.

These are just some the treasure hunter will come across, and there are possibly many more. The turtle sign is found as a carved sign on a rock or inside a cave, or as carved rock or cement shapes, and will be found on mountain ranges, near to lakes, streams, or rivers, either as pointers or have a deposit of gold or precious stones buried inside or underneath them.

Example "A": is telling the treasure hunter to follow the direction in which the head is pointing. This is the same as Example "L".

Example "B": is asking the treasure hunter to follow its tail to the treasure or the next treasure marker.

Example "C": Notice here the right front leg is bent, pointing towards the treasure or next treasure marker.

Example "D": The head of the turtle has been removed; this means that the treasure has already been taken.

Example "E": The head, legs, and tail are all hidden from view; this means danger to the treasure hunter, but also the objects are hidden, possibly underneath the turtle or nearby.

Example "F": The turtle has no legs or tail; this means that the treasure is here! If the turtle is made of stone or pink man-made concrete a hole will be drilled into the shell; the diameter of the hole will be approximately one in diameter and approximately 3 inches deep.
This tells the treasure hunter that the treasure is either inside (pink cement) the turtle or underneath it. Sometimes the heart has been carved onto the back of the shell with the hole drilled in the centre of the heart. This means: **"rich object inside or below"**.

Example "G": The turtle has distance markers showing a distance to the treasure, or the next marker on the treasure trail. These markers vary, and will depend on who buried the treasure in the first place. Some generals used diamonds to signify distance, others bars.

Example "H": The turtle is telling us that the treasure is buried to the right, and will be found at a depth of 3 metres.

Example "I": The turtle is climbing an incline or hill, which means "change direction".

Example "J": The turtle has his head turned to the right, towards the treasure, but also means "DEATH!"

Example "K": The turtle is where the treasure lies, underneath.

Example "L" The turtle's head is pointing towards the treasure, similar to Example "A".

Stone turtles have been found near to known old Japanese communal washing pools in rivers or pools pointing towards the entrance to the treasure or tunnel wealth entrance.

(See Section 9.43 River & Waterfall Burial Locations)

9.54   Photographic Analysis Of Stone Turtles

This turtle has been weathered by many years of rain and wind, but it still can tell us much about what is buried nearby and beneath it. The head is pointing north.

The turtle has hearts too, meaning "rich object below". The fish is pointing towards a water deposit.

9.55 More Photographic Analysis Of Stone Turtles

9.56 Photographic Analysis Of A Stone Turtle Shell

Shell: No Head, Tail or Legs

This is an example of "E": meaning danger, deposit either under the turtle or nearby.

The shell doesn't have any treasure markings on its back, but was found very near to a river. Therefore, the deposit will be in the river, inside an underwater cave or tunnel or inside the riverbank itself. The danger could be a water trap inside a vertical shaft or a tripwire inside the cave or tunnel itself.

To the Japanese, hexagons represent the divisions of a sea turtle's shell. These creatures, which return yearly to Japan, are an integral symbol of Japan. According to legend, Japan itself sits on the back of a gigantic sea turtle. Like the beloved Japanese crane, turtles represent long life, as they were both thought to live up to one-thousand years.

9.57   **Treasure Faces**

 A FACE WITH EYES LOOKING DIRECTLY AT OBJECT.

 A FACE WITH NO EYES: NO TREASURE HERE.

 A FACE WITH CROSSED EYES IS FACING TREASURE.

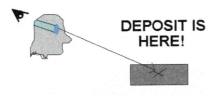

A ROCK STATUE OF A HEAD OR HUMAN SKULL POINTS TO THE TARGET. SOMETIMES THE LEFT OR RIGHT EYE HAS A HOLE DRILLED RIGHT THROUGH SO THAT THE TREASURE HUNTER CAN LOOK THROUGH TO SEE WHERE THE HEAD IS LOOKING.

Here the eyes are looking at the location of the treasure deposit; note the right eye socket is deeper than that of the left, suggesting that it is this eye that is looking directly at the precise location of where the treasure is buried.

This site is waiting excavation in late 2013.

9.58 How To Find Treasure Inside Tunnels

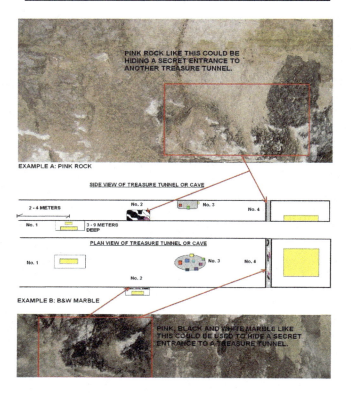

The treasure deposit shown in yellow can be buried at the entrance of the tunnel or cave as shown in location No.1. The treasure hunter will find a giveaway at approximately 3 meters deep. Below this target expect at a maximum depth of 9 meters the main treasure cache to be buried, usually in a sealed concrete vault. Location No.2 is a concealed tunnel entrance marked by black and white marbling or pink coloured rock. No.3 is a fall rock treasure, and No. 4 a false constructed wall which hides the main treasure deposit.

Sometimes the treasure hunter will break through this false wall and find nothing behind, but he should look very carefully, because the Japanese may have buried the deposit, as explained in Example No.1, or concealed the treasure in one of the walls, as in Example No.2.

You, as the treasure hunter, must be open minded and become very aware of the Japanese military art of total concealment. Use your cunning eye over places that will need closer inspection, and remember: seek and ye shall find.

9.59 How To Find Secret Tunnel And Cave Entrances

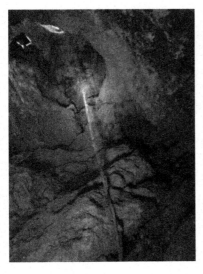

A secret tunnel entrance can be identified by the treasure hunter simply by looking for pink or black and white marble colouring on the walls of the tunnel, or a secret cave or tunnel entrance in a sheer rock face. The Japanese military put Japanese ceramic specialists from Ishikawa in northern Honsu in charge of sealing treasure entrances.

Using special clay from Northern China, mixed with washed marine sand, cement and local crushed rock and colouring, would help blend and camouflage these entrances. This technique meant that the cement would not shrink as it cured over time, leaving no visible trace to where the concealed opening was, but some kind of marker pointing to the entrance would be left behind. This would be a face, a turtle, an arrow pointing at the secret entrance or even a large "A" or a "3" or a number "5" to the left or right near to the closed entrance.

Large rocks may also be used to mark the location, positioned in front of the entrance to further conceal its location.

These secret tunnel entrances would be blocked up by a concreted wall 1-2 meters thick, and coloured in such a way as to blend in with the natural rock formations.

If these techniques were not used, then look for a very large boulder concealing the entrance, behind which smaller boulders would have been used to block up the tunnel or cave entrance.

What To Look For

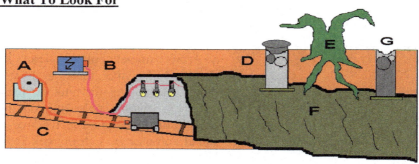

Key:

A: Motorized winch and steel cable used to pull mining carts out of the tunnel system.

B: Electrical generator to power lighting, power mining drilling equipment and telephone communications deep underground.

C: Narrow gauge railway tracks and wooden sleepers.

D: Vertical ventilation shafts for airflow underground. Expect these to run the whole length of the tunnel complex, and spaced every 4-6+ meters apart.

E: Dead tree, a tell-tale sign that the tree died because of a lack of water. The main tap root found no water in a dry tunnel system below, or was cut off when the tunnel was being mined.

F: The tunnel itself.

G: A depression in the ground, a sign of a collapsed ventilation shaft or a soldier's entrance into the tunnel below.

Treasure hunters have found that the motorized winches and the electrical generators have disappeared from old buried tunnel entrances. The items that remain, however, are the old narrow railway tracks, the steel cable, and the electrical power and field telephone cables located just under the surface of the ground. These items can easily be detected using metal detectors mentioned in sections 8.70 and 8.90. Once these metallic items are detected they will help lead you in the direction of the buried tunnel entrance and ultimately down into the tunnel complex itself. See link: http://www.geofizz.co.uk/products/rover-c2.htm

9.60 Construction of a Japanese Treasure Tunnel System (Luzon)

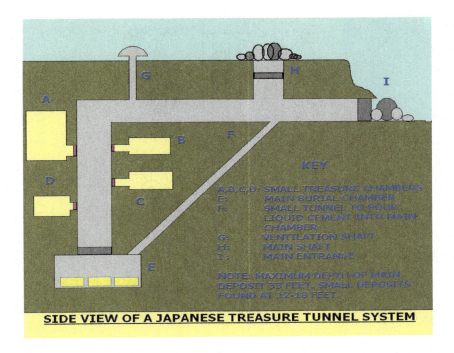

SIDE VIEW OF A JAPANESE TREASURE TUNNEL SYSTEM

This diagram shows the side view construction of a military Japanese treasure tunnel system excavated recently in Luzon. This was found on the eastern side of a steep ravine.

You can see how rocks and boulders have been used to conceal entrances and the main shaft ("H"). Secret treasure rooms "A", "B", "C", and "D" have been made off the main treasure shaft leading the main treasure burial chamber "E". Further excavation of this site is still continuing as I write this book. It is interesting to see the complexity of this particular treasure tunnel system and I can only imagine the hundreds of hours of digging that must have taken place in order to create such an elaborate structure underground.

9.61 Types Of Tunnel Layouts

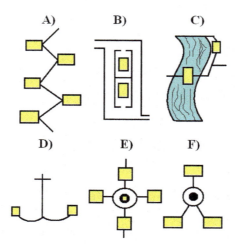

Key

A) Zig-Zag tunnel with chambers full of gold bars: Northern Luzon.

B) A basic tunnel bunker design: General Santos: Mindanao.

C) River tunnel system: Buddha deposit buried in the river bank, tunnels running under the river to the main deposit chamber, and existing on the other side of the river: Crow Valley: Luzon.

D) Anchor tunnel system: deposits opposite each other: Panay Island.

E) Central shaft used to lower deposits inside four chambers situated at different depths, and holding different precious items. For example, chamber 1: gold bars; chamber 2: loose diamonds; chamber 3: gold coins in barrels; chamber 4: jewellery. Location: Cagayan De Oro, Mindanao.

Never assume that tunnels are just straight; they were not. The Japanese military made them zig-zag and wind in different ways for defensive purposes. Many tunnel floors hide secret trapdoors to other tunnel systems running below the first. Always check for hidden passageways either in the tunnel floor or in the walls of the tunnels themselves.

9.62 Feel Your Way To Find Gold Deposits

The temperature of the walls of the tunnels always remain constant, but in the case of a false wall the temperature of the material used – clay, cement and crushed rock colouring – will be warmer in temperature to that of the surrounding natural rock face. The reason is simple: airflow behind false walls or sealed doors will cause a temperature difference of between 3-6 degrees centigrade that will be detected by the palm of your hand.

By looking for the pink and black and white marble colourings, as mentioned in section 9.58, and using your hand placed on the surface of the tunnel or cave, you should be able to feel the temperature difference and identify the area where the secret entrance starts and ends, revealing the secret tunnel. Other techniques include the use of a laser thermometer, which fires a laser at the wall and reads the reflected beam temperature via an LCD screen for you to note. By scanning the walls in this way you can quickly identify these hot spots.

If you are a very rich treasure hunter, then the use of a thermal image camera will greatly help in finding both secret entrances and areas of ground where the temperature is hotter that the surrounding ground temperature. These devices are very expensive, but will cut treasure hunting time in finding hidden treasure.

Once you have found the "hot spot" on the side of the tunnel wall, tap the area with a large hammer and see if you can hear an echo behind the secret entrance to the treasure tunnel. The ceramics have been known to break away easily due to old age. One Filipino was leaning on the tunnel wall, which collapsed under his body weight; he fell backwards into the secret tunnel entrance simply by accident and discovered ancient Chinese vases, and plates worth thousands of dollars.

Therefore, always look, then look again; explore places that you have visited before, and try using my search techniques; you may be very surprised with the results. Use as much light in darkened tunnels as possible to have the best chance of discovery. Very good bright flashlights are a must for seeing the differences in colours on walls and looking above at tunnel ceilings. Another technique to find hidden tunnels and gold deposits is by using laser guided infrared scanners.

Laser guided infrared scanners work by recognizing that all objects radiate infrared energy. This energy travels in all directions at the speed of light. Objects store and dissipate this energy in different ways and concentrations. For example, if treasure were hidden in a cave on the side of a mountain, and the mouth of the cave was filled in with rocks and rubble, the treasure would be hidden from sight.

However, when an infrared scanner is pointed and fired at the side of the mountain, it would read the typical surface temperature. The trapped air in the cave keeps the mouth, even though covered over, slightly cooler, and this difference can be detectable. Buried treasure (gold and silver) will absorb and store more heat than the ground surrounding it. As the ground cools, the treasure retains a higher degree of heat, which is indicated on the infrared scanner.

Using laser guided infrared scanners to locate physical things such as treasures, caves, tunnels, mines, and wells will shorten your site survey time. When an infrared scanner is used at a treasure site at ground level, or scans the side of a hill, the guided infrared scanner lens collects and focuses the energy onto an infrared detector.

Then the information is sampled by an onboard computer and is instantly displayed on an LCD screen, thus showing the temperature of the target area. By taking different readings of an area, the scanner will be able to determine temperature changes caused by buried metals, caves, tunnels and old mine shafts. Many treasure hunters have reported that infrared scanners have been instrumental in helping to locate many **new** treasure sites. Sometimes the ground is covered by heavy vegetation and it is almost impossible to take in larger metal detectors. In many cases the infrared scanners would locate the hot spot or disturbed area, making it easier to locate the treasure.

See link: http://www.kellycodetectors.com/laserscan/lasersca.htm.

9.63 Examples Of Excavated Treasure Shafts

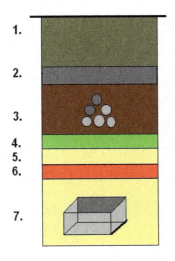

KEY:
1. Shallow Layer of Soil
2. Layer of Ceramics, Coral and Sea Shells 12 inches Thick.
3. Pyramid Rocks 3" in dia. Middle 6 inches in dia.
4. Green Planks of Wood.
5. Layer Of Fine Sand.
6. Red Planks of Wood.
7. Concrete Vault Found at 12 Feet Down Measurements: 24" Long 20" Thick & 20" Wide.

NOTE: BETWEEN THE GREEN AND RED PLANK A GREY JELLY SUBSTANCE WAS FOUND BELIEVED TO BE POISON. PLEASE BE AWARE!

Example 1

A side view of a shaft excavated in Negros Occidental; it gives the treasure hunter a detailed explanation of what to expect and what to look for as the excavations progress.

Example 2

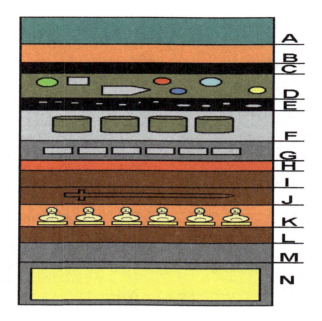

Key

A: 23 Meters: Top soil.
B: 26 Meters: Mud brown soil mixed with sawdust.
C: 27 Meters: Black soil or black sand.
D: 30 Meters: Brown soil with square, round coloured balls & marker stones.
E: 35 Meters: Gravel mixed with black soil or black sand.
F: 45 Meters: Brown soil: drums of gold coins.
G: 47 Meters: Concrete bar layer.
H: 49 Meters: Red soil layer.
I: 52 Meters: Brown soil layer.
J: 54 Meters: Japanese sword pointing to treasure vault.
K: 57 Meters: Golden Buddha layer.
L: 59 Meters: Brown soil layer.
M: 60 Meters: Concrete layer 0.5-5 meters thick.
N: 63 Meters: Golden bullion bars vault 1-10 metric tons.

9.64 An Actual Treasure Site Found In Rizal (2006)

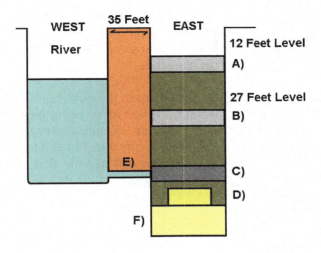

Key

A) 12 feet thick concrete slab.
B) 12 feet thick concrete slab.
C) 12 feet thick concrete slab or gold inside a concrete jacket.
D) Main gold deposit on top of fine sand.
E) Water trap expected at 55 feet or at the depth C) is located.
F) Fine sand to a depth of 30 feet.

As we can see from the above diagram, the deposit can only be recovered in a safe manner when the water source is cut off completely at E).

As I write this book, the excavations have stopped due to lack of finances, this group of treasure hunters have managed to reach a depth of 45 feet without having any problems with surface water. This is because the concrete layers have acted as giant hydraulic plugs, keeping the water table back at a lower level than that of the surrounding area. Once they remove the last concrete slab at a depth of 48 feet, water will either rush into the hole from the river water trap shown in position E), or the last hydraulic seal at position E) will be broken, releasing ground water deep inside the hole that will flood the gold and the diggers inside the shaft within a few minutes. The weight of the gold will then sink deep into the surrounding fine sand shown at position F).

This is another example of how the Japanese buried treasure hoards and has been included in this book just in case other treasure hunters come across a similar site in the future and can use these diagrams, for guidance purposes only, as to what to expect. At a depth of 55 feet, water traps, gas and bomb traps were placed as per the Japanese Engineering Battalion Code in order to protect Imperial treasure hoards from treasure seekers such as ourselves.

Please be aware that, as you get nearer to the gold deposit, the danger of the shaft collapsing, flooding, explosions or being gassed becomes all too prevalent and the threat to human life increases enormously. Yes there may be danger signs prior to a booby trap, but as a treasure hunter you must assume the worst scenario and assume that the Japanese forgot to tell you of the forthcoming danger. In this case, the Rizal group had no indication that a water trap was directly below where they had been digging.

Two solutions to bypass many of these dangers could be resolved by excavating a second vertical shaft(s) alongside the original excavation. As shown below:

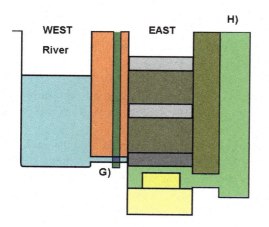

Key

G) Small bore pipe to plug water flow into the main shaft.

H) Larger vertical shaft to bypass all major traps and concrete slab obstacles.

9.65   Triangle Treasure Signs

The triangle is a symbol of light, a symbol of masculine virility, a sign of God, or harmony, a sign for the Buddha, and a sign for the Holy Trinity: The Father, Son and Holy Spirit. The code writers have used this sign in many ways; the triangle represents where an object has been buried, and has links to golden Buddha's, jewels and other golden objects. Some generic examples of this treasure symbol are shown below:

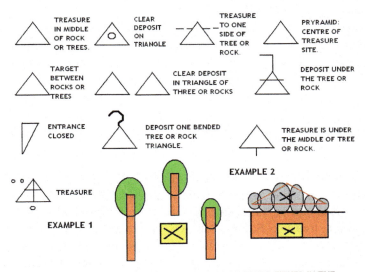

THE TRIANGLE: THE TREASURE OR TARGET WILL BE FOUND EITHER IN THE MIDDLE OF A 1) TRIANGLE OF TREES, INSIDE A TREE WITH A TRIANGLE AND A HOLE IN THE CENTRE OR 2) BETWEEN THE ROCKS (LOOK FOR PINK ROCK OR PINK HEART SHAPED ROCK OR BELOW THE ROCK PILE UNDER THE GROUND WHERE X MARKS THE SPOT. LOOK FOR OTHER SIGNS LIKE:

The above examples show where an object is expected to be buried. The pile of rocks may be shaped in a pyramid arrangement on top of each other, or large rocks in a triangle with the target situated in the centre, as Example 1 shows.

Sometimes there will be three deposits on each corner of the triangle. This can be a triangle of trees or rocks. The interpretation of the triangle largely depends on how the site has been laid out by the person(s) hiding the item(s) in question.

9.66   Treasure Mound Shape Identification

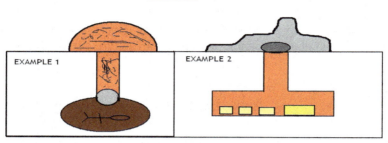

EXAMPLE 1: GRAVE SITE WITH DEAD INSIDE MOUND IS USUALLY SAND DEPTH 18-21 FEET DEEP DANGER OF METHANE GAS.

EXAMPLE 2: SALAKOT SHAPED MOUND, THE TREASURE IS BELOW THE MOUND AGAIN AT A 18-21 FEET DEEP COULD HAVE A BODY GUARDING THE ENTRANCE OR A SMALL BOOBYTRAP.

CARE AND PRECAUTIONS MUST BE TAKEN. EXPECT THE UNEXPECTED ALWAYS!

In the diagrams above we can see the differences between example 1 and 2.

In example 1, the mound is made up of earth and sand. As the shaft becomes deeper, the sand content becomes more prevalent. Such a mound was found in Mariveles, Bataan. The diggers had mistaken the mound as a treasure **Salakot** shown in example 2, and one of the diggers was nearly killed when he removed the boulder at the bottom of the shaft and methane gas escaped from the mass grave chamber beneath, so please beware: not all mounds are treasure mounds!

The **Salakot** is the one to look for; its shape shown in grey is easily recognisable and will stand out silhouetted on top of a mountain, hill or a river bank.

The **Salakot** is a traditional wide-brimmed hat worn in the Philippines. It is usually made of either rattan or reeds, and may be regarded as the Filipino counterpart of the conical straw hat found in East Asian and Southeast Asian countries.

9.67 **Tunnel Signs**

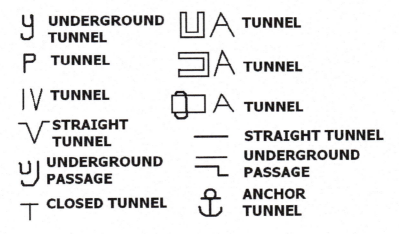

If you are looking for a secret tunnel entrance, these symbols above may help you locate it!

9.68   **Mirror Images**

The Japanese produced strange sculptures that had treasure markings on them. These were left as landmarks or a representation of what could be buried close by or directly underneath where they lay. The treasure symbols give us a clue of what these two *Buddha-type* sculptures represent.

If we analyse the picture, we will see that these stone objects are telling us what is buried, and where.

"Beneath here you will find golden artefacts such as a Buddha and statue-type relics".

9.69   **Mirror Images Underground**

Looking at the first eight-shaped symbol in both of these treasure sign examples, we can see that they look very familiar to the shape shown on the right side of the photograph above. These treasure symbols mean: gold bars, Buddha's and jewels buried below this place.

9.70 **The Riddle Of Broken Rocks**

These uncut stones represent items that are buried underneath the ground, so what could it be?

A true story: A Filipino finds a coconut tree with a triangle carved into it. He knows that the treasure code for a "triangle" states that treasure is between the trees, or the treasure is to be found between the rocks that could also look like a pyramid made up from a pile of small rocks.

He looks around and observes that there are no other trees or rocks in the area of the tree, and thinks to himself that the treasure must be below the tree that has the triangle marking. He starts to dig, and when he reaches 5 feet he finds a blanket of uncut rocks. As he makes the excavation wider, he gradually uncovers a 5 by 5 feet square area of small rocks 5 feet deep in the ground.

The rocks are laid out just like a carpet, and he thinks to himself: someone has taken great care in making sure that this square of rocks is perfect in every detail. Our man looks at the square of uncut rocks, and decides to shovel all of the rocks out of his squared hole.

He digs another 3 feet down, then to 8 feet and finds nothing! He picks up his metal detector to check the hole for a positive bleep, but no "gold" target is registered on his metal detector. He becomes angry and frustrated and decides he is wasting his time. He spends the rest of the day filling the hole in and walking away.

Why?

Because he did not know what the rough rocks represented, and the significance of the 5 x 5 feet square.

So What Is The Answer?

He had to dig to a depth of 25 feet and there he would have found hundreds of uncut diamonds.
There would have been marker stones at varying depths to show he was on the right track. So the moral of the story is never ever give up, always expect the unexpected, always think in a creative way, and always ask yourself "why would someone go to the trouble of creating such an exact square 5 feet down in the earth?"

"What does the dimensions of the square mean and what do the rough rocks represent?"
The Filipino who dug the hole still does not know the solution to this mystery; now you know what to look for when you come across a similar situation.

9.71   **Pyramid-Shaped Rock**

The Pyramid Rock: This was found in a shaft excavated in southern Luzon in August 2008, at a depth of 21 feet. The pyramid rock is a very good sign for the treasure hunter; it means that the target is directly below this marker! Before this marker a small piece of blue porcelain was found at a depth of 15 feet. This particular site was started in the rainy season. The hole has since filled with water and won't be restarted until the beginning of the dry season in early January. The items expected to be found here are ten 6.2 kg bars and 1 kg of uncut diamonds. Because the soil is now saturated with water, the sides of the shaft can collapse at any time; it is therefore too dangerous to continue, unless the sides of the shaft can be supported, and the water pumped out. The depth of the shaft is now 28 feet deep. The targets should be found at a depth of no more than 35 feet. A tunnel system will also be found running to a defensive hill some 15 metres to the north of this excavation.

Note:

During the early 1940s, Japanese military stole an unknown quantity of pyramid-shaped gold ingots from Burma.
These ingots weighed 6.2 kg and had the following dimensions:
15.5 x 5.5 x 3.8cm. The pyramid-shaped rock marker could be a representation of what is buried below this pyramid rock, mirroring the exact dimensions of these lost Burmese gold pyramid-shaped ingots.

9.72 **<u>Water Well Secret No.1</u>**

As you look at the photograph above, what do you see?
The answer is that half of the top of the well has been re-rendered using a mix of pink cement, a favourite of the Japanese to signify ***Cherry Blossom Luck***, with "treasure".
Now look more closely…can you see the "5" in the bottom left corner, just off the centre of the picture?
This is a treasure symbol meaning **"start here"** or **"object underneath"**.
I believe the Japanese soldier who carved the "5" symbol wanted to write more and used pink cement to identify this particular well as "special" so that it could be found easily at a later date. Simply because when we look at the next photograph we see:

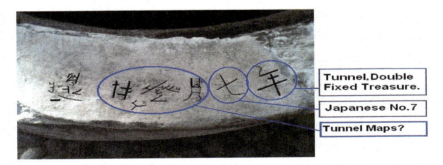

Many symbols, some worn off over the years, but "Tunnel, Double Fixed Treasure" and the number "7" are visible. This old well needs ***further investigation***. See why on the next page.

9.73　Water Well Secret No.2

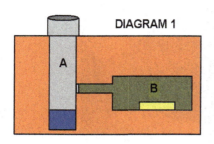

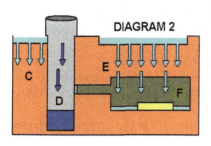

Key

Diagram 1:
A: Old well shaft.
B: Secret treasure vault.

Diagram 2:
C: Water dissipates into the ground.
D: Well water.
E: Ground water finds its way into the vault.
F: The surface water falls into the treasure vault below.

These treasure vaults would have been excavated from inside the shaft of the well itself during the Japanese occupation, well away from prying eyes. These water wells would have been near or adjacent to Japanese military garrisons where the Kempeitai military police or a group of Japanese officers were living, usually inside old Spanish colonial houses or buildings situated near to major road and bridge crossings. The well shaft entrance will be bricked up or concreted over to hide the tunnel entrance into the vault. As mentioned in section 9.72, the wall of the well may have treasure or Japanese Kanji markings that will give you a clearer clue in helping identify such a treasure deposit.

Carry Out A Basic Experiment:

By pouring water around the well and observing how it sinks into the dry earth, you can judge whether the water is draining into the ground or into a secret treasure chamber below. The water will disappear at a faster rate above the chamber entrance, and you may find that you can hear the water drop sounding like a waterfall as it pours through the roof of the vault, falling to the floor below. Once you have established that this is the case, then further tests may be needed, using ground-penetrating radars, or bore holes can be drilled above the area of interest to further explore and verify your findings.

9.74 Water Pump Secret

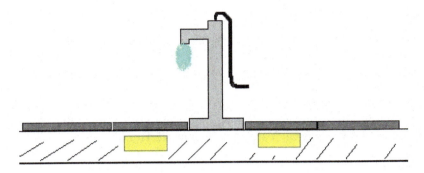

Under the flagstones of the old hand operated water pump that serves the Filipino villages in rural areas gold bars have been found.

A simple place to hide a few gold bars, especially during the conflict; the communal water pump was the ideal place to hide a bar or two, and very easy to retrieve at a later date. Who would think of looking here for a gold bar?

These old hand pumps are still found in remote villages throughout the Philippines, and are still used today by the local population for drinking water and for washing themselves and their clothes. I used one of these water pumps to wash myself on a recent trip to Glan in Mindanao.

9.75 "X" Marks the Spot Symbols

We have all read about the treasure being found on the big "X", where this symbol represents the spot where the treasure is hidden. Pirates, thieves, and very bad men throughout history marked treasure maps with an "X". When the time was right, the hidden loot could be retrieved once again.

In the case of the vast wealth buried in the Philippines, the "X" symbol has many definitions and explanations. Here are some of the common ones used by General Yamashita, General Homma and the Tanaka Group.

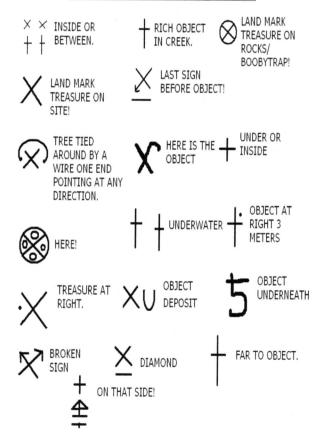

9.76 "Z" Symbol Meanings

The "Z" symbols taken from various code books are shown below:

ZKC = Deposit Under   Zhc = Deposit Under

Z = Under The Tree Or Under the Stairs

Z = Gold Deposit Here $Z\dagger$ = In Front Of Here

$\mathcal{y}Z$ = Towards Another Sign $Z + \mathcal{C}$ = Infront

$\mathcal{y}Z$ = Golds Bars And Jewels Z = There 15 Yards

10.00   Hidden Dangers: Toxic Gas

The Japanese Imperial Army generals did not want to use gas against the enemy, simply because they knew that the American forces would retaliate with an even larger quantity of gas, which would probably have resulted in the death of most of the Imperial forces and many thousands of innocent civilians. This, however, does not mean that supplies of such deadly gas were not shipped to the Philippines in preparation of an all out attack. Treasure hunters have in the past been killed by gas capsules filled with hydrogen cyanide, which give off their deadly vapour when accidently trodden on inside tunnels and caves. These capsules are placed just under the soil and are invisible until the hapless victim comes along.

10.10 Japanese Germ Warfare

A treasure hunter therefore must be aware of the type of gases and poisons that were used at this time in history, and be able to recognise the letters and symbols used on barrels and other improvised containers. Most are not aware that the Japanese also had a germ warfare team called **Kyodo Unit 371** during WWII, which *could have* carried out experiments on prisoners of war on the Philippine islands and left a nasty legacy of old chemical drums or infected material behind inside a hole, a tunnel, or indeed inside a cave system on one or more of the islands. This is probably not the case with respect to germ warfare, but it is very important to recognise the symptoms of a person that has come into contact with either a gas or a poisonous liquid, left as a booby trap or simply discarded in an old tunnel during the war. You, as the treasure hunter, must know how to administer first aid to the patient. In this section of the book I explain some of the dangers you may encounter and what every serious treasure hunter should be aware of before and during excavation activities.

Kyodo Unit 371: Germ Warfare Team

The Imperial Japanese Army's germ warfare unit planned to stage germ attacks against U.S. troops in Japan just after Japan's surrender in World War II in August 1945, citing a memorandum left by the unit's commander, **Lt. Gen. Shiro Ishii**.

Unit 731 gave up the plan after being told by the top commanders of the Imperial Japanese Army, "Do not die in vain," the historians said. It is unclear how Ishii planned to carry out the attacks, because statements of the memorandum are very fragmented.

Unit 731 was already known to have made preparations to stage "*Tokko*" suicide germ attacks against U.S. forces just before Japan's surrender. Commander Ishii, who was a medical officer, had handwritten the memorandum that stated that his unit planned germ attacks even after the end of the war.

It was analyzed by a well-known Japanese authority on biochemical weapons, Professor Keiichi Tsuneishi, at Kanagawa University in Yokohama. The memorandum, written in a large notebook, depicts developments involving the germ unit during eleven days from Aug. 16, 1945 – the day after Japan's surrender. It states: "Will transport to the home country '*Maruta,*' *PX* as much as possible." "*Maruta*" was the unit's code word for prisoners of war on whom germ weapons were tested, while *PX* means *pest bacillus-infected fleas*, the researchers said.

The expressions mean Ishii apparently planned germ attacks against United States troops and studied transporting germ warfare personnel and their equipment to Japan, they said. Entries on Aug. 26th, two days before the arrival of an advance team of the U.S. forces, carry instructions from top army generals that state: "Don't die in vain" and "Wait for next opportunity calmly".

The instructions were issued by **Gen. Yoshijiro Umezu** and **Gen. Torashiro Kawabe**, then chief of staff and deputy chief of the Imperial Japanese Army, respectively.

Professor Tsuneishi of Kanagawa University said it is unlikely that Unit 731 planned to send prisoners of war to Japan. He later stated that the unit may have tried to send specimens produced through human experiments to the homeland in preparation to attack allied forces. The Imperial Japanese Army established Unit 731 in 1936 as an anti-epidemic and water supply division of the Kwantung Army. But its real mission was to develop biological weapons using plague, anthrax and other bacteria to kill the enemy with. The Kwantung Army was part of the Japanese Imperial Army stationed in northeastern China, which was under Japanese control.

Headquartered in the suburbs of Harbin in Heilongjiang Province, the unit conducted germ warfare in various places in China and mainly used Chinese as subjects in human experiments. Historians believe that some 3,000 people died in the human experiments conducted by the unit before and during the war years.

Japanese military chemists were in charge of protecting treasures buried by the Imperial Japanese family.

Smaller deposits were also protected in much the same way; not with deadly germs but with chemical warfare. Here are a few of these deadly gases and devices that need to be considered and planned for prior to starting any excavation in haste. Gas masks, gas detectors are a basic requirement for your and the digger's safety. The gas detector will detect leakage of methane gas or indeed other gases long before you or your diggers will. Be prepared with gas masks too; once the gas

detector alarm sounds you have less than thirty seconds to protect yourself with your gas mask.
Have it will you at all times, and readily at hand if the occasion arises that you need it quickly in an emergency.

Do not compromise here. Death due to exposure to gas is preventable and must be taken very seriously at the early planning stage of any treasure hunt. These gases kill a few people in the Philippines every year; please do not become another casualty yourself, or indeed any members of your excavation team.

Unit 731: Japan's Dirty Secret:

See:
http://www.youtube.com/watch?v=D7yDOXGmtro&feature=related

Ghosts of Unit 731:

See:
http://www.youtube.com/watch?v=7KPxyPv2d4c&feature=fvw

On the subsequent pages I mention some of the nasty things that you may expect to find under the ground.
This is not a definitive or indeed a complete list, but it gives you the reader a good idea of what you must be prepared for and how to administer first aid to any member of your team that may be affected by gas or chemical poisoning. Always be prepared and have a good first aid kit and other protective equipment available at all times. Make sure that members of your team can use gas detectors, gas masks, and can administer first aid to any member of your team if the situation ever arises. It also pays to have an emergency evacuation plan worked out just in case of accidents underground. Know where all of the entrances and exits are before blindly digging your "new hotspot". See the appendix at the rear of this book for gas detectors and gas mask suppliers.

10.20 Sarin Gas

Important Notes:

1) Known as **"GB"**. The liquid is clear, colourless, and tasteless.
2) There is **NO ODOUR** or **SMELL** given off.

CONTACT SYMPTOMS

3) Runny nose, watery eyes, excessive sweating, coughing, diarrhoea.
4) Confusion, drowsiness, weakness, headache, vomiting and low blood pressure.

REMEDY

Rinse eyes with plenty of water.
Wash skin with soap and water.
Seek medical attention immediately.

10.30 Methane Gas (CH4)

Important Notes:

This gas is found inside tunnels and shafts that have been sealed for a very long time. The methane gas can be a result of rotting vegetation, or in many cases the decomposing of human or animal flesh buried in sealed tunnels, where the air has become stagnant due to the lack of air flow. The smell of rotting flesh is very strong and will make the treasure hunter very sick until he vomits; this putrid smell is usually mixed with the methane gas that has been produced by the rotting process of flesh over a long period of time.

This gas itself is odourless but kills very quickly and many treasure hunters have died unaware that the gas has been released around them; while digging and standing in a deep hole, the shaft will fill with methane gas within seconds, starving the digger of fresh air and killing him within twenty-five seconds.

Methane gas detection units must be employed inside tunnels and in deep shafts to monitor the quality of the air at all times; before, during and after work has ceased for the day. The gas detector must monitor these excavations constantly for the build up of methane gases.

This type of methane gas detector will give off an audible alarm when the methane gas reaches unacceptable levels of toxicity for humans.

Appropriate methane gas masks must be supplied to all workers who are working inside the tunnel system. These precautions, and proper forced fresh air circulation using surface electrical fans attached to ventilation ducts rooted down to where the diggers are located, is a must in order to give the digging group better protection against this deadly gas. (See appendix for further details.)

The gas is odourless and explosive when mixed with air, and therefore very dangerous. No digger should be smoking, as a precaution while working inside any tunnel or shaft, or indeed while digging new excavations, as an added safety precaution.

Treasure sites and grave sites have been excavated where a layer of charcoal has been placed around and over buried bodies, sealing in the decomposing remains, smell and methane gas. If this layer is broken by digging, the methane seeps out into the excavation hole and kills the treasure hunter instantly by cutting off his air supply. (See section 9.19, Gate guard.)

CONTACT SYMPTONS

Eyes are red and painful, feel giddy and the patient's lips turn blue, resulting in confusion, drowsiness, respiratory failure, unconsciousness, and death.

REMEDY

Remove the patient well away from the gas and administer artificial respiration in a well-ventilated area; wash eyes with plenty of water for several minutes and seek medical advice immediately.

10.40 Hydrogen Cyanide (HCN)

Important Notes:

An HCN concentration of **300 mg/m³** in the air will kill a human within a few minutes.
The toxicity is caused by the cyanide ion, which prevents cellular respiration. Hydrogen cyanide (under the brand name Zyklon B) was most infamously employed by the Nazi regime in the mid-20th century.

This gas was used by the Japanese as a deterrent, and was used in various forms to protect the openings of caves and tunnels. Some booby traps involved small glass capsules under the earth 1-3 metres inside the entrance, and positioned in such a way that space and a quick exit would be restricted in order to achieve maximum casualties in a very small area. Also known to have been used to protect Buddha's, where a pressure plate was connected to a drum containing the gas; the removal of the Buddha activates a small detonator placed on the side of the gas-filled drum, killing the treasure hunter within seconds.

Small glass HCN capsules were mixed with backfill soil on many large Imperial treasure sites. You may come across these capsules used to deter treasure hunters excavating smaller sites. Be aware; look for them in the soil and clay, or just under the cave or tunnel floor, ready for someone to tread on them, or in the backfill soil that has been used to backfill old defensive tunnels.

Important Note:

According to the Japanese Engineering Battalion treasure code, poison capsules were placed at **7, 10, 13, and 17 feet**.

CONTACT SYMPTOMS

This gas poisons within seconds of coming in contact with the ambient air surrounding the victim, or being swallowed.

This gas has an odour of **"BITTER ALMONDS"** and the victim will feel giddy, experience headaches, have a weak heartbeat, his eyes will be dilated, and won't react to a bright light. His mouth will be covered in foam, he will have red coloured skin, and be vomiting. His eyes will be protruding, and will experience stiffness in his lower jaw.

Other symptoms include: hyperrnea, palpitation cyanosis, unconsciousness, asphyxia convulsions, and death.

REMEDY

None.

10.50   Mustard Gas (C4 H8Cl12S)

IDENTIFICATION NUMBERS: "CAS" OR "505-6-2"

Important Notes:

This gas is a powerful irritant, which targets the eyes, skin, the respiratory tract, lungs, larynx, pharynx, bone marrow, oral cavity, and sexual organs. Will cause cancer, but symptoms are not shown in the patient straight away. The liquid is colourless or yellow in colour and **must not be touched or inhaled**.

CONTACT SYMPTOMS

A powerful irritant; exposure leads to convulsions, coma and death. The symptoms can include the following: nausea, fatigue, headaches, eye inflammation, eye pain, and skin blistering.

REMEDY

Wash eyes with copious amounts of water, or saline solution, for at least fifteen minutes.

Wash the skin all over using a neutral soap. Administer antibiotics containing sulphite 20% solution, and midrates. Liquid contamination: use fullers earth and wash with paraffin, soap and water. If the gut has become contaminated, give the patient 100/200ml of milk or water. Seek medical advice immediately.

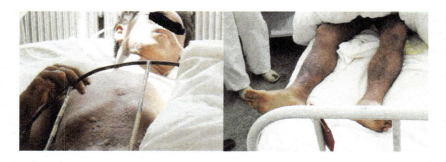

This Chinese man dug up some drums containing mustard gas in China on a building site quite recently. They had been left by the Japanese military during WWII. He emptied the drums containing the liquid into the ground.

Soon afterwards he was hospitalised with blistered skin, swollen eyes and had problems breathing. He later died of his injuries. The liquid mustard gas still killed him after being stored underground for over sixty years. So be very aware of this danger when you find 55 gallon drums; remember not all of them have gold coins stored inside them.

10.60 **Poison Gas Symbols**

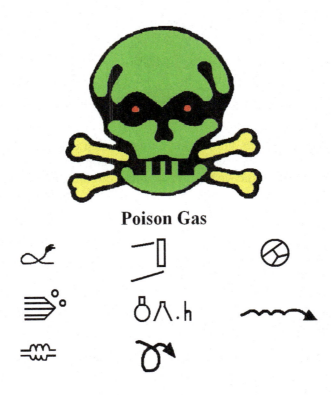

Important Note:

As stated previously, according to the Japanese Engineering Battalion treasure code poison capsules were placed at **7, 10, 13, and 17 feet**.

10.70   Itchy Skin

Many Filipino treasure hunters have told me that once they have dug a hole they get to a point where the digger complains that his skin has become very itchy and very sore; in some circumstances the exposed skin was burnt, especially on bare elbows, arms and knees, where the digger has crawled into a tunnel where the earth had been infected with sodium hydroxide powder.

In this case two alkaline powders were mixed into the soil and the contaminated soil was used to backfill the tunnel or shaft excavation in order to protect the hidden hoard from unwanted treasure seekers.

Sodium Hydroxide (NaOH) powder

Persons whose clothing or skin is contaminated with solid sodium hydroxide or its solution can secondarily contaminate their rescuers by direct contact; therefore it is very important that the rescuers wear the recommended rubber-type gloves, as prescribed on the following page, when handling infected person(s).

Sodium hydroxide is a **white** non-combustible solid that absorbs moisture from the surrounding air. When this solid is in contact with water, it may generate sufficient heat to ignite combustible materials. Sodium hydroxide **compound** has no smell; therefore no odour provides any warning of hazardous concentrations. Sodium hydroxide does not produce systemic toxicity, but is very **CORROSIVE** to the touch, causing itching and skin irritation, possibly burns or red patches to any exposed skin. Scratching infected areas will lead to skin and blood infections. Inhalation of sodium hydroxide dust, mist, or aerosol may cause irritation of the mucous membranes of the nose, throat, and respiratory tract. When this occurs the worker must get out of any confined area into one that has fresh air and seek medical help immediately.

Potassium Hydroxide (KOH) powder

Elemental potassium is a soft **silvery-white metallic** alkali metal that oxidizes rapidly in the air and is very reactive with water, generating sufficient heat to ignite the hydrogen emitted in the reaction.
Eye contact: Immediately flush the eye with plenty of water. Continue for at least ten minutes and call for immediate medical help.

Skin contact: Wash off with plenty of water. Remove any contaminated clothing. If the skin reddens or appears damaged, call for medical aid.
If swallowed: Drink plenty of water and call for immediate medical help at once.

Protective Equipment: <u>ALWAYS</u> wear safety glasses when handling potassium hydroxide or its solution is thought to be in the soil. Safety glasses are needed because when the chemical gets in the eye it causes irritation; by contrast, potassium hydroxide can cause you **serious eye damage**.

Wear gloves made from neoprene, nitrile or natural rubber; all are suitable for handling soil containing solutions with concentrations of up to 70% potassium hydroxide or sodium hydroxide powders.

Wear wellington boots and clothing that will protect you from direct contact with these powders and contaminated soil.
The way to avoid this is to wear a shirt, trousers and cover your skin with Vaseline™ (petroleum jelly), which will act as a barrier against the "ITCHY".

If you experience irritation while digging you are probably close to the target! Wear rubber gloves and old shirt, trousers and boots to protect your exposed skin. Yes even when you are working in 40°C heat and high humidity.

Note:

The poisonous powders can be burnt off by immersing the object in gasoline or kerosene, then set a light to burn the powder residue off the surface of the recovered gold object. This should be done in a well-ventilated open area to avoid inhaling the resulting smoke or fumes that will be given off when carrying out this process. If no kerosene is available then wash the object thoroughly in soapy water and rinse off with fresh clean water before handling.

It has been noted that green and red balls have been found on smaller sites at various depths ranging between 8-15 feet. These balls are a little larger than a tennis ball and very light, similar to bath ball salts. These balls contain two different types of poison, which dissolve into the surrounding soil when it becomes saturated with water.

These balls should **NOT** be touched with bare hands; always wear rubber gloves for you own protection. These poisons are easily absorbed into the skin just by picking them up!

Even planks of wood coloured green, red or even blue at various depths can also be impregnated with poison, and should be disposed off in a safe and thoughtful manner.

Burning these items may lead to respiratory failure if the smoke is inhaled; therefore a better way of disposal must be found to protect other people and livestock that may innocently come into contact with these deadly poisons. Re-burying them will only re-contaminate the surrounding soil, poisoning grass and land, killing the cows, goats and sheep that may graze there. Store above ground, wrapped in heavy duty plastic bags as a temporary measure, until a better way to dispose of these dangers can be found.

Some Filipino treasure hunters have found a grey jelly-type substance covering a cemented vault at depths of between 18-21 feet. This substance is there to protect the treasure and will poison anyone who comes into contact with it.

10.80   **<u>Grey Powder And Danger Signs</u>**

A treasure hunter recently wanted to know what a grey powder was when he found it laying on the floor of a tunnel system entrance in Luzon.
He stated that the strong smell inside the tunnel smelt of carbide, and had given the diggers a headache while they worked in such a confined space inside an old tunnel passageway.

This grey powder was used as a fuel to illuminate the tunnel passageways while the miners worked using carbide lamps to light the way.

Carbide lamps, also known as **acetylene gas lamps**, are simple lamps that produce and burn **acetylene** (C_2H_2), which is created by the reaction of **calcium carbide** (CaC_2) with **water**, producing acetylene gas (hence the smell of carbide).

Carbide lamps were developed in the 1890s. They were first used for carriage lamps, and were quickly adapted for underground mining operations. The lamp has a removable base, which would be unscrewed and filled with small grey pellets of calcium carbide.

A small amount of water was poured into a reservoir in the top part of the lamp. A tap controlled the amount of water which would flow slowly from the reservoir into the carbide chamber below. The water reacted with the carbide to form acetylene gas, which rose to the top of the carbide chamber into a small tube, which led out of the chamber to a burner tip. This could be lit with a flint, and the flame produced was focused by a shiny reflector to give a bright white light between four and six times brighter than that of an oil lamp or flame safety lamp.

The rate of water flow could be adjusted with the tap to vary the amount of gas produced and hence the amount of light, which would last for several hours. A miner would carry spare water and carbide pellets so that he could refill the lamp whilst underground. Carbide lamps were easy to use and to maintain and were very popular in iron ore mines where there was minimal risk of explosion to the build up of methane gas.

Danger Note: As explained on the previous page, carbide is a grey powder or grey pellet which, when mixed with water, gives off acetylene gas, which can become very explosive when mixed with air inside a tunnel or cave system.

Calcium carbide must be kept dry and well-ventilated and removed from the excavation site before further digging can resume.

Do not smoke inside old tunnels or have naked flames, such as candles or burning torches, in close proximity to this substance. If the digger can see a quantity of grey powder lying on a wet or damp floor, or if the smell of carbine can be detected as you enter an abandoned tunnel or cave system, do not approach the area with a naked flame!

Silicon carbide is grey in colour and occurs naturally in nature. Discovery inside a tunnel or cave entrance could point to previous coal, iron ore or gold mining activity from the distant past, and may not be connected in any way to Japanese treasure hoards. Not all tunnels in the Philippines were made by the Japanese military occupation during WWII.

Footnote:

The Philippines is one of the world's most highly-mineralized countries in Southeast Asia, with untapped mineral wealth estimated at more than $840 billion. Philippine copper, gold, and chromate deposits are among the largest in the world. Other important minerals include nickel, silver, coal, gypsum, and sulfur. The Philippines also has significant deposits of clay, marble, limestone, silica, and phosphates.

Despite its rich mineral deposits, the Philippine mining industry is just a fraction of what it was in the 1970s and 1980s, when the country ranked among the ten leading gold and copper producers worldwide. Low metal prices, high production costs, and lack of investment in infrastructure contributed to the industry's overall decline. A December 2004 Supreme Court decision upheld the constitutionality of the 1995 Mining Act, thereby allowing up to 100% of foreign-owned companies to invest in large-scale exploration, development, and utilization of minerals, oil, and gas. Some local government units have enacted mining bans in their territories; this may include **_banning treasure hunting activities_** into old abandoned mine tunnels due to safety concerns.

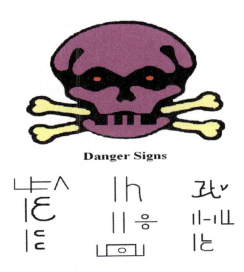

Danger Signs

The danger signs are warning signs of immediate danger ahead, which could be followed by a booby trap sign, as seen in section 11. Always be aware and very cautious and proceed with extreme caution.

10.90 Black Water

Many treasure hunters speak of "black water", where rivers, streams, lakes, ponds and old water wells are places where treasure hunters have become very sick while either swimming in such places or trying to drink the water.

We could argue that the water has been polluted in modern times by man and chemical leaching of nitrates from the land, or from human or animal waste that, over time, has washed into this particular water source.

I want to make you, the reader, aware of another theory that may solve the black water problem once and for all, and may explain why so many local people, for over sixty-five years, have had problems in one area where the river or lake is named "black water" and will not go near or drink from this particular water.

According to Charlie Ryrie, who has written *The Healing Energies of Water* (ISBN: 1-856751-05-8), water has an extraordinary gift of memory, which means that its structure can be transformed in such a way it can either help heal or make someone very sick. The water passes this memory onto every water droplet and will continue holding this memory until someone re-programmes the water source with another memory.
"Black water" will stay negative and will make people sick until someone changes the negative vibrations to positive vibrations.

The Japanese military and Shinto priests knew this about this phenomenon very well, and asked the water to guard buried treasure that was either in the water or very close by.

Akuba Meaning Curse

All they had to do was take a small amount of this water and place a curse onto it, then pour it back into the water source where it came from. Within a few hours, the river, lake or pond became "black water", thus guarding the treasure forever.

Recently, a Japanese scientist called Dr Emoto conducted an experiment to see if "The Power of Words Over Water" actually worked.

His question was simple: Can water be affected by our words or prayers by directing our energy behind the words we use? The answer was yes of course. Dr. Emoto took water droplets and exposed them to various words, music, and environments and froze them for three hours. He then examined the crystal formations under a dark field microscope. He took before and after photographs of the water droplets under experiment. The results on the following pages are in fact totally mind-blowing and prove without doubt my point that water DOES hold a memory.

Next, Dr. Emoto stuck a piece of paper with these words: "You make me sick. I will kill you." Here's how the frozen water droplets looks like under the microscope:

See how "black water" could easily be made to guard hidden treasure in water.

Unless the curse is lifted from the water source by the person who placed it there in the first place, the water will remain black and negative forever.

The results on the following pages are in fact totally mind-blowing..

On the left: A water droplet exposed to classical music and folk dance music.

Left: how water looked like after the word "love" was spoken over water; the result is totally amazing.

This is water from Lourdes, France, beautiful in its cellular structure, resulting in healing and vitality given to those who drink it.

Prayers are said over water to make it "holy" and positive. The power of the spoken word does affect water as we can clearly see here.

As a treasure hunter, must therefore be aware that the water surrounding a treasure hoard may have a memory that can harm you. If this is the case, then praying over the water will change this "old" memory from negative to positive, which will help you, the treasure hunter, and the surrounding environment and wildlife that relies on this water source for its survival.

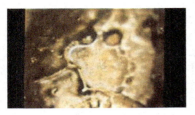 This is polluted water.

We must know whether the water we come into contact with during our treasure activities is a danger to our health prior to any excavations or exploratory adventures in water begin.

There are many tests that can be carried out to check water quality for drinking and whether it is safe to swim in. We as treasure hunters want to know how practically we can test contaminated water that can risk our health and our well-being, as we are digging or searching flooded sites that may have become polluted by past and present human activity.

We therefore must know how to recognize these unseen dangers and be able to test water samples for waterborne bacteria and pollutants before exposing ourselves and others to potential danger.

Basic Water Quality Tests: 1) pH Level

The acidity of the water will affect your ability to explore rivers, streams, man-made lakes, water tanks, water wells and ponds. It is therefore very important to test the pH level before you jump in and become exposed to a potential danger of high levels of acid water, which will result in terrible skin burns. On the pH scale, zero indicates extreme acidity, 14 will indicate extreme alkalinity and 7 indicates a neutral state. Most swimming pool experts recommend a pool pH should be between 7.2 and 7.8. To raise or lower pH, a pool custodian simply adds acids or alkalis into the water. For example, adding **sodium carbonate** (soda ash) or **sodium bicarbonate** (baking soda) will generally raise the pH, and adding muriatic acid or sodium bisulfate will lower the pH.

The pH of water is important to aquatic life. If the pH falls below 4 or rises above 9 everything is dead. If there are no water plants or fish living around your water treasure site, then assume that the water has a very high pH level or is badly polluted and hazardous to marine life and of course your own.

To test the pH levels of water purchase a good pH tester:

See links: http://www.digital-meters.com/Complete-Water-Testing-pH-Meter-Kit-GOnDO-PHB-1
And:
http://www.maudesport.com/waterproof_pocket_ph_tester_and_solution-hanna-7231747-18628

Sewage Contamination

This nasty stuff has bacteria that propagate in the digestive tracts of humans and animals. They coexist with other bacteria so they are often used as indicators of possible pathogenic contamination. These deadly germs include hepatitis and Escherichia coli (E. coli), and are a group of bacteria that can cause a variety of illnesses in humans, including diarrhea, urinary tract infections, respiratory illnesses, pneumonia and other problems. The obvious tests that can be performed to check for sewage contamination is to use your senses of sight and smell; look for sewage discharge pipes into the water nearest to your site, and smell the water for freshness.

Weil's Disease

Other unseen dangers also come from infected rat or animal urine which causes leptospirosis (Weil's disease). It most often affects teenagers and adults and is more common in men swimming in contaminated water. The bacteria are absorbed through the skin or mucous membranes of the mouth and eyes. It gets into the bloodstream very easily if you have a minor cut on your skin or feet if you become immersed in infected water.

Recent outbreaks

An outbreak of leptospirosis was reported from the Philippines in July 2011 after widespread flooding, causing more than 2000 cases and 156 deaths by October, chiefly in Western Visayas, National Capital Region, Central Luzon, and Davao. A fresh outbreak was reported in January 2012 from the island of Mindanao after flooding caused by tropical storm "Washi". Symptoms may include fever, chills, headache, muscle aches, conjunctivitis (pink eye), photophobia (light sensitivity), and rashes. Most cases resolve uneventfully, but a small number may be complicated by meningitis, kidney failure, liver failure, or hemorrhage. Those engaging in high-risk activities may consider taking a **prophylactic 200 mg dose of doxycycline**, either once weekly or as a one-time dose.

Hepatitis

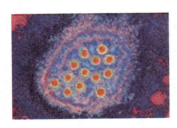

Hepatitis, a broad term for inflammation of the liver, has a number of infectious and non-infectious causes. Two of the viruses that cause hepatitis (hepatitis A and E) can be transmitted through water and food; hygiene is therefore important when controlling what you eat and drink.

Prevention

Check for high pH and sewerage contamination before entering the water

Injections for Hepatitis A and E prior to visiting the Philippines

Do not enter the water if you have open cuts or wounds to your skin

Protect your body with a good waterproof barrier cream and wear a wet suit.

Avoid direct water contact with your eyes, ears and mouth if at all possible; wearing a scuba mask would help reduce eye infections.

Wear rubber gloves and wellingtons and avoid bare feet in muddy infected water at all times. Wash your hands regularly and before eating any food.

Lists of vaccinations needed for the Philippines will be found using this link:

http://www.mdtravelhealth.com/destinations/asia/philippines.php

Further in-depth sewage tests can be carried out using portable testing equipment.

See link: http://www.palintest.com/products-details.aspx?id=16

11.00 Japanese "Katashiro" (to curse a human being)

A physical object used as an emblem of the presence of a spirit in rites of worship. The term also refers to **an** object representing the human figure (*hitogata* or *nademono*), used in rites of purification (*misogi* or *harae*) to represent the subject of the rite, in which case the subject rubs the object on his body or blows breath upon it, thus transferring transgressions and pollutions (***tsumi*** *and kegare*) to the object, which is later cast into a river or another body of water.

Katashiro were also used when casting spells or curses. Most *katashiro* seen today are made of paper, but in the past they were also made of gold, silver, iron, wood, rice, straw or miscanthus reeds. From the Heian period, a *hitogata* was presented to the court by a Yin-Yang divination master (*onmyōji*) each month for the performance of a rite called *nanase no harai* ("seven tides purification").

A similar rite called the ***jōshi*** *no harai* (lit., "first-day-of-the-snake exorcism") was performed on the third day of the third month, and this custom led to the practice of casting adrift dolls displayed for the third month's nodal festival (*sekku*).

These dolls later came to be preserved and displayed as decorations rather than discarded. Shinto priests were used to protect large Imperial treasure sites, and could have asked the elemental earth spirits to guard such sites against intruders and treasure hunters. Please be aware of these curses when you happen to come across such a treasure site.

Shinto Symbolism

Shintoism is the term for the indigenous religion of Japan, based on the worship of spirits known as **kami.** Founded in 660 BC, at the time of Buddhism, it was Japan's state religion until 1945.

The Torii Gate: A Japanese religious symbol that marks the entrance to a sacred place or space, representing the finite world and the infinite world of the gods.

Kami is the Japanese word for the spirits, natural forces, or essence in the **Shinto** faith. Although the word is sometimes translated as "god" or "deity," some Shinto scholars argue that such a translation can cause a misunderstanding of this term.

11.10 **Booby Traps and Japanese Bombs**

Booby traps: Most of the Japanese booby traps encountered during the early stages of the war were constructed with ordinary hand grenades with friction-type fuze igniters or improvised electrical fuzes. Later, machine-made fuzes were also used.

These fuzes were rigged to an explosive charge, which would easily detonate when pressure was applied or when an electrical circuit was closed.

Ingenious methods were used, where hand grenades were often trip-wire-operated and either buried just below the surface or left lying on the ground in brush or rubble where troops could step on or kick them. Others were found attached to coconuts by means of a string.

When the coconut was picked up, the grenade exploded. Bamboo poles were similarly fixed with the expectation that troops would pick up the poles to make huts. Common objects such as fruit cans, toothpaste tubes, flashlights, umbrellas, pipes, pistols, and soap were also booby-trapped.

The Japanese were even known to place hand grenades or packages of picric acid in the armpits or underneath bodies of their partially buried dead to explode when the bodies were moved.

Bangalore torpedoes, used by the Japanese to demolish barbed wire entanglements, were occasionally also used as booby traps. The torpedo consisted of an explosive charge placed into a piece of common iron pipe capped on both ends.

To operate, the caps had to be removed and a fuze inserted in one end. Casualties resulted when American soldiers tried to use the pipes as crowbars or fire grates.

11.20   **Booby Trap Signs**

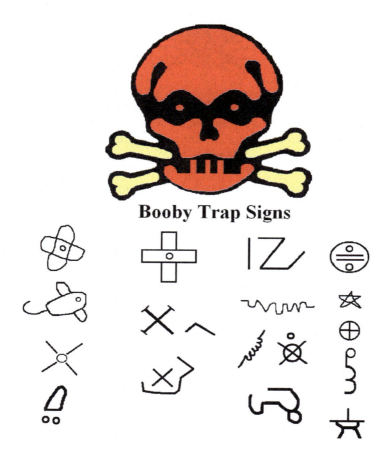

Booby Trap Signs

Above are symbols that were used to convey booby traps. These include aerial bombs, tripwires, poisonous gas tubes, canisters, and water traps. If you find one of these, stop the excavation immediately and carry out a risk assessment on the hidden danger which will be found just a few meters away.

11.30   The German-Made Teller Mine

This device was buried just under the surface of the ground and rigged to a tripwire. Once tripped, the mine would jump 3 feet into the air and explode at waist height, cutting the soldier in two with hundreds of red hot ball bearings flying in all directions.

11.40   The Italian-Made Thermos Bomb

This device has a small ball bearing inside which rolls about and will make contact with the detonator circuit if picked up or disturbed. Usually found near old airfields, roads, and sometimes in cities, rice fields and inside tunnels. **Do not touch it.**

11.50 German-Made Stick Grenade

The Japanese did use German-made stick grenades similar to this one below:

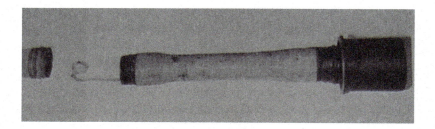

11.60 Left to Right : Japanese Stick Grenade, Japanese Hand Grenade & Japanese Knee Mortar Grenade

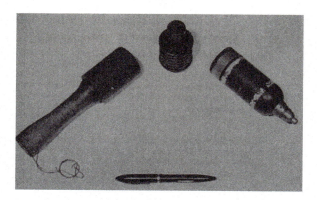

These devices can be found anywhere while digging on a site or inside caves or old Japanese tunnels; I agree they will be very rusty and old, but still could explode due the explosive chemicals inside being very unstable and highly explosive. So please be aware and be careful.

11.70 <u>Land Mines Used By The Japanese Forces</u>

From left to right:

Anti-vehicle type: contains two pounds of high explosives.
Anti-personnel: Dutch-made, captured in Java, dome-shaped, 8 1/2 inches in diameter.
Anti-tank magnetised mines: looks like a khaki hot water bag in a brown cover. The four legs are square magnets designed to attach onto metal, whether it be a tank or an anti-aircraft gun. Once armed and the fuze set, this device will explode five seconds later.

I have only included Japanese munitions here, but remember where battles took place with American and Allied forces. Other types of explosive devices belonging to the Allies could just be buried a few feet under the surface of the ground. Please do not assume that age and rust has made these explosives harmless. The explosive chemicals inside will be highly unstable due to age and likely to sweat in the hot sun and will explode if touched or disturbed by fresh excavation activity.

11.80 Booby Traps in Tunnels and Shafts

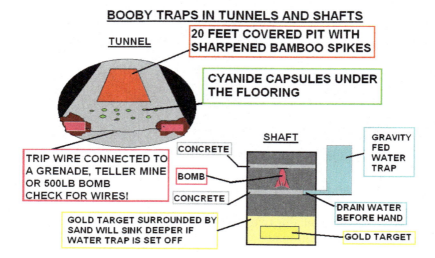

Booby traps inside newly-discovered caves and tunnels that were closed by the Japanese or blocked by deliberate explosion during WWII were done for a reason. The cave or tunnel systems were used either for defensive and military storage or for treasure burial purposes, the latter being the case.

The Japanese would have booby-trapped the entrances to stop or slow down the advancing Americans as the Japanese soldiers inside used other escape routes.
As the war was coming to an end, the American infantry found that chasing Japanese soldiers into caves and tunnels was too time-consuming and costly in lives. It was easier to blow up the entrances, burying the Japanese soldiers inside alive.

Today more Filipinos are discovering these old tunnels and caves in their quest to find riches and many entrances remain booby-trapped by the Japanese military and must be treated with great care and caution.

Note: Some blocked tunnels have wires coming out of the entrances; these may be old power cables for tunnel lighting or military telephone land lines, or could be connected to explosive stored inside a 55 gallon drum just inside the closed tunnel, waiting for the Filipino to pull to see what is on the other end, and suddenly **BOOM** up it goes. I have heard of two such cases, so please don't add your life to this recent *death list*. Be careful out there, and think "safety" before you act.

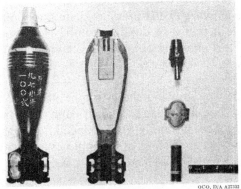

FIGURE 10.—Model 100, 81 mm. HE mortar shell, showing ignition cartridge, propelling increment, and Model 100 fuze.

FIGURE 12.—Model 91 (1931) hand grenade.

11.90 Imperial Japanese Bombs Used During WWII

It is important to recognise the types of bombs that were used during WWII; a treasure hunter may find himself in a situation where a bomb is excavated at a site which is very much alive and wired to explode if the unwary digger activates the tripwire or the pressure plate the bomb is sitting on. What type is it? Is it real or a dummy bomb? Here is a pretty comprehensive reference list showing colour codes and types to study before you tackle the problem!

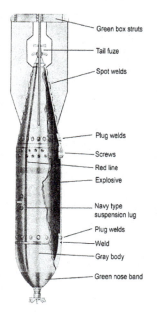

Left: The drawing shows a type 98 No. 25 land bomb, for use against land targets. They were normally not produced to a high standard, consisting of a simple cylindrical case riveted or welded to a cast steel nose.

Below: A Japanese motorized aerial bomb carrier found near to the old American military housing quarters at Clark Air Force Base Luzon. This photograph was taken at the rear of Clark Museum in 2005.

Imperial Japanese Bomb Table

High Explosive Type	High Explosive Type
Type 92 15 kg High-explosive bomb	Type 99 30 kg High-explosive bomb
Type 94 50 kg High-explosive bomb	Type 94 100 kg High-explosive bomb
Type 3 100 kg High-explosive bomb	Type 94 Mod. 50 kg High-explosive bomb
Type 94 Mod.100 kg High-explosive bomb	Type 1 50 kg High-explosive bomb
Type 1 100 kg High-explosive bomb	Type 1 250 kg High-explosive bomb
Type 92 250 kg High-explosive bomb	Type 4 250 kg Anti-shipping bomb
Type 3 100 kg Skipping bomb	**Fire Bombs**
Type 4 100 kg Anti-shipping bomb	1 kg Thermite Incendiary bomb
Type 4 500 kg Anti-shipping bomb	5 kg Thermite Incendiary bomb
Smoke Bombs	Type 97 50 kg Incendiary bomb
Type 100 50 kg Incendiary bomb	**Gas Bomb**
Type 100 50 kg Smoke bomb	Type 92 50 kg gas bomb
Flares	**Flares**
Type 90 parachute flare	Type 1 12 kg parachute flare
Type 3 parachute flare	Type 97 concrete bomb
Type 94 substitute bomb	Type 1 30 kg substitute bomb

Listed are just a few of the bombs the Japanese manufactured during the Second World War. Assume that many different types are still buried with treasure deposits in the Philippines and are still a danger to life today as they were during the 1940s. If you dig up such a bomb listed above, mark the area with red barrier tape and evacuate immediately. Inform the local police and, if you can, the local army bomb disposal team.

12.00   **Explosive Danger Signs**

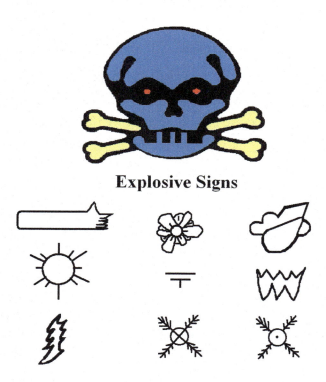

Explosive Signs

Explosive devices are still a major danger to treasure hunters even though these devices have been buried for over sixty-five+ years. Therefore, explosive sign recognition is so important in keeping you safe as you dig deeper towards your treasure target. According to the Japanese Engineering Battalion Treasure code, bombs were buried at 12, 35 and 45 feet deep.

12.10 Water Traps

Water traps are a hazard that all treasure hunters must be aware of, and can creep on you unawares. Usually there will be a danger sign in the form of a two pieces of wood nailed together in the form of a large "X". Our diggers mistook this to mean "Big Deposit"!

The shaft was over 120 feet deep; the water gushed into the shaft when the side was slightly widened and caused havoc. We were lucky no one drowned. There will be more water in the reservoir feeding the water trap in the rainy season if the reservoir is fed off the high mountain springs.

If the water trap is fed from the river, then usually the deposit is buried 1 meter below the water table. The best time to recover therefore will be in the middle of the dry season, on the second day of the full moon, when the river and water tables will be at their lowest.

If the source of the water reservoir is up the mountain or hill, then it must be found quickly and the flow into the shaft cut off, or the stream or river that flows into the natural pool storage area diverted, then the pool can be pumped dry. Look higher up the hill or mountain for a natural pool or lake either outside in a small hidden valley, between rocks, or hidden in a cave system not too far away from where you are digging.

12.20 Water Trap Solution No.1

TO STOP THE WATER POURING INTO THE SHAFT.
1) BUILD A CONCRETE WALL 8 INCHES THICK AND BRACE IT WITH BAMBOO POLES

2) FIND THE SOURCE OF THE RESERVOIR HIGHER UP THE HILL AND BLOCK OFF THE WATER, OR DIVERT THE FLOW.

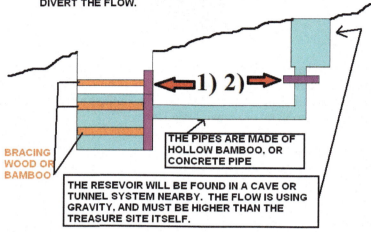

12.30 Water Trap Solution No.2

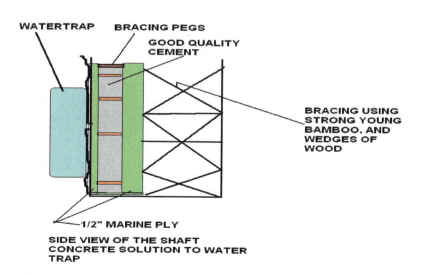

SIDE VIEW OF THE SHAFT
CONCRETE SOLUTION TO WATER TRAP

This was our solution to the problem: wooden bracing down the length of the shaft while the cement cured. Some of the bracing was taken away once the concrete had hardened or "cured" over a period of five days.

Note: If the water source feeding the water trap is not located and cut off, the water pressure behind the concrete wall will continue to increase and will, over a short period of time, burst through the concrete wall, flooding the shaft instantly and drowning all the diggers working at the bottom of the hole.

13.00 Where Did The Japanese Bury The Gold And Precious Items That They Looted?
Answer: Places Listed Here Where Treasure Has Been Found:

Major road and river "Y" and "T" junctions.	Inside old Spanish-style houses behind or below the bathroom or "CR".
Bottom of old WWII cesspits. Check pit base is not false, concealing treasure.	Under old Japanese and other military flag posts.
Under old military accommodation huts, under floors of aircraft hangers, and under military finance buildings.	Under military parade grounds, military flag poles, military observation posts high on hills and mountain ranges.
Buried in the corners of rice fields in concrete vaults (4L x 3W x 2D feet).	Under airport runways at either end. (look for old Japanese flag pole hole).
On top of hills where the Japanese had a look out post or military camp. Under the foundations of anti aircraft guns, and inside old ammunition bunkers.	Inside river banks; behind, and under waterfalls. On natural springs, and near small creeks. Under large water fountains.
Under water inside cargo, military ships, submarines, and sunken aircraft.	Under cemeteries or grave stones or inside old crypts.
Japanese military compounds where POWs were kept prisoner.	Underwater cave systems, in man-made tunnels, ponds and lakes.
At the base or foot of the mountain.	In the roof spaces of churches, also under the stone floors of mosques.
Under Old WWII Bomb Dumps.	Under school buildings, under river, road and railway bridges.
Man-made tunnel systems, and drainage culverts, ditches and storm drains.	Inside natural cave systems. (look for limestone or chalk caves).
Inside military trucks buried in road ditches, or old bomb craters.	Inside treasure mountains that resemble mount Fuji in Japan.
Inside fake rocks, and coral rock found on beaches and hill site locations.	Major road "Y" and "T" junctions found outside small towns in rural locations.
Under concrete roads which were patched up due to WWII bomb craters. Gold in the crater and new concrete poured on top.	Under old bus station buildings and under the floors of cellars in old houses too.
Under old road and railway bridge foundations and even railway tracks.	Inside old water wells and mine shafts.
Inside coral reefs and rocks.	Under historical monuments such as forts, cathedrals, churches and monasteries.
Under military gates leading to the military camp, or very near to this location.	Main railway stations and sidings off the main branch line, old r/w tunnels too.

13.10 Untouched Treasure Sites Compiled Over 20 Years Research
By: Mr G. Santchez

In this section of the book I include over 90 sites that require further investigation by a serious dedicated treasure hunter. I have included listings of areas that may surprise you. I have not used his real name for security reasons.

Treasure Sites (Luzon) Cave & Waterfall Sites		Buried Treasure Land Sites (Luzon)	
Location:	Tons:	Location:	Tons:
1. Dumagat Secret Treasure 1	50	1. Zapote Tree Secret	2
2. Dumagat Secret Treasure 2	50	2. Mango Tree Secret	4
3. El Sombrero Treasure 1	50	3. Santolan Tree Secret	5
4. El Sombrero Treasure 2	30	4. Tamarind Tree Secret	2
5. Secrets of Digoyo	50	5. Lamp Light Treasure 1	2
6. Mt. Billionaire	100	6. Lamp Light Treasure 2	3
7. Gen.Tamaso Cache	20	7. Market Crossing Treasure	1
8. Gen.Tanaka Cache	50	8. Peroz Road Treasure	1
9. Snake Cave Treasure	50	9. Triangle Bridge Treasure	6
10. Padlock Cave	20	10. Japanese Flag Treasure	1
11. Caged Buddha	20	11. Japanese Executive Camp	2
12. 3 Buddha Cave	20	12. Fr. Terreno's Treasure	6
13. Killer Buddha of Digoyo	10	13. Mango Hill Treasure	8
14. Underground Temple	20	14. Colocol Creek Treasure	7
15. Underwater 2 Metal Box	1	15.Masoc/Grandfather Treasure	25
16. Chained Underwater Buddha	1	16. Skull Tunnel Treasure	30
Sierra Madre Mountain Range (Luzon) Deposits Inside Cave Systems		**Sierra Madre Mountain Range (Luzon) Deposits Inside Cave Systems**	
1) DUMAGAT SECRET TREASURE 1 Cave inside waterfalls full of gold (approx.50 tons). 48 x 6kg gold bars were recovered in 1986. More available, but require proper climbing equipment & funding.		**2) DUMAGAT SECRET TREASURE 2** High cliff wall cave with big log bridge in the mouth of the cave: full of gold bars coated with black asphalt 50 tons spotted by local natives in 2003.Require funding.	
3) EL SOMBRERO TREASURE 1 Cave with gold stockpile (est. 50 tons) and fatigue big box with big padlock. Spotted by local native 1986. Still there. Project requires funding.		**4) EL SOMBRERO TREASURE 2** Cave with gold stockpile (30 tons, gold) in 7 chambers with golden Buddha's and box full of precious stones, spotted in 1991 by local natives. Project requires funding.	

Sierra Madre Mountain Range Luzon Deposits Inside Cave Systems	Sierra Madre Mountain Range Luzon Deposits Inside Cave Systems
5) GEN. TANAKA & TAMASO TREASURE A 12 meters by 12 meters gold stockpile in hidden cave chamber. The relatives of the general went to the Philippines looking for treasure cave. Inside our remains of the late general who is buried on top of a gold stockpile.	**6) CRASHED JAPANESE CARGO PLANE** Spotted by natives in 1995, several boxes cargo is still intact...suspected to contain a precious cargo.

Mindanao Island Cave Tunnel Treasure Sites

Location:	Tons:	Location:	Tons:
1. Seven General Treasure	30	9. Col. Oshihiro Hansawa Treasure	50
2. Three General Treasure of Tagurano	20	10. Col. Yamaguchi Treasure	50
3. Gen. Murakami Treasure	5	11. Lt. Ohata Treasure	20
4. Gen. Teruya Treasure	15	12. Secret of Carmen	50
5. Adm. Nakone Treasure	20	13. Secret of Lake Venadu	50
6. Gen. Kutamura Treasure	50	14. Secret of Makilo Ranges.	50+
7. Treasure of Panabo	20	15. Djakarta Tunnel	80
8. Treasure of Mundo Hill	80	16. Crown of Cambodia	50

Mindanao Underwater Treasure Sites

Location: (Photo: Siwa Maru Merchant Ship)	Tons:	Location: (Photo: Japanese Midget Submarines)	Tons:
1. Siwa Maru (Island Ship)	500	8. Underground Submarine Base	20
2. Tikang Maru Merchant Ship	100	9. Underwater Cement Vault	20
3. Sakima Maru. Merchant Ship	100	10. Runway Edge Sea Vault	10
4. Maru of the Orient 3	100	11. Missing Sea Plane	4
5. Capt. Kimura Ships (6)	500	12. Daibatsu of Ginoog	20
6. Mini Submarine	6	13. Daibatsu of Davao Gulf	20
7. Camouflaged Submarine	20	14. Cliffwall Submarine	20

13.20 Philippine Map Showing Buried Gold Deposits

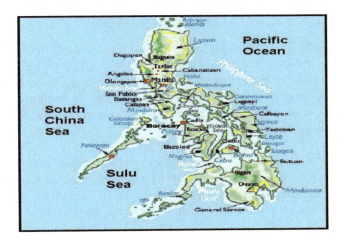

The map gives you the reader a ***rough indication*** of where to look for treasure hoards; the gold is shown on the map in yellow. This map is a useful reference tool when looking at areas that you may consider visiting in your quest to find buried gold in the future.

This map shows my dowsed locations of buried Au deposits scattered all over many of the islands. Each yellow pin represents a deposit or something of great interest. This dowsed map was built up from my dowsing activities carried out between the years 2006 to 2010. There are still lots of buried WWII gold deposits still awaiting discovery.

If you do not believe me, ask a good gold dowser to dowse your map and confirm whether the area is positive prior to excavation. This will save you time and a lot of money!

You may ask why I have included this gold map location above in my book. The answer is very simple: I cannot recover all of these sites myself, and also it is to prove to you, the reader, that I have spent many hundreds of hours dowsing areas of the Philippines for buried gold to show you and myself that *even today* many deposits still remain **untouched**, awaiting discovery!

The only question is: will you rise to the challenge and recover some of these treasures yourself, or will you let others, such as governments, secret societies and mining companies, do the finding? If you are serious in locating your own golden treasure, then contact a talented dowser, such as Mr Matacia from the USA. Maybe he will be able to help you dowse your map or photographs and give you a precise GPS location of your own buried gold.

See link: http://www.louismatacia.com/

Note:

Treasure hunting activity in sensitive areas such as military camps, nature reserves, graveyards, battlefields and private land is strictly forbidden or strictly controlled by the landowners or by local government agents. All treasure hunters must have up-to-date treasure permits, landowner contracts and permission to carry out site investigation or digging activities.

Please be aware that you cannot go onto private land and dig without due regard to Philippine laws and regulations. If you do, then expect to be arrested by the local police and jailed. (See section 7.60 and 7.70 for information on permits and agreements needed before any excavations can begin).

Be Honest:

Many treasure hunters are not honest when it comes to informing the relevant authorities of their intentions and start illegal excavations on private land, expecting that they can carry out "secret activities" without telling anyone what they are doing. The local population is not naïve, simple or stupid. They are watching your every move, day or night; therefore, communicate with the authorities beforehand.

Being honest about what you would like to do, and where, is paramount in fostering good relations with the local authorities and the local population in your area. Over the years, many foreigners have used all sorts of cover stories to try to cover up illegal treasure hunts and excavations.

One Japanese businessman claimed to be constructing watering pools for a new crocodile farm. This sounded plausible, until you know that this site was half way up a mountain! He later recovered a box that was cemented into the base of one of the mountains nearby containing uncut diamonds. One of the local Filipino diggers he had hired found one of the uncut diamonds near to the impression the box had left in the rock face.

So think very hard if you intend to tell a white lie about your treasure hunting activities. I suggest you do not use these tired excuses listed below:

We are building a swimming pool	We are building a new fish pond	We are building a new house (plausible I guess)
We are building a sunken Japanese oriental garden	We are drilling for water (yeah sure!)	We are building a crocodile farm

Ask Permission First.

Dishonest treasure hunting activity will not make you rich; it will bring you much pain and a lot of heartache, and possibly a jail sentence for illegal mining or even trespassing on private land. There is no point in finding a gold target and not having the necessary legal permits or permission to retrieve the items you have found.

Many treasure hunters do not think about how these heavy items will be transported away from the recovery site safely either! Why place yourself in this crazy position in the first place? There is another important consideration that is also overlooked time and time again – that of heavy lifting winches for recovery, transportation, and armed security plans for safe transportation from your site to a secure location.

Always plans A, B, and C! Always backfill any excavations after you have finished; **DO NOT** leave deep holes that will be a constant danger to the local children or population. Always factor an amount of money in your excavation budget to pay for this activity, and make sure your diggers finish the job properly and to the satisfaction of the landowner so he is happy the ground is stable and safe before everyone leaves the site.

Heavy Lift Recovery and Transportation:

If you have the necessary permission from the authorities, and the owner of the land, to recover buried precious items from the land, then a comprehensive recovery plan must be known well in advance in order to safely recover these buried items with the necessary heavy lift block and tackle and winch equipment ready at your disposal.

These items were buried by one or many men, and possibly transported by truck(s) to the site. If it took an army and heavy machinery to place the gold target into the ground in the first place, it will take an army and heavy lifting equipment to get it out, and modern trucks that can carry the heavy loads safely to a secure location.

Have a good solid "secret" recovery plan with the necessary heavy-lift equipment and transport readily on hand when it is needed, and recover at night, when many eyes watching your progress will be asleep. Transport the recovered items away during the night-time, in total secrecy, to ensure your group's safety at all times. VHF and UHF Radio frequencies are monitored by the police and by the army, so be aware of this fact. Ask: how will you communicate with your group?

13.30   <u>Sea Treasure Sites</u>

During WWII, it is estimated that 296 vessels were sunk around the coasts of the Philippine Islands. There are 124 ships in Manila bay alone and 145 vessels in other parts of the Philippine archipelago. In recent years, the Japanese have helped the Philippine Navy sonar scan the entire seabed around most of the islands for one reason only: to map where these vessels are located, and to identify known treasure ship locations from Japanese military archives. In the early part of May 1942, a U.S. Navy ship carrying 350 tons of silver pesos worth, at the time, approximately $8 million, was dumped into the South China Sea, south of the island of Corregidor by the retreating Americans. Was this the ship *USN Harrison*, mentioned below, or another ship?

In April 1942, U.S. minelayer **Harrison** dumped hundreds of boxes of Filipino coins, to the value of five million, into *Manila Bay at a depth of 18 fathoms to avoid them falling into Japanese hands. The Japanese military did in fact recover 2.25 million after they captured the Philippines. Today, approximately one million pesos remain and are awaiting salvage from the South China Sea.

In 1955, the Japanese Foreign Ministry had an agreement with the Philippine government to salvage fifty-seven ships off the coasts of Manila and Cebu, which has now been completed, with the provision of recovering an additional one-hundred-and-seventy-five ship wrecks. Why would this be? The answer is ***not*** to recover WWII human remains, even though this limp excuse may be used by the modern IJN. It was to salvage the hundreds of tons of war booty still lying on the seabed around the Philippine islands. Out of one-hundred-and-seventy-five Imperial treasure sites, thirty-four are reputed to be under water. Remote deep anchorage bays around the Philippine Islands were used to sink military and merchant vessels in water depths that ranged between 280-320 feet of water. Sea caves were another favorite hiding place of the Japanese, only accessible at low tide and completely submerged as the tide returned.

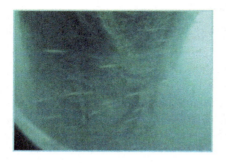

In 2006, a large underwater tower structure has since been found by two divers in 220 feet of water, south east of Corregidor, which may be the lost depository for such a large quantity of silver. The cylinder-like structure is 45 feet high, 11 feet wide and buried deep into the sandy seabed. The assumption is that whatever is inside this massive tube is so heavy that the structure has withstood countless heavy seas and many typhoons that batter the south west coast of Corregidor during the rainy season.

This structure is covered in discarded fishing nets, and possible steel WWII anti-torpedo netting, wrapped tightly around the structure protecting its inner skin against sea water erosion. I have watched the film taken at the time of the dive in 2006, and I have spoken to both of the divers who, when asked, could not tell me whether the structure was an aircraft fuselage or a submarine.

This mysterious cylinder could just be an underwater refueling station or an anchor point for passing ships, waiting under the ocean for an intrepid diving team armed with an **ROV and cutting equipment to find out once and for all. See on the following page a map showing the approximate location of this cylinder, labeled "F".

Left: a view of the top of the underwater structure wrapped in fishing nets.

Source: www.shipwreckregistry.com//index10.htm:
**Remotely Operated Vehicle

13.40 Locations Of Japanese Ships Sunk During WWII

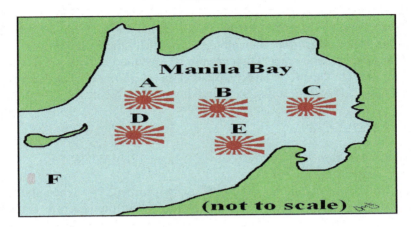

Key
A: **Destroyer Satsuki**
B: **Destroyer Okinami**
C: **Destroyer Akishimo**
D: **Cruiser Nachi**
E: **Unknown Supply Submarine**
F: **Unknown Underwater Vertical 15 M Cylinder Fixed to the Seabed**

A: <u>Destroyer Satsuki</u>

Approx location: Lat:14°35'01.01"N: Long:120° 44' 58 00"E. Approx depth: 25 meters.
On September 21st 1944, after escorting a convoy from Singapore via Miri and Brunei to Manila, *Satsuki* was attacked by aircraft of **Task Force 38** in an air raid on Manila Bay. *Satsuki* took three direct bomb hits, killing fifty-two crewmen and injuring fifteen others, and sunk.

B: <u>Destroyer Okinami</u>

Approx location: Lat: 14° 34'56.30" N: Long: 120° 49'56. 74"E. Approx depth: 21 meters. On the 13th November 1944, *Okinami* was sunk in a U.S. air raid on Manila. Suffering one direct bomb hit and several near-misses, she sank upright in shallow water 8 miles (15 km) west of Manila.

C: Destroyer Akishimo

Approx location: Lat 14° 35' 00.58" N: Long: 120° 54'55. 75"E.
Approx depth: 11 meters. On the 13th November 1944, a U.S. air raid on Manila struck *Akishimo*, then alongside another ship called the *Akebonoat* at Cavite pier. Direct bomb hits resulted in both ships being set ablaze. On the 14th, a large explosion on *Akishimo* further damaged both ships; *Akishimo* rolled over onto her starboard side.

D: Cruiser Nachi

Approx location: Lat:14° 31'02.14" N: Long:120°43'57.89" E.
Approx depth: 31 meters.
The *Nachi* was in Manila Bay on 5th of November 1944 when she was attacked by three waves of U.S. planes from the aircraft carriers *USS Lexington* and *Ticonderoga* of *Task Force 38*. In this engagement, *Nachi* was hit at least nine times with torpedoes as well as rockets. She was broken in two by two big explosions and sank in the middle of a large oil slick. Of the crew, eight-hundred-and-seven were lost.

E: Unknown Supply Submarine

Approx location: Lat:14° 31'13.35"N: Long: 120° 49'08.22" E.
Approx depth: 24 meters.
When this submarine was sunk is a total mystery. Further research will be needed to ascertain whether she was sunk in U.S.N. attack or deliberately sunk by the Japanese Navy.

F: Unknown Underwater Vertical 15 M Seabed Cylinder

Approx location: Lat:14° 17'36.48" N: Long: 120° 33'40.36" E.
Approx depth: 55 meters.
Is this a secret Imperial treasure site? This huge cylinder towers above the ocean floor near to a submarine wreck.

Partial List Of Japanese Shipping Losses During The 1942-45 Conflict

Type Of Ship Sunk	Name Of Ship	Where It Sank
Merchant Cargo	Tatsuhiro Maru	Luzon
Merchant Tanker	San Pedro Maru	Luzon
Merchant Cargo	Hozan Maru	Luzon
Merchant Cargo	Toyohi Maru	Luzon
Merchant Cargo	Santos Maru	Luzon
Merchant Cargo	Hakushika Maru	Luzon
Merchant Cargo	Azuchisan Maru	Luzon
Japanese Mil. Cargo	Minryo Maru	Luzon
Merchant Tanker	Akane Maru	Luzon
IJN Destroyer	Tamanami	Luzon
Japanese Mil. Cargo	Shiroganesan Maru	Luzon
IJN Escort Vessel	Kusagaki	Luzon
Imperial Army Transpt.	Shin'yo Maru	Luzon
Imperial Army Transpt.	Makassar Maru	Luzon
Imperial Army Transpt.	Ejiri Maru	Luzon
Imperial Army Transpt.	Toko Maru	Luzon
Imperial Army Transpt.	Kinugasa Maru	Luzon
Imperial Army Transpt.	Toan Maru	Luzon
Japanese Mil. Cargo	Arabia Maru	Luzon
Merchant Cargo	Chinzei Maru	Luzon
Merchant Cargo	Hakushika Maru	Luzon
IJN Destroyer	Akizuki	Luzon
IJN Seaplane Vessel	Kimikawa Maru	Luzon
IJN Destroyer	Fuyo	Luzon
Merchant Cargo	Ushio Maru	Visayas
Merchant Cargo	Himeno Maru	Visayas
Merchant Cargo	Tonan Maru	Visayas
Merchant Cargo	Himeno Maru	Visayas
Japanese Mil. Cargo	Taishin Maru	Visayas
Japanese Mil. Cargo	Odatsuki Maru	Visayas
Japanese Mil. Cargo	Chuka Maru	Visayas
Japanese Mil. Cargo	Olympia Maru	Visayas
Japanese Mil. Cargo	Sydney Maru	Visayas
Japanese Mil. Cargo	Shanghai Maru	Visayas
Japanese Mil. Cargo	Taibin Maru	Visayas
Hospital Transpt. Ship	Kamakura Maru	Visayas
IJN Destroyer	Inazuma	Mindanao
IJN Destroyer	Akigumo	Mindanao
IJN Destroyer	Tanikaze	Mindanao
IJN Destroyer	Shiratsuyu	Mindanao

13.50　The Imperial Japanese Navy Symbols

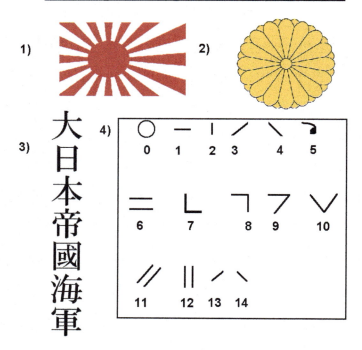

Key

1) Japanese Imperial Navy flag 2) Imperial Family Seal 3) Imperial Japanese Navy written in Kanji 4) Japanese Imperial Navy numbering system: these numbers were used on one treasure site near Glan, Mindanao to indicate the depth of the buried deposit. In this case the depth would be in fathoms and not in meters. (A fathom is equal to: 2 yards (6 feet) in an imperial or U.S. fathom. Originally based on the distance between the fingertips of a man's outstretched arms, the size of a fathom has varied slightly depending on whether it was *defined* as a thousandth of an (Admiralty) nautical mile or as a multiple of the imperial yard. Formerly, the term was also used to describe several units of length, varying in length from 5-5½ feet or 1.5-1.7 meters.)

13.60 How Do I Apply For A Treasure Hunter's Permit To Dive On Shipwrecks?

In the Philippines the **SHIPWRECK/SUNKEN VESSEL** Permit was previously issued by the office of the President in 2004, and became known as: **Administrative Order No. 2004-33** and is issued by the **Department of Environment and Natural Resources**, with office address as follows:

DEPARTMENT OF ENVIRONMENT AND NATURAL RESOURCES

Visayas Avenue, Diliman, Quezon City.

APPLICATION FEE: 12,000.00 (PHP)

SHARING AGREEMENT:

Fifty/Fifty (50/50) as follows: **After** an audited report of expenses has been evaluated and approved by the Oversight Committee.

LICENSING PROCEDURE:

Survey/Salvage Permit: You will receive this within thirty working days after all documentation is evaluated and approved by the Technical Review Committee.

Upon discovery of valuable items, the National Museum shall be called upon to determine whether or not they are considered to have a cultural interest and/or historical value.

All treasures found shall be allowed for export only upon approval of the National Heritage Commission and other concerned government agencies.

SURVEY/SALVAGE AREA:

The area given for SEA sites is twenty (20) hectares. Once you have the permit that means no one can work within your licensed area.

PHILIPPINE PARTNER COMPANY:

As with most Southeast Asia countries, no foreign company can work in the Philippines without having a written Joint-Venture Agreement with a local Philippine Partner/Company. All licenses issued in the Philippines are issued in the name of the local company. All documentation is printed in English.

Note: During the battle of Manila Bay on May 1st, 1898, the American naval fleets, led by George Dewey, fought against the Spanish fleet under General Patrocinio Montojo and destroyed over 15 Spanish galleons. These ships lay alongside many WWII wrecks in the Bay. This action signaled America's colonization of the Philippines.

In 2004, these Spanish silver doubloons were salvaged from a Spanish wreck in shallow water near Mariveles Bataan, Luzon.

 Many more underwater riches are awaiting discovery, including the *true* whereabouts of the **real** Japanese treasure-laden merchant vessel The Awa Maru. There were stories that the ship carried treasure worth approximately US$5 billion: 40 metric tons of gold, 12 metric tons of platinum, and 150,000 carats (30 kg) of diamonds and other strategic materials

The ship departed Singapore on March 28th 1945, but on April the first the ship was intercepted late at night in the Taiwan Strait by the American submarine USS Queenfish (SS-393), which mistook her for a destroyer.

The Awa Maru was sailing as a hospital ship under the protection of the Red Cross, and under the agreed rules, she disclosed to the Allies the route she would take back to Japan. Her original route was planned through a minefield, but her final route avoided the mines.

The torpedoes of the *Queenfish* sank the ship, and only one of the 2,004 passengers and crew, Mr Kantora Shimoda, survived. He was the Captain's personal steward, and it was the third time in which he was the sole survivor of a torpedoed ship.

The commanding officer of the *Queenfish*, Commander Charles Elliott Loughlin was ordered by Admiral Ernest King to an immediate general court-martial. As the Awa Maru sank "she was carrying a cargo of rubber, lead, tin, and sugar. Seventeen hundred merchant seamen and 80 first-class passengers, all survivors of ship sinkings, were being transported from Singapore to Japan. The survivor later stated that no Red Cross supplies were aboard, they having been previously unloaded.

In 1980, the People's Republic of China launched one of the biggest salvage efforts on a single ship in history. They had successfully located and identified the wreck site in 1977 and were convinced that the vessel was carrying billions in gold and jewels.

After approximately 5 years and $100 million spent on the effort, the search was finally called off. No treasure was found. However, several personal artifacts were returned to Japan.

In the aftermath of the salvage attempt, the NSA scoured thousands of intercepted communications to determine what exactly happened to the treasure. From the communications, they determined that the treasure was not to be taken back to Japan. It was to be sent from Japan to Singapore where it would then be delivered to Thailand. The gold was successfully delivered and the Awa Maru was reloaded with a cargo of tin and rubber for the return trip to Japan.

A second ship called the Awa Maru 2 was the real treasure laden ship, and she was never found. Simply because she was deliberately scuttled in deep water near to islands far from the South China Sea by members of a secret Japanese Army intelligence unit during the end of WWII.

Then in 1986, Mr Takaki found this ship. Two-thirds of the ship was buried under 30 feet of sand but most of it is still there laying on the bottom of the sea bed.

While diving the wreck Takaki found laboratories, medicine containers and hospital equipment inside the wreck itself. What struck him was the inscriptions on the cabin doors were in English and not Japanese." I believed then that I found the Awa Maru 2" he said, the Awa Maru was of European make, he stated.

Takaki removed the letters molded in Bronze on the side of the ship and had the Japanese letters translated. The letters read: "Maru" which means ship.

Takaki conducted a small salvage operation on the site of the wreck. This very limited part time salvage effort resulted in the recovery of over 2,000 items, including 800 pieces of Chinese plates, cups, dishes and other ceramics from the Ming, Ching and Sung Dynasties. During the last three years he also recovered 11 small gold bars each one weighing about 100 grams and contained in small wood boxes. He also found dozens of other antiques such as large brass burners, some of them almost 1,000 years old.
Diving for gold Takaki also brought up thousands of bars of tin, brass, lead, and zinc as well as at least three 62-kilo bags of platinum group metals. Much more is still awaiting recovery today!

13.70 List Of Japanese Prisoner of War Camps In The Philippines During WWII

Japanese Prisoner of War Camps in the Philippines	
Bataan: Luzon	Fort Hughes: South West Luzon
Batangas: Southern Luzon	Las Pinas: South West Luzon
Casisang : Central Mindanao	Los Baños: Laguna, Luzon
Cabanatuan #1 & #3: N. Luzon	Nielson Fields: South East Luzon
Capas: Northern Luzon	Nicholas Fields: South East Luzon
Clark Field: Northern Luzon	O'Donnell: Northern Luzon
Corregidor: Luzon	San Fernando: North East Luzon
Davao: Southern Mindanao	Palawan Island: Puerto, Princesa

The above list is not complete in that there were unofficial internment camps set up by the Japanese military. Some buildings changed in use during the Second World War, from fortifications, to hospitals, and then to POW camps as the war progressed. One such place was situated in Sioton Naga in Cebu, where many Japanese and Filipinos lost their lives.

A detailed listing of many of these military and civilian internment camps and current GPS locations can be found using the following website link.

See: http://www.west-point.org/family/japanese-pow/POWSites-Philippines.htm

Many of these sites are official war grave sites, where digging is strictly forbidden. Always seek written permission before carrying out any search or recovery activities on land where many people were held, tortured, and murdered. Human remains are still being found today on these sites. Therefore, have respect and use caution when carrying out your field research and treasure hunting activities.

You do not know what is buried where, and what grim items you may uncover. A group called: "Moores marauders" are now looking for some of the *78,000 **American servicemen missing in action who are still unaccounted for from WWII.** Many volunteers give their time to recover human remains and repatriate lost servicemen back to their living relatives. If you do find human remains, please contact this organization for advice and further guidance.

See link: http://www.mooresmarauders.org/index.htm

13.80 Airfields Occupied By The Japanese During WWII

A good place to look for possible war booty would be sites where the Japanese constructed airfields. A map on the following page was compiled by the U.S. Military Intelligence and issued on the 30th of September 1944. It shows fifty-eight occupied airfields throughout the Philippines Islands.

Many are still in use today, and by cross-referencing military camps, airfields, military movements, and my Imperial treasure site listings, the treasure hunter will be able to identify hot spots that will require further field investigation, together with the appropriate permission from the landowner to visit potential sites.

Gold bullion was recovered by Allied forces at either end of runways and by the sides of runways, under taxiways, even in the middle of the perimeter track that runs all around the airfield, under the concrete floors of aircraft hangers, and in ready-made bomb craters, which were then filled over with rubble and earth.

(*Reference: United States Department of Defense 2003 report).

13.90 Japanese Airfields 30th September 1944

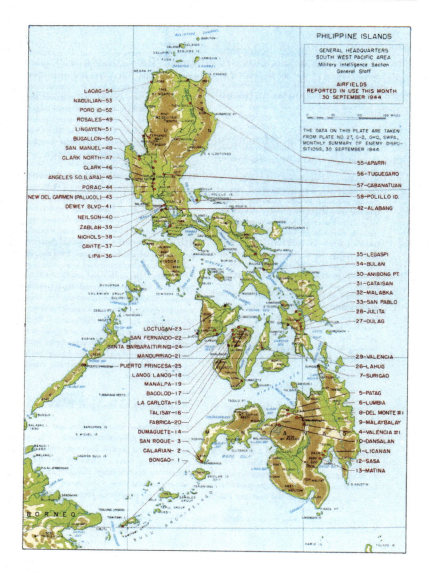

For further information on WWII airfields please see:

http://www.pacificwrecks.com/airfields/philippines/clark/index.html

14.00 Building Up A Picture Of A Beach Treasure Site

What Do I look For?

It is important to become a master at drawing your site accurately, showing the rocks, rivers, hills, mountains, trees and old buildings in order to help you get a feeling of the hidden energy and past history of your site. Do not assume anything until you have completed a detailed drawing and mapped out positions of all of the geographical features in relation to each other. When it is completed, look at your map closely and with an open mind and ask yourself: where would I bury treasure here? Your first assumptions may not always be the correct ones; always look and look again.

Never assume you know all the answers; in time you will have flashes of inspiration, and pictures of what happened in the past will come to you as you sit quietly in the energy of the place.

When this happens, write your thoughts down. This will help you build up a snap shot, frozen in time, of how the site was long ago, and how the treasure could have be concealed by the Japanese military long ago.

We are now going to look at a real treasure site that I helped survey in Mindanao six years ago. This should help illustrate my point about building up your map and having an open mind until it is complete in every little detail.

We found three different treasure symbols carved on three differently shaped rocks:

If we look at each symbol, reading from left to right, we have an arrow pointing down into the ground, the middle symbol is another arrow pointing to the first rock on the left, and then the famous triangle sign that was explained in section 9.62.

As we look at these signs, they do not make any sense until you draw a basic sketch of the whole site, which helps put these three symbols into context with their surroundings.

A very old tree with a mark on the right side.

14.10 Do Not Assume Anything Until You Have The Whole Picture!

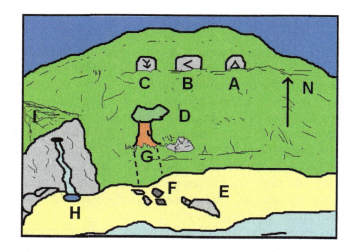

Can you see what has now happened to the rock markings? These have now been placed at the top of a hill, in a row, overlooking an isolated beach and facing out to sea where they can **easily** be spotted by the returning Japanese military forces. The rocks and geographical features can **easily** be recognized by their different shapes by telescope by returning Japanese sailors far out to sea. Every feature shown is totally **unique** to this site, making it **easy** to locate even many years after the war was over.

In fact this site has stood here for over half a century, waiting for the Japanese to return and recover the treasure. Even now it remains untouched, because the locals do not understand the meaning of the symbols. They have missed my point: **you must have the whole picture** before you can understand what is buried where, and by whom. Now can you see where the treasure is buried?

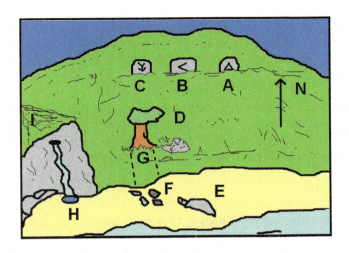

No Please Explain This Picture To Me

In order to understand the rock markings on (A), (B), and (C), we must read these symbols from left to right and **NOT** from right to left, in the conventional "western" way. The triangle symbol on (A) is saying: "Treasure will be found between rocks or trees". This also mean between trees and rocks together, or in the middle of three rocks or trees found in a triangle shape.

The arrows shown on (B) and (C) are pointing to (D), the tree, and we have flat broken flagstones on the beach at (F) and another rock situated by the right side of the tree.

The tree (G) has a marking on the right side of the tree trunk. This means that on the right side there is an opening to a cave or tunnel, possibly under the tree or under the rock on the right marked (D).

The turtle's head (E) is pointing to the flat broken flagstones (F) cast in concrete into the sandy beach, which is marking an entrance to a tunnel system, but also the turtle could also be pointing towards the waterfall (H). This area needs to be investigated more thoroughly.

(G) Shows the suspected underground route of the tunnel where the treasure is possibly stored running from the beach up the hill towards the tree (G).

(H) Is a waterfall where the Japanese could have buried treasure. A potential site for treasure is below the waterfall in the dark blue pool below the falls, behind the falls, on top of the falls, or to either side of the falls.

My field notes near the location (I) mentions that the water flowing out of the waterfall itself comes from an old copper mine on the far side of the hill. This would need further investigation as a possible place to hide military supplies or even a treasure hoard.

Plan of Action

Once I have studied my finished "Treasure Map", I would investigate the site more fully by firstly using my metal detector to detect 1) the tunnel and 2) the gold deposit. I would start at point (E), the turtle, just to make sure no giveaway bars were buried inside the turtle or underneath it. Then I would start metal detecting at point (F) and scan the path (G) that leads towards the old tree (D). I would also scan all around the tree and check out the rock to the right of the tree for any treasure marks on the side or on top of the rock to see if there was a shaft under the rock leading to the treasure hoard.

I would mark hot spot areas that I found with the metal detector and review the data before selecting a target to be excavated. This would depend upon where the hot spot was located and the relative ease of recovery, such as size, depth and tools available at the time of the site investigation.

I suggest you should recover the easy giveaways first before tackling the larger targets buried at deeper depths. The small recoveries finance the larger ones and **not** the other way around. Start small and work up to the more complicated burial sites, simply because these will take more time to excavate and will cost more in labour, additional time and heavy equipment costs.

The deeper the excavations, the more that has to be spent on shoring up the sides of the shaft with wood and bamboo. Flooded holes become a major problem, and generators together with water pumps have to be used to pump water out. This becomes an expensive operation when the generator is working twenty-four hours a day, trying to keep the bottom of a 30 foot flooded shaft dry for your diggers.

Probe Your Way

If you don't have a metal detector then this could be a solution to finding lost gold bars buried by the Japanese soldiers.

One way to find a target in soft earth or sand is to use a long iron rod or a rigid steel cable about 20 feet long and 20mm in diameter. This can be used to probe the sandy earth to locate a buried box. The length of the probing rod could be marked off in 1 meter lengths so that depth measurements can be noted once a hot target is located under the soft sandy ground.

The probe can enter the ground at various angles so that areas under trees or under rocks can be probed for hidden tunnels, caves or treasure hoards before any excavations are started. Once you have "hit" a target that you feel needs further investigation, the depth will be known and, if probing under a rock, the angle at which to dig towards the target.

14.20 Why Did The Japanese Military Bury Gold Deposits On Beaches?

Many deposits were buried on beaches simply because the Japanese Navy were about to go into action against the American Navy or Allied forces. Any Japanese naval or merchant ships would have been unloaded of their precious cargo prior to any naval battle commencing if there was time to do so, or if an American blockade stopped merchant ships delivering their precious cargo to Tokyo, Japan.

Many unofficial gold deposit sites are scattered along deserted coast lines where sea battles took place, and where greedy Japanese officers decided to bury some of the cargo for themselves, sometimes murdering their own men to keep the buried locations secret and known only to the ship's captain and a few of his "loyal officers" onboard.

Usually a basic hole was dug to a reasonable depth of 18-21 feet and the treasure hoard deposited into the shaft or a natural limestone cave and filled in with stones or wet cement if there was some available, thus concealing the entrance. The location would have been noted on a basic map and a secret pact would be made between the officers and the captain that one day, after the war was over, they would return to recover the blood gold and all retire rich and very happy.

In reality, many Japanese sailors, soldiers, and officers would die in the ensuing sea and land battles, and the locations of where the gold was buried would also be lost forever as these men lost their lives for the great Japanese Emperor.

Note: Look for islands located near to where major WWII sea battles were fought between the American Navy and the Japanese Imperial Navy, such as the Battle of the Sibuyan Sea, part of the larger Battle of Leyte Gulf.

Battle of the Philippine Sea: 18th of June, 1944

The Battle of the Philippine Sea was the largest carrier battle of the war, and the United States pilots called it *"The Great Marianas Turkey Shoot"* because there were so many Japanese aircraft shot down during this time. On the 15th of June, there were 20,000 American troops ashore Saipan, an island east of the Philippines.

The odds of the battle were two to one in the American's favour, thus outnumbering the Japanese forces considerably. Out of sixty-nine Japanese aircraft in the first attack, forty-five were shot down. The second attack was even worse when the Japanese sent one-hundred-and-twenty-seven dispatched aircraft to shoot at the United States forces stationed on Saipan, and only twenty-nine of these safely returned.

The Japanese suffered massive destruction, and the Americans lost very few fighters and bombers. Aside from the disaster in the air for the Japanese, their hidden fleet was discovered and mostly sunk by American forces, and although the United States succeeded in destroying a large part of the Japanese task force, they did not achieve the total Japanese naval destruction they had planned until later on in the war at the Battle of Leyte Gulf.

Battle at Leyte Gulf: 23rd to the 26th Of October, 1944

The battle occurred over an area of over 500,000 square miles of sea and included every type of vessel, from submarines to aircraft. On the 6th of October, Moscow informed the ambassador from Japan that the U.S. 14th and 20th Army Air Forces had been ordered to make attacks intended to isolate the Philippines.

The Denver fired the opening gun, beginning the battle on the sea. Toyoda, the Japanese admiral in command, had the disadvantage in that his fleet was scattered over such a large distance. This would be the end of the Japanese Navy in the seas surrounding the Philippine islands.

14.30 Markers And Clues To Look For On Beach Sites

If time was precious, due to a forthcoming sea or land battle near to the area in question, the buried treasure site would be accurately marked onto the appropriate topographical map of the area and at least one underwater concrete sea marker would have been used as a marker and pointer to the land-based treasure just offshore by using weighed concrete blocks. In the isolated beach areas of Southern Mindanao, this method of marking was used.

I was involved in looking for such an underwater marker, which we knew pointed to the location of a large beach treasure that my team of local fishermen had already identified.

This marker had already been discovered sitting on the bottom of the sea at a depth of 2 meters by a local fisherman whose boat had accidently hit it at low tide, thus damaging the bow of his boat. The position of this marker was to the right of a small river estuary that flowed into the sea.

This geographical feature would have been used as a good reference point and marked on the topographical "treasure map"; a reference point to aid future identification if approaching the site from the sea. Pinpointing the exact position of the beach treasure site would have been done by the use of such a concrete marker.

This marker was a large concrete rectangular vault measuring 4 feet long by 2 feet wide and 1 foot high.

On the top of this maker there is a giant capitol "A". This symbol means "Gold" or "Wealth Entrance".
The tip of the "A" pointed in the direction of the treasure site buried on shore. Sometimes these markers would contain a number of gold bars for additional weight in order to stop the marker itself drifting out to sea. The number of 6 kg gold bars used as ballast vary in number from 4-10 bars cast inside a very hard cemented jacket encased around the bars themselves.

Many of these markers have been recovered already in this area of Southern Mindanao, but many still exist around sandy coastal beaches just under the water, awaiting discovery. Some may be anchored by chains to the sea bottom or chained to large underwater rocks or coral. Look for the letter "A" or "V" on these man-made concrete structures lurking just under the water awaiting discovery.

Sadly we did not find our cement vault, simply because the water was very murky due to monsoon rains and muddy river water run- off from the land. One day I will return to look for this lost marker and hopefully recover the gold bars, which will enable us to fund the recovery of the main hoard of treasure just behind the beach front.

14.40   **Our Beach Treasure Site**

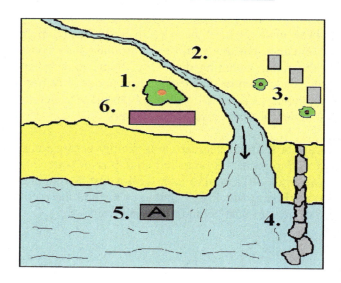

Key:

1. Very old acacia tree.
2. River estuary flowing into the sea.
3. Old Japanese bases where nipa huts once stood during WWII.
4. Old Japanese pier destroyed by the Japanese military when they left the area.
5. The concrete vault marker pointing towards the main treasure site labeled No.6.
6. The main treasure site.

As you can see from the layout of my drawing above, there were many clues left to suggest that Japanese military used to live here, and used the long pier to bring goods ashore from large merchant vessels.

14.50   <u>Treasure Site Layouts</u>

The Japanese military were very cunning in the way that they buried treasure deposits.
Here are some of the examples and treasure layout patterns that were used for small and larger treasure sites. These site layouts must not be ruled out for the larger Imperial sites.

The "Giveaway Deposit"

The first example and most commonly known is where two to six bars of gold are buried at a depth of between 3-9 feet. The treasure hunter finds these and is very happy. He walks away from the site.

Directly below the "giveaway" there could be a larger deposit buried at say 18-21+ feet, which would consist of 20-50 gold bars. Therefore, if you were lucky and found the giveaway, always check the bottom of the hole before you leave the site with your metal detector just in case a larger deposit is buried at a depth of up to 21+ feet below the first.

Site Layouts

The Japanese military followed a theory and this was: Do not bury all of the treasure in one place; spread it around a planned "prepared treasure site" layout, so that even if one deposit is discovered at least the other deposits will remain untouched. Always bear this in mind when looking for treasure deposits.

An example of a large treasure deposit being divided and buried in two separate locations can be seen in section 16, "Analysis of Sliding Rock Treasure Markings" where the treasure symbols tell us this occurred on this site in Mindanao.

14.60 The Pentagon Treasure Deposit Layout

The pentagon is a five-sided shape where the five angles are 108°, and on each of the points a treasure deposit has been buried. Some treasure hunters have uncovered a pentagon-shaped rock that is a scale model of the layout of the treasure site. Using a protractor and a ruler, the treasure hunter can measure both the angles and the distances between each deposit.

All you need is either an old WWII map showing the locations of the five deposits, or a number 5 carved on a large rock stating "START HERE". This symbol will help locate the first of the five burial sites, by finding another burial sign close. Sometimes large rocks will be placed in a pentagon pattern ten to twenty feet apart. Under each rock there will be a treasure deposit.

A perfect pentagon shape like the one shown the diagram below, will have the same angles as mentioned above and lengths of lines AB are the same as AE. ED lengths are the same as BC.

The deposits were buried on points A, B, C, D, and E. Smaller treasure deposits will be found at points B, C and D, at depths ranging from 3-21 feet. At Point A the largest gold deposit will be found at 21-100+ feet.

Remember that the distances between deposits will vary on each treasure site, and so will the angles. Do not assume that the distances between deposits are miles apart. In some cases the deposits have been found a few feet from each other.

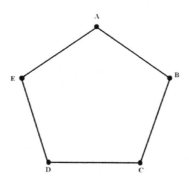

14.70 Types Of Pentagon Markers

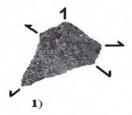

Key:

1) The rock marker: pointing to the five deposits.

2) The second marker is found on a rock, five holes are drilled into the rock showing five deposits of loose diamonds, gold coins, jewelry and gems, and the largest deposit will be gold bars. These deposits will be near to this marker; follow the theory that each point is pointing at the five deposits as described in example 1.

14.80 An Example Of A 5 Arrow Pentagon Deposit Marker

─── Treasure has been divided and buried in **5 seperate** locations. The Yellow lines suggest that the distances are the same or similiar in length. This distance could be in meters or yards. The yellow lines measure 5- 30 yards or meters ─────── This distance is 30-50 yards/ meters away.

The unit of measurement will depend where this particular marker is situated, and whether the Korean treasure code was used. If in Davao, for example, yards would have been used. Other Japanese treasure codes would have used meters as a distance measurement.

Once you have measured these distances out in the direction of the five arrows, you need to look for the other five markers on rocks or trees situated some distance away from this sign that will show you the exact spots where the deposits have been buried.

14.90   Pentagon Treasure Site Layout

Looking at the map above, you should be able to identify the pentagon pattern and identify where the most valuable deposit was hidden, and which deposit may have a booby trap attached to the treasure deposit. All is revealed below and on the subsequent page.

Key To The Treasure Symbols

 A mature tree is used as a reference point, and reading the treasure symbols from top to bottom we have: heart-shaped rock marker buried above treasure deposit, found at depths of between 3-15 feet; two boxes below the heart marker containing gold and diamonds, amounts or weight not known, will be found at depths of 9-27 feet.

 A second mature tree is used as the second reference point. The first symbol represents a coiled snake, meaning treasure is buried below here and will be found at depths of between 3-15 feet. The second symbol, two circles and a black dot in the centre, means money deposited here. The rectangular box

below these two signs means treasure in a box. Therefore, the money is buried inside a box below the roots of this tree, or will be found very close to the tree itself at a depth of between 3-15 feet.

 The symbols are telling us to look at the island situated in the middle of the river; here you will find a large quantity of fifty bars of gold. This treasure is hidden under the island rock, inside a concrete vault.

 2 meters to the right of this tree, (**NOT left**) under the "D"-shaped marker you will find gold coins in a box under the ground.

 Jewelry has been buried under the Salakot-shaped rock with a booby trap.

15.00   Lightning And Gold Theory

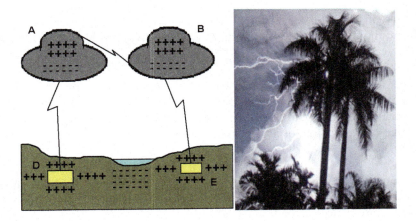

Lightning & Gold Theory

The top parts of clouds A and B are positively charged and the bottom of the thunder clouds are negatively charged. The theory is that lightning discharging from the clouds to the ground will happen when an area on the ground is more positively charged than the surrounding terra firma (mother earth).

It seems that lightning does not always strike the highest point when we are dealing with buried metal hoards in the Philippines. On more than six separate occasions I have come across lightning striking the same areas many times over a prolonged period spanning many years, all of which are suspected treasure sites, where it was rumoured that over 2 metric tons of gold had been buried by the Japanese.

We all know that gold is a very good conductor of electricity and will let current flow very easily through it. But when such a large mass is buried and is in direct contact with mother earth, its resistivity is going to be lower than that of the surrounding earth or sand that it is buried under and will allow current to flow freely through to metal into the surrounding earth above and below the buried object.

The buried metal will have a greater **positive** charge than that of the surrounding area and will act as a good electrical grounding conductor plate to mother earth. Lightning is more likely to discharge millions of volts on this particular spot than the less positively charged areas surrounding the buried gold hoard. (See diagram D and E shown above.)

The lightning therefore will strike this same area again and again, whether half way up a mountain or on the beach. It is therefore very dangerous to camp around an area that you know has multiple lightning strikes, where a tree or area of the ground has been scorched by burning marks.

It is also important to note that lightning can fuse metal together under ground, and make steel and iron objects electromagnetic! This will affect any compass readings and could point the way to a buried truck, or a steel reinforced bunker hiding treasure. Use a compass or your Casio watch as described earlier in this book to locate this hidden secret treasure.

15.10 <u>An Example Of Lightning and Gold Theory</u>

Above is a photograph of a beach where lightning continually strikes the same place month after month, and year after year. It may not surprise you to know that during WWII this whole area was a Japanese military camp.

I have dowsed this photo and found that 5 meters inland from the eroded sand bank there is a tunnel only 15 feet deep. Inside the tunnel there are four Japanese Military Type 94 6-wheeled trucks touching bumper to bumper.

In the photograph above, I have drawn four trucks similar to the one on the right. The roots of the coconut trees are touching the old metal framework of all the trucks, and the tyres have perished through time. Each 5.3 ton truck had sunk into the ground, making good electrical contact with mother earth.

This area under the coconut trees is now more negatively charged than anywhere else in the surrounding area.

The coconut tree trunks now act as "lightning rods", attracting lightning to strike the tops of the trees, which results in the millions of volts flowing down the tree trunk and through the mass of metal underground which is more negatively charged than the surrounding area.

This process will continue to happen until the "earth connection", i.e. the trucks remain buried underground. Cutting down the coconut trees will not solve the problem of future lightning strikes; they will continue until the trucks are dug up out of the ground and taken away.

This is same for buried gold dumped into pits or stored in underground concrete bunkers or inside concrete blocks; lightning will be attracted to these more negatively charged areas, both on land and under water.

Lightning will strike land and sea sites if the area is more negatively charged by a mass of metal. Gold is a perfect conductor for massive electrical discharges of millions of volts to earth from these frequent thunderstorms experienced all over the Philippine islands.

15.20   Does Buried Gold Give Off An Aura?

The answer to this question is yes, gold and other metals give of an ionic plume that can be seen either early in the morning or at dusk.
One man in particular used his psychic ability to actually see the aura floating above the buried and sunken gold on land and at sea. His name was **Olof Jonsson**,* a gifted psychic who was born in Sweden in 1918.

He helped President Marcos locate the Japanese Battle Cruiser **Nachi** in Manila Bay by seeing the "yellowish plume" hovering over the wreck on a calm day. When the divers went down to investigate, they found to their surprise Olof had indeed put them right on top of the wreck's location.

This idea of buried gold giving off an aura or a plume, similar to smoke from an open fire, is not new. The ancient Incas in Mexico found gold by "seeing" the aura plume described, usually in the early morning when there was no wind and the weather was calm.

Not all of us have these gifts of seeing or feeling the presence of gold, however a very successful British treasure hunter has come to your aid and has mastered the art of photographing gold, silver, copper and other metal auras buried in the ground. This has taken him three years to perfect the process and to recognize the different colours that represent various types of metals buried under the earth.

Now using modern digital cameras with infrared filters fitted to the lens, the camera can capture these auras, and by using Photoshop software, the treasure hunter can verify where precious metal is buried prior to any excavations taking place. Steel, iron, copper, gold, silver, can also be identified using this technique to verify treasure deposits before you start expensive excavations. Identifying steel or cast iron objects beforehand is useful, for example if you think old bombs or other hazards may be around a buried gold cache.

David Villanueva has written an exciting book on this very subject, called *The Successful Treasure Hunter's Secret Manual: Discovering Treasure Auras in the Digital Age.* (ISBN 978-0-9550325-5-4). Please see link: www.truetreasurebooks.com

In September 2012, David reported to me that one of his followers used the techniques described in his book and found thirteen gold coins weighing 110 grams at a depth of 1.85 meters. The infrared photo showed a massive aura on the surface of the sand. This technique works! I therefore suggest you invest in this fascinating book and use it to find your own hidden gold. Treasure hunting discussion links to photographing treasure auras:

See link:
http://treasurehunters.yuku.com/topic/494/ARE-TREASURE-AURAS-FOR-REAL?page=2#.TztxYMXUN_c

To watch a practical demonstration of David Villanueva with his digital camera photographing a gold aura and recovering four buried gold sovereigns using his metal detector:

See link:
http://www.truetreasurebooks.net/products-page/e-book/the-successful-treasure-hunters-secret-manual-discovering-treasure-auras-in-the-digital-age

*Olof Jonsson (October 18, 1918, Malmo, Sweden-May 11, 1998, Las Vegas) was a well-known clairvoyant whose abilities were similar to the extraordinary powers attributed to advanced yogis (*sidhis*, in Sanskrit). As a young man, he was tested extensively in Europe. When he immigrated to the US in 1953, J. B. Rhine, Director of the Parapsychology Laboratory at Duke University, conducted many experiments with him. Olof Jonsson was also involved in other high profile ESP tests, including one with Astronaut Edgar Mitchell on the Apollo 14 mission to the moon.

He also was chosen to be the psychic on the team which recovered approximately two billion dollars of gold buried in the Philippines by the Japanese during World War II. Two books were written about Olof, the first published in Sweden, and *The Psychic Feats of Olof Jonsson*, by Brad Steiger, in 1971. (ISBN 0137320167)*

15.30 Infrared Images Of Buried Gold From Known Treasure Sites

This picture (left) was taken of an area of ground where an old Japanese map and my dowsing told the owner of the land where the gold was located.

The owner decided to check the area out using his digital camera and an infrared filter, just as David describes in his excellent book *Treasure Auras in the Digital Age*. We can see clearly two gold deposits; the darker one will have more mass than the smaller aura on the right of the photo. The owner is planning to excavate this site in August 2009.

In this picture we can see the infrared aura coming from an object buried in the ground. By using experimental infrared photography, using three different filters of varying light spectrums, you photograph known metal objects above the ground you can successfully identify which infrared light colour spectrum matches gold, silver, diamond, copper and iron..

You build up a library of these colours on a database, which will enable you to easily identify these "matched" infrared colours of known metal objects above ground with infrared auras giving off metal objects buried below the ground as you photograph areas of interest with your digital camera.
This photographic technique works both on land and over water sites.

Image A: Nazi Gold Bar   **Image B: The Negative Image**

Image A is a "known" Nazi gold bar, and image B the negative image.

We now can identify an inky dark blue colour matches gold, both above ground and below ground.

This technique can be used to verify a gold aura when an infrared image is converted into a negative image. See C below.

Image C: A Bluish Gold Aura: 100% confirmation that gold is buried here.

This process of taking a series infrared digital photos of an area means that you can survey a lot of ground quickly and efficiently. Infrared photographs can be taken in rapid succession, transferred into a laptop and viewed on site within minutes, and areas with buried metal will be identified instantly, saving many hours in searching rough terrain in the baking hot sun with a metal detector. The other advantage is that these photographs can be taken early in the morning, or at dusk, when the surrounding temperature is not unbearable. Remember: the longer the metal object has been in the ground, the better the infrared aura. In the case of gold, this aura will be at its best when the sun has warmed up the ground all day, and the sun's rays have penetrated the ground during the day. The gold will retain this heat and will increase the infrared aura around the object at dusk and early in the morning when there is little wind and when air humidity is low.

15.40 Spiritual Activity At Potential Treasure Sites

Becoming Aware Of Your Surroundings

In some cases potential treasure sites are situated where WWII battles took place, and in many circumstances these old "battle sites" still hold a negative energy and many dangers to anyone thinking about starting new excavations. Sometimes your psychic senses will make you aware of such negative vibrations, and will result in the feeling of sickness or feeling nauseous. Maybe you will feel that someone is watching your every move. This supernatural activity can be detected in photographs taken of these sites. I want to share this phenomenon with you so that you are more *psychically aware* of what to expect and how to counter-act these invisible negative forces.

Use your own psychic abilities that we all have to *see* or feel the unknown hidden dangers that are waiting to catch us off guard. We must "wake up" and "tune in" before we start digging holes blindly here and there.

Look at this photograph below and tell me what you see through your third eye.

What can you "see" in this picture? I want you to really look and experience the spiritual energy here…what are you feeling, what do you think happened here during WWII?

Would you want to visit here for example? Would you start using a metal detector or carry out excavations?

I hope you have written down in truth what your psychic senses are telling you and how you actually "feel" about this photograph; it could save your life on future WWII battle sites.

Now Let Us Now Compare Notes:

This is this email message I wrote to a Filipino who wanted to know if there was any gold buried in the photograph.

"Hi Jako, how are you??
Regarding the photo you sent me of Sioton Naga, Cebu: When I first looked at the photo, I had a bad feeling and said to myself "Yuk". The spiritual energy here is not good here, even after so many years have passed. I feel that many were killed here both Japanese and Filipino fighters.

Please tell Bert this. I would not detect or dig until the area is prayed over. Also watch for WWII land mines, and possibly unexploded bombs. Personally I would not excavate or even think about metal detecting here."

In less than twenty-four hours I had this reply: **"Sioton, Naga, Cebu was a concentrated camp of JIA. And many Filipinos were killed in this area, together with many Japanese. That is what living witness says. You're right Aquila this area is very dangerous for the current owner. He said that there were a group of treasure hunters showed her a treasure map and said that the treasure site contains two bombs before the treasure deposit can be excavated. That's why they didn't touch it and many treasure hunters have failed to recover gold bars in this area."**

I told Jako to keep well away; it is not the dead that hurt you, it's the unexploded munitions that have been left in the ground, and I feel that there are many dangers here for an ill-prepared treasure hunter to deal with safely. After all, a little piece of gold is not worth the risk of dying for is it?

15.50   What About This "Orb" Picture?

How do you feel about these pictures? I took these photographs inside a Japanese tunnel on a known treasure site in Luzon, where over two-hundred-and-twenty souls were buried alive by the Japanese military.

Eleven trucks full of gold went into a tunnel system below this one, then dynamited it shut, killing all inside, including Filipino civilians, British POWs and Japanese military.

What do you see? Would you want to go inside this tunnel and explore, or would you stay away?

I decided to explore, and I even switched off my flashlight to get a feeling for the place!
I did not feel scared, but warm and safe. I prayed for the many dead that lay under this tunnel complex. The orbs of light were not visible to me when I took this photograph, and no, they are not water marks or dust specs on the camera lens either!

The lens was covered and the camera was turned on when I entered the tunnel. This was the second photo that was taken inside the tunnel. There was a firefight here between Japanese and American forces. We found bullet holes above the entrance.

On the left we can see that the camera has captured a very clear image of a large orb on this digger's left leg in the same tunnel system as shown in the photograph above.

Over a three day period I photographed many orbs surrounding the digging team inside this tunnel.

It seemed that, where we were digging, these orbs would only appear on photographs and when our digging team were active, as though they were very interested in our digging activity.

Were these spirits trying to tell us something? Did they want us to know that many years ago they were like us, blood and flesh, and died here before their time in a hail of bullets and explosions?

15.60 <u>**Orbs That Spell Danger And Disaster**</u>

Let us say that you have taken a series of photographs of a potential treasure site, and on a few of the photos you observe orbs similar to those shown in the photograph on the previous page.

The orbs that you see are perfect spheres, some of which are clear and see-through; others may be coloured blue, pink, or brightly lit by pure white light.

We will now assume that near to where you took these photos you start your excavation, and after two to three days, you decide to take another set of photographs of the same area.

Now you notice that the shapes of the orbs have changed, and now they appear to be misshaped and appear over or inside your excavation hole or newly-dug tunnel.
This is when alarm bells must start to ring with you. Some treasure hunters have experienced life-threatening dangers just after they had taken these types of photographs. The orbs are a warning of imminent danger. The timescale is not specified, but if you ignore this warning you do so at your own peril.

Whether you believe in spiritual activity or not, it would be unwise to continue any excavation without seeking out any unseen dangers or booby traps that lie underneath the earth. The orbs could be the spiritual energy of the dead. Please observe and look closely at your photographs as your excavations progress for any changes in the orb appearance from normally round circles to misshapen orb shapes like the examples shown on the previous page.

Photograph A: Taken by myself on a recent hunting expedition. I saw this through the camera lens as I took the picture.

Photograph B: If you look closely you will see an orb at the bottom of this shaft.

15.70 Japanese Military Isuzu Type 94 6-Wheeled Transport Truck

Introduced in 1934, this lorry weighed 5.3 tons, its top speed was 60km per hour, and could carry 1.5 tons of equipment, or gold bars for that matter. Isuzu produced two models, the petrol engine version called the Ko Model 70PS, and the diesel version called the Otsu Model 70PS.

Both these models were built to meet high standards of transportation requirements set by the Imperial Japanese Army who demanded a good reliable truck with performance to match. The type 94 was produced in very large numbers and used extensively throughout SE Asia until the Second World War ended.
Dimensions: 5.4 meters long: 1.9 meters wide: 2.2 meters high.

15.80 Why Is this Information Important to a Treasure Hunter?

Popo Reported this in 2009:

"We have a treasure recovery operation right now in Davao, Mindanao. This is the BASE CAMP OF GENERAL NAKAHARA. We have a living witness who has already penetrated inside the tunnel in 1992 at the depth of 300 to 350 feet below ground. **He saw five six by six wheeled trucks parked in the main road of the main tunnel. Three of those trucks were covered with canvass we expected that the loads on these trucks are still onboard because the cargo is covered over with canvass.**

The other two trucks are parked in different positions. The canvass covers are missing from these two trucks. We think that their precious cargo has already been deposited inside the treasure room just off the main tunnel. Our eye witness saw also many human skulls and bodies inside the tunnel, helmets, swords of Japanese soldiers". The particular site is currently awaiting a serious investor as I write this book.

As we can see from the above reputedly true statement, six by six wheeled trucks were buried inside tunnels fully laden with boxes of gold bars on the flatbed of these types of military vehicles. Also trucks were buried in bomb craters, in ditches along the side of roads, or just inside the entrances to tunnels systems as large underground metal "markers" that could be detected by metal detectors at the end of the war by returning Japanese nationals.

If you are aware of this information and know the dimensions of the truck that was used during WWII, then identifying what you have found aids "recognition" and gives you a clear "picture" of what could be buried underground before excavations begin. You would also expect to get a "hotter" gold target on the rear of the truck than the front with your metal detector. Therefore you can pinpoint where the rear of the truck is located in relation to the front, saving excavation time. The total carrying capacity of the truck was not large compared to today's standard of 40+ tons, but when you hear stories that twenty trucks arrived over a two-month period at a treasure site, it gives you an idea of how many tons were potentially offloaded (20x 1.5 ton = 30 tons).

15.90 How Do I Tell If A Buried Truck Is Under The Ground?

As the soil has settled, a depression around the outline of the truck would form over time. Where the truck is situated, treasure hunters have found that the grass and vegetation has become stunted in height compared to the surrounding vegetation.

The colour of the grass has a washed out appearance, simply because of the metal content leeching into the soil over the surface area of where the truck is laying beneath the ground, which has contaminated the surrounding soil. By using a deep search metal detector similar to the one described in earlier chapters, the outline of the truck can be mapped out and the area pegged and roped off before any excavations begin.

The photo (left) clearly shows the outline of the truck that I dowsed for a treasure hunter on a site in Mindanao. When we compared the dimensions with the Isuzu Type 64 truck of 5.4 meters long and 1.9 meters wide, they were a virtual match to our detected area. Excavation of this historical vehicle is due to start very soon.

16.00 Analysis of Sliding Rock Treasure Markings

This photograph was taken from a treasure site in Mindanao, which shows that the treasure deposit was so large it had to be divided and buried, or hidden, in two locations. The rock that had these markings was slid into place, and butts up against another rock, which acts like a sliding door.

The gold sign is the Japanese Tanaka sign for gold. The site needs further investigation, and funding is needed to recover what is behind these sliding rocks shown in the photograph, and also to find the location of the second treasure deposit which will be found in another location up to 50 metres away.

Further markers or arrow pointers carved on large rocks or trees would have been used to further aid the treasure hunter finding the precise location of this second hoard.

16.10 River Rock Treasure Analysis

In this photograph we see a site that has been marked with treasure codes (top left hand side) and a hollowed out rock in the shape of a heart. This heart is telling us that there is a rich object directly below the rock, as the yellow arrow indicates, or that the entrance to the treasure tunnel is directly beneath this rock. The large "5" tells us to start our excavations here, and the green line is showing the direction in which the tunnel is heading.

16.20 Treasure Items Recovered In The Philippines

A small golden Buddha found in the mountains north of Davao, in Mindanao.

Manufactured in Burma in 1932, and showing 99.8 percent pure.

The black bitumen was probably applied by the Japanese soldiers to disguise the fact that the Buddha was indeed made from gold. Many gold items were covered in bitumen before they were buried.

16.30 <u>**Recovered Gold Bars**</u>

A nice example of a 6.3 kg five-star Sumatra 24-karat gold bar, (999.9) recovered from an unknown location. Again it was bitumen coated. Gold bars were never this pure in the 1930-40s; therefore this bar is probably a fake.

A recovered 24-Karat Cambodian gold bar is shown here.

In a Japanese-made tunnel measuring over 500 meters long, these 12.5 kg gold bars were found in the westerly part of Mindanao. They were stacked 1 meter high and lined the whole length of the tunnel system.

16.40 Gold Bars And A Small Buddha

What a Find! Over thirty 6.5 kg bars and a small golden Buddha. Wow!

In June 1994, twenty 75 kg dore bars were excavated from a secret treasure site. The assay report at the time valued each 21-Karat bar at US $900,000.00.

16.50   **More Recent Finds**

This fantastic hoard of gold bars was found inside a tunnel complex somewhere in *Zambales in Western Luzon circa 2003.

A closer look at one of the bars reveals a Cambodia five-star bar. According to the late Robert Curtis, these bars are Japanese re-melted bars to disguise the fact that this gold probably belonged to British, Dutch and French gold reserves sent to Singapore, Indonesia and French Indochina before the Second World War.

(Left): Using an accurate locator imaging system and an SSP 2100 pulse induction detector, these treasure hunters were able to locate gold bullion! The treasure hunters located the tunnel system firstly from an image that had been created by scanning the potential treasure site after much research, and then the SSP pulse induction unit was used to discriminate and pinpoint the gold bullion. The picture below shows two of many gold bars found at a depth of 80 feet. **See:** http://www.accuratelocators.com/findsph.html
(Photo submitted by: D. Langston in 2008).

(Right): These beautiful gold bars were found in a natural cave system in the hills overlooking Surigao City, Surigao del Norte in October 2011.

These bars are being offered for sale through a local priest intermediary as I write this book.
Were these bars part of a larger gold consignment still waiting discovery deeper inside this cave system?

* Zambales is a province of the Philippines located in the Central Luzon region. Zambales lies on the western shores of Luzon Island. Its shoreline is very ragged, and features many coves and inlets; ideal places for Japanese merchant ships to unload rich cargoes and hide treasure hoards in caves and man-made tunnels.

16.60 Treasure Supposedly Found In The Mountains South Of Cagayan de Oro

Here is a copy of an email I received in late 2006 describing a massive treasure tunnel system, still guarded by Mr. Fukurawa, a ninety-two-year old Japanese Imperial Army soldier, and how he wanted someone to buy some of the treasure hoard so that he could provide for his Filipino family before he died.

The question you must ask yourself is this: Would you travel to a remote mountain and pay for a small part of this treasure? I certainly thought long and hard about it; now judge for yourself:

"Dear Aquila,

We understand you. We make judgments through the internet for we both don't know each others group. Treasure scams in the Philippines as you have mentioned are true and are so rampant but not with our group. This is the only treasure that we are trying to negotiate because we are the only group authorized to negotiate. We are happy with our family and we are contented with our present lives and we rather live this way or rather choose poverty rather than riches gotten by fraud. Loyalty and honesty is not a problem with us, we always make sure that everybody is safe.

The terrain covers mountains, rivers and forest is most safely reachable only by trail-hike for 18 days in good weather. No land vehicle can reach the area, the river cannot be used to transport the stuff because it is already populated, and aircraft such as helicopters are not good to be used since it will call the attention of the people near the area.

Sorry we cannot give you the detailed location of the mountain tunnel, and even if you have a Japanese friend who can pay much more than the PHP 2 million, the instruction to us was clear **"No Japanese national should be involved in this transaction"**. If your group wants us to take another picture of the treasure and focusing on each item with a measurement we will do that if your group will shoulder the financial expenses needed to go the area.

We are not military, NPA or any kind of armed group. We may not be able to put completely what is in our minds because of our language differences but we believe that you are intelligent and better people than our group.

Only **one** person is allowed to go to the area to assay the stuff, it will be accompanied by 2 other person one is a member of our group and the other is a trustee of the old man and no other company.

I am attaching eight of the latest photos taken prior to our communication, the image is not so clear here but you can see here the 24,6, and 1kg of gold bars in fact some the bars are still covered by that black substance.

I think it's a type of asphalt. As you can also see there the 3x 6kls bars are so soft they are bending out of shape to only 30 minutes sun exposure.

Photograph 1

History about this site

About 3 years ago, one of the two closest friends of my dad who stop searching for treasure showed up again in the compound where my dad is working with the news that, he happened to helped someone by saving his life and this someone in return to my dads friend's kindness brought him to the place where that picture I sent to you was taken. The tunnel was **one** of the six *Jakarta* tunnels; the tunnel is full of treasures coming from 60 different countries and holds a Japanese armoury.

You can find different kinds of money here from coins to paper bills from 30 different countries.

A big Buddha (Left). With a revolving head full of diamonds and the golden cup is full of big diamonds and rubies.

Photograph 2

This picture (Left) shows the diamonds inside the head of Buddha shown above in photo3.

Photograph 3

19 Life sized golden Buddha's shown here all in a row.

Photograph 4

Gold bars are stored here and form all sorts, shapes and sizes. For example the cube size gold bar that you saw in the photo with a mark BCMC.

Photograph 5

The Canadian 24 Kilo gold bar marked CANADA= 999.9 with a 3 star. Cambodia made 6 – 75kls gold bars are marked with 5 stars. The others are marked HKB with a 3 star marked, there are lots other's we can't read the writing or the marks on these other bars.
The 75kls Canadian gold bar has a dimension of: $4 \times 4 \times 14^{1/8}$.

Photograph 6

The tunnel has train railroad inside, there are other metals inside the tunnel that they can't be identified. 6 Wells Fargo boxes are in the tunnel each box is worth $50Million each.
We can offer you the following deal: 2 Million pesos is the payment for:
*100 bars of AU 6 or 6.1 kilos each
*1 Small Golden Buddha weighing 2 kilos (See Photographs 5 and 7).
*Half jar of Gold Coins
*Half jar of Gems of 12 different colours (not jewelries)
*1 piece of diamond

Mr. Fukurawa the 92 year old Japanese Imperial Army struggler who guards this site only wants 2 million pesos cash before we can bring the merchandise out of his place and **no Japanese** can be involved in this deal because he will be considered as a ***traitor to his homeland***. 18 days walk that is already back and forth to the area, that is if the weather is not good but if we have a good weather it will be shorter than 18 days.

6 Wells Fargo boxes are also inside the tunnel, each box is worth $50 Million USD each.

Photograph 7

The gold bars are genuine. Aquila, we are not players here (players are what we termed for people who fool their buyers by selling fake gold and it is common here in the Philippines). You can test or assay the gold for yourself in the mountain and you can choose any bars you wish to test".

Q: What would you do reader? Would you risk trekking through a mountain range for 18 days to possibly "buy" these items, and risk being murdered as you came down the mountain path on your return?

16.70 Nickel Babbitt Bars Found

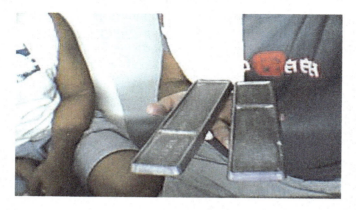

Nickel Babbitt bars found inside an old Japanese bunker near General Santos; they were over three-thousand bars stored inside. These particular ones were made by the American Smelting Company of Detroit U.S.A.

Babbitt Metal: Also called white metal, is an alloy used to provide the bearing surface in a plain bearing. It was invented in 1839 by Isaac Babbitt in Taunton, Massachusetts, USA. The weight of these bars varies from 1.2 kg up to 8 kg.

Common compositions for Babbitt alloys Are:

90% tin, 10% copper
89% tin, 7% antimony, 4% copper
80% lead, 15% antimony, 5% tin

Originally used as a cast in place bulk bearing material, it is now more commonly used as a thin surface layer in a complex, multi metal structure. These bars would therefore have been very useful in the manufacture of bearings for aircraft, vehicles and machinery for the Japanese war effort if they had been exported back to Japan during WWII.

16.80 I Found Some Metal Is It Valuable?

Treasure hunters find bars of metal under the ground and think they have found something of value. Many times they like to think that they have found some platinum or other "valuable" rare metal. On many occasions this has been proved not to be the case. In order to find out what the metal is, we will need accurate measurements of the length, the width and the height of the metal bar that you have found in centimeters. We will also need an accurate weight of the bar in grams or kilograms to carry out our calculations.

Once we know these, we can multiply (L) x (W) x (H) in cm multiplied by the specific gravity to find the calculated weight of the metal. Once we have done this, we can compare this calculated weight with our measured weight of the bar taken previously to see if there is a match. If these two weights match we will know the type of metal that has been found.

How Is Specific Gravity Calculated?

The mass of over thirty different metals and alloys are listed on the next page. While individual samples of metal and alloys differ, impurities will often have an influence on the specific gravity. A 1000 kg of pure water equals 1 cubic meter. Pure water was chosen as the 'base line' for specific gravity and given the value of 1. The specific gravity of all other materials is compared to water as a fraction heavier or lighter in density.

For example, beryllium has a specific gravity (sg) of 1.84 (1840 kg/cu.m) (see specific gravity table on the following page). As specific gravity is just a comparison, it can be applied across many units. The density of pure water is also 62.4 lbs/cu.ft (pounds per cubic foot), and if we know that a sample of aluminium has a specific gravity of 2.5 then we can calculate that its density is 2.5 x 62.4 = 156 lbs/cu.ft. Note: kg/cu.m divided by 16.02 = lbs/cu.ft

A Practical Example:

A metal bar measuring 20cm (L)ong, 6cm (W)ide and 4cm (H)igh weighing: 4.1 kg was found 2 meters underground on a potential treasure site. Find out by calculation what this metal could be.

Using the specific gravity values listed on the next page, we can find out the answer by trial and error. Therefore let's try some of the metals:

1) Copper: 20 x 6 x 4 x (8.93) = 4286.4 grams or 4.26 kg.
2) Lead: 20 x 6 x 4 x (11.34) = 5443.20 grams or 5.44 kg.
3) Nickel: 20 x 6 x 4 x (8.8) = 4224 grams or 4.224 kg.
4) Brass: 20 x 6 x 4 x (8.4) = 4032 grams or **4.032 kg**.

The only result that nearly matches with our weighed weight of 4.1 kg is brass, casting at 4.032 kg. If we look at the Specific Gravity Table for brass casting, we can see that the value of brass castings vary between 8.4 and 8.7, depending upon the impurities that were inside the metal when the bar was made.

Always remember: impurities make a difference in weight. This technique of calculating the weight gives an approximate value for comparison purposes only, but will help you identify the type of metal that has been recovered, and not be tricked into buying "fake" gold bars or cheap platinum bars that are worthless. On the next page is an example of how to spot a fake platinum bar using the specific gravity of the metal multiplied by its volume.

16.90 I Have Heard That Some Counterfeit Johnson Matthey Platinum Bars Are In Circulation, And Offered For Sale In The Philippines. Is This True?

Johnson Matthey is aware that over a number of years there have been numerous fraudulent offerings of large quantities of purportedly platinum bars, made in various styles, in particular bars purportedly manufactured by Johnson Matthey, bearing an inverted horseshoe mark.

Usually the offers (or even bids) have originated in Asia and have centered around Indonesia. The common thread has generally been the "horseshoe" brand and **AZL18.**

It is impossible to accurately estimate the number of "horseshoe" bars in circulation. However, the quantities offered are often out of all proportion to the amount of platinum that could possibly be in existence in the entire world. Commonly they have been for tens, hundreds or even thousands of tonnes. Mostly, the offers are routed through small traders and individuals unfamiliar with precious metals or platinum. Forged certificates, mostly of a poor and amateurish nature, have been provided, and a variety of different methods and forms of contracts have been proposed attempting to arrange a "deal".

Whenever Johnson Matthey has had the opportunity to make a physical examination of this type of bar, they have always been manufactured of a base metal, typically what is, in effect, a **high grade stainless steel.** The degree of technical skill shown in manufacturing the bars is considerable. To avoid purchasing counterfeit platinum products, Johnson Matthey recommends that you always make a purchase from a reputable source and that you always verify hallmarks and serial numbers wherever possible with the company, especially if a "JM" hallmark's stamped into it and the bar has a serial number.

A quick and very approximate test you can perform to check the genuineness of a platinum bar is to measure the dimensions of the piece in centimeters.

Multiply together to give the volume, then **multiply the volume by the density of platinum, 21.45 gm/cc. This will give you the theoretical weight that the bar should be if it** is really platinum. **If the actual weight is less than 85% of theoretical, it is probable that it is not platinum**. For example a bar of given dimensions: ½"x 2.5"x 3" is offered for sale. Calculate the theoretical weight using the *density of platinum of 21.45 gm/cc.*

Answer: Convert inches to centimeters: 1.3 x 5.7 x 7.6 = **56.316 9(Volume) x 21.45 gm/cc. = 1207. 97 grams**

(1.207 kg) Calculated weight of this bar's dimensions should now be compared to the bar's measured weight using accurate weighing scales, and its weight should match. If not, the weight of the bar will be at least 85% of this theoretical weight of 1.207 kg OR (85/100x1.207 kg) = 1.0259 kg and used as a check to see if the bar is genuine. An assay test will also be needed to verify that the bar is indeed 100% genuine.

Platinum (Pt) Properties

- **Color** is a white-gray to silver-gray, usually lighter than the platinum color of pure processed platinum.
- **Luster** is metallic
- **Transparency** is opaque.
- **Crystal System:** Isometric; 4/m bar 3 2/m.
- **Crystal Habits** include nuggets, grains or flakes, rarely showing cubic forms.
- **Fracture** is jagged.
- **Hardness** is 4-4.5
- **Specific Gravity** is 14-19+, pure platinum is 21.5 (**extremely heavy even for** metallic minerals).
- **Streak** is steel-gray.
- **Other Characteristics:** Does not tarnish, is sometimes weakly magnetic and is ductile, malleable and sectile meaning it can be pounded into other shapes, stretched into a wire and cut into slices.

17.00 Specific Gravity Table For Metals

Metal or Alloy Type	kg/cu.m
Aluminium – Melted	2560 - 2640
Beryllium	1840
Brass – Casting	8400 - 8700
Copper	8930
Delta metal	8600
Gold	19320
Iron	7850
Lead	11340
Magnesium	1738
Mercury	13593
Molybdenum	10188
Monel	8360 - 8840
Nickel	8800
Nickel silver	8400 - 8900
Platinum	21400
Plutonium	19800
Silver	10490
Steel - Rolled	7850
Steel - Stainless	7480 - 8000
Tin	7280
Titanium	4500
Tungsten	19600
Uranium	18900
Vanadium	5494
White metal	7100
Zinc	7135

Always remember that this technique of identifying metal types should also be used in conjunction with assay testing the metal, especially when you are trying to confirm the purity of say platinum, gold or silver bars.

17.10 I Can't Melt The Metal!

On many occasions treasure hunters tell me that there are no markings on the metal, and when they have tried to melt the metal by heating it in a fire or taking it to the blacksmith's shop, the metal has not melted even though red hot heat has been applied for many hours. When the metal reaches a red glow, the temperature of the metal has reached 600° centigrade. Hot enough to melt tin, lead and zinc, but not the precious metals listed in the table below.

Many precious metals have very high melting points, and will not be melted without the use of a proper smelting furnace that can reach temperatures of up to 1800° centigrade.

Why Does the Temperature of the Furnace Have To Be So High?

Simply because some metals have a very high melting point, and the furnace must be able to reach this temperature in order to smelt the metal in question.

In the case of platinum, the melting point is 1772° centigrade. Unless you have your very own furnace, in the case of ex-President Marcos, there is no way you would be able to find out whether you have found platinum by trying to melt it. That is why the specific gravity calculation is a better and preferred way to find out what the metal could be before trying to sell it.

Here are a few examples showing the melting point in centigrade of metals that may be useful:

Metal	Melting Point	Symbol
Gold	1064.43°C	Au
Platinum	1772.00°C	Pt
Silver	961.93°C	Ag
Titanium	1660.00°C	Ti
Tin	232.00°C	Sn
Lead	327.46 °C	Pd
Zinc	419.58°C	Zn

17.20   <u>A Recovered Gold Certificate</u>

Above: a Wells Fargo gold certificate series 1934 for 7000 metric tons of gold bullion.

17.30 A Recovered J.P.MORGAN Gold Bullion Liberty Bond

A J.P. Morgan gold certificate: *"Payable to bearer on demand as authorized by law".*

"This is to certify that the secretary of the Department of the Treasury of the United States of America has required John P. Morgan to deposit a volume weighing Three Point One Hundred Ninety Seven Metric Tons in Gold Bullion particularly at Fort Knox, Kentucky, the official Gold Bullion Depository of America.

The volume served as guarantee to the emergency loan for the LIBERTY BOND to be corresponded with a printed Federal Reserve notem with a portrait of Woodrow Wilson, Series 1934.

The undersigned acknowledge receipt that this volume in Gold Bullion in the vaults of the depository at Fort Knox, Kentucky. This volume can only be retrieved by the depository John P. Morgan upon all payments of the loan by government of the United States is completed.

Signed and sealed and acknowledge receipt these bars in Gold Bullion this 12th day of January 1942 in Washington, District of Columbia United States of America".

It is interesting to note that **only** J.P Morgan could redeem his gold, and no one else, and that the United States Treasury do not state when the "loan" will be paid back to J.P. Morgan, if at all. The multi-millionaire, J.P. Morgan, Jr. died the following year in 1943.

Today, the merchant bank, J.P. Morgan serves one of the largest client franchises in the world and their clients include corporations, institutional investors, hedge funds, governments and affluent individuals in more than one-hundred countries. J.P. Morgan is now part of J.P. Morgan Chase & Co. (NYSE: JPM), a leading global financial services firm with assets of $2.2 trillion.

The firm is a leader in investment banking, financial services for consumers, small business and commercial banking, financial transaction processing, asset management, and private equity funds. Without this certificate and the $100,000 notes, there is no way the current J.P. Morgan bank can redeem their gold bullion from Fort Knox, (even if they were allowed too). With assets of $2.2 trillion already, an old gold certificate has some historical interest to them, simply because it is part of the bank's history.

I wonder, nonetheless, whether the company would like to have this certificate back so that it can be exchanged for hard cash by the current J.P. Morgan Chase & Co. for gold bullion taken by the U.S. government in 1942, presumably to fund the war effort.

17.40   Historic U.S. Gold Certificates (1934)

Series 1934 $100 Gold Certificate, front.

Series 1934 $100,000 Gold Certificate, front.

The largest denomination of currency ever printed by the Bureau of Engraving and Printing (BEP) was the $100,000 Series 1934 **Gold Certificate** featuring the portrait of President Wilson. These notes were printed from December 18th, 1934 through to January 9th, 1935 and were issued by the Treasurer of the United States to Federal Reserve Banks only against an equal amount of gold bullion held by the Treasury Department. These notes were used only for official transactions between Federal Reserve Banks and were not circulated among the general public.

17.50 Woodrow Wilson Series 1934 Gold Certificate

17.60 Recovered Woodrow Wilson Series 1934 Gold Certificates

These $100,000 notes were with the J.P. Morgan Gold Bullion Liberty Bond seen in section 17.30.

17.70 When Were Gold Certificates Used?

The gold certificate was used from 1882 to 1933 in the United States as a form of paper currency. Each certificate gave its holder title to its corresponding amount of gold coin. Therefore, this type of paper currency was intended to represent actual gold coinage,

In 1933, the practice of redeeming these notes for gold coins was ended by the U.S. government and until
1964 it was actually illegal to possess these notes (in 1964 these restrictions were lifted, primarily to allow collectors to own examples legally, with no connection to gold).

When U.S. paper money was modernized in the year 1928, gold certificates ceased to be issued.
When the U.S. was taken off the gold standard in 1933, gold certificates were withdrawn from circulation. As noted above, it was *illega*l to own them. That fact, and public fear that the notes would be devalued and made obsolete, resulted in the majority of circulating notes being retired. In general, the notes are very scarce and **valuable,** especially examples in *"new"* condition.

The history of United States gold certificates is not too clear. They were authorized under the Act of March the 3rd 1863, but unlike the United States Notes also authorized, they apparently were *not printed* until 1865. They did not have a series date, and were hand-dated upon issue. "Issue" meant that the government took in the equivalent value in gold, and the first several series of gold certificates promised to pay the amount only to the ***depositor***, who was explicitly identified on the certificate itself. The first issue featured a vignette of an eagle uniformly across all denominations.

Several later issues (series 1870, 1871, and 1875) featured various portraits of historical figures. The reverse sides were either blank or featured abstract designs. The only exception was the $20 of 1865, which had a picture of a $20 gold coin. The series of 1882 was the first series that was payable to the bearer; it was transferable and anyone could redeem it for the equivalent in gold. This was the case with all gold certificate series from that point on, with the exception of 1888, 1900, and **1934.**

Gold certificates, along with all other U.S. currency, were made in two sizes; a larger size from 1865 to 1928 and a smaller size from 1928 to **1934**. The backs of all large-sized notes, and also the small-sized notes of series **1934, were orange**. The backs of the series 1928 bills were green, and identical to the corresponding denomination of the more familiar Federal Reserve Notes, including the usual buildings on the $10 and $100 designs and the less-known abstract designs of denominations $500 and up. Another interesting note is the series of 1900. Along with the $5000 and $10,000 of the series of 1888, all 1900 bills ($10,000 denomination only) have been redeemed, and no longer have legal tender status.

Summary of Gold Certificate Series.

To the depositor variants were:
1865: eagle on front, abstract design on back.
1870, 1871, 1875: portrait on front, same abstract design on back.
1888: similar to 1875, except blank on reverse side.
1900: similar to 1888.

To the bearer variants were:
1882: slightly modified front from 1875, with offset portrait. New rear design featuring eagles.
1905–1913: new design, similar to modern currency, central portrait, Great Seal of the United States on reverse.
1922: design elements taken from 1882 or 1905–1913.
1928: similar to Federal Reserve Notes, green back.
1934: similar to above, gold back, for bank use only to settle gold balances, not legal to privately own.

17.80   Wells Fargo U.S. Dollar Notes

Old U.S currency was used to pay U.S. soldiers their wages in the Philippine Islands during World War II. These are commonly known as "Wells Fargo" because the bank donated safes to the U.S. Army to store the old US notes inside prior to distribution to the U.S. Allied forces. Wells Fargo themselves did not have banking facilities in the Philippines during the Second World War.

Some of these Wells Fargo safes were stolen as "war booty" by the Imperial Japanese forces during this time in the Philippine Islands. Many safes were recovered by Filipinos after the war, and most of them have been opened and the money redeemed.

The serial numbers on these safes are meaningless now, because so many of them have been opened, emptied, and refilled with newspaper, and resealed. If you have a safe, examine the bottom of it and look for signs of resealing, such as new welding seams.

What Are These U.S. Notes?

This is simply old U.S. currency, most of which are dollar notes that will either be series **1934** or **1935** with some dated **1928**.
Note that "Wells Fargo" is **not** printed on these notes. They are old U.S. dollar notes once stored inside Wells Fargo safes. Also, the notes were supplied in Wells Fargo metal boxes. These boxes contained 25, 50, 75, 100, 125, and 150 million dollars.

17.90 Can These Old U.S. Notes Be Redeemed?

At the time of writing this book, the answer to this question is yes.
Below is a sample of the different types of notes that buyers in the Philippines will purchase:

It seems that these notes can be redeemed and will be exchanged by the U.S. Treasury for one-one value; one old dollar for a new dollar. (http://www.ustreas.gov) One buyer in Manila is giving the seller 60% of the face value of each note. The percentages are split thus: 10% to the seller's agent, 10% to the buyer's agent and 20% for the buyer.

Please see appendix in the rear of this book for further details.

How Does This Help Us When We Find Old Dollar Notes?

The table shows you below what notes can still be redeemed at the U.S. Treasury or at any Federal Reserve Bank in the USA.

Series	$1	$2	$5	$10	$20	$50	$100	$500	$1000	$5000	$10 000	Obligation clause	Remarks
1928												Redeemable in gold on demand at the United States Treasury, or in gold or lawful money at any Federal Reserve Bank.	Branch ID in numerals.
1934	*	*	*	*	*	*	*	*	*	*	*	This note is legal tender for all debts, public and private, and is redeemable in lawful money at the United States Treasury, or at any Federal Reserve Bank.	Branch ID in letters; after the Great Depression in 1929.

18.00 Japanese Treasure Maps and Locations

Panabo Del Norte: Nr Davao, Mindanao

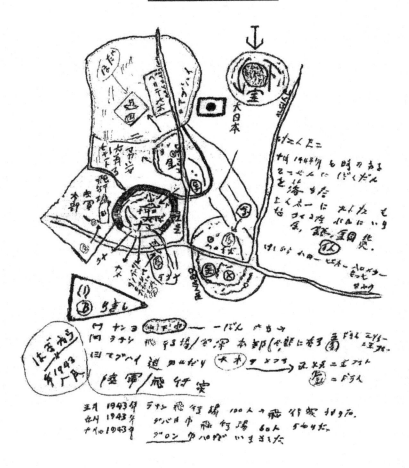

Panabo Del Norte. GPS Location: (Lat: 7°18'28.70"N Long: 125°41'1.91"E). At least four deposits were buried here during the years 1943 and 1944 also mentioned on this map.

18.10 Untouched Treasure Site: Southern Mindanao

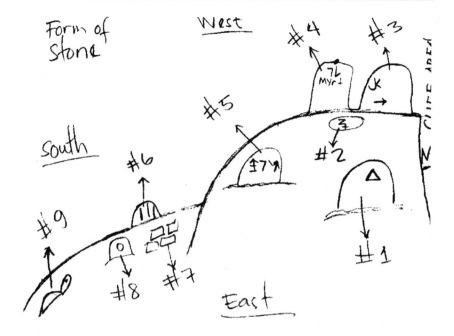

I have studied this particular site in depth over many months and have solved most of the treasure markings on the rocks and the stone turtle shown on the left of the drawing. This site has gold bullion buried inside a large rock. It also hides a large cache of gold that was separated and buried in two locations, one of which is behind a massive sliding boulder. On one of these rocks, it tells us that precious gems have also been buried in another location.

One day I will return to this site with the necessary tools and financial funding to recover what was buried by the Japanese Imperial forces in late 1944.

18.20 A Japanese Treasure Map Of Southern Cotabato Mindanao

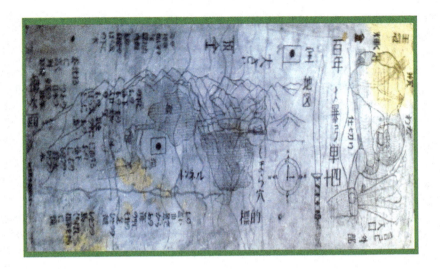

This treasure map shows a river system flowing from the east to the west coast somewhere south of the Cotabato City (GPS location: Lat: 7°13'0.80"N: Long: 124°14'59.63"E).

Two possible locations for where the river mouth meets the sea are located at:

1) Datu Odin Sinsuat (Lat: 7°11'18.82"N: Long: 124°11'2.44"E) where the river runs from west to east towards Kabuntalan. (Lat: 7° 6'59.65"N: Long: 124°22'59.80"E).

2) GPS Location: (Lat: 7° 6'16.04"N: Long: 124° 2'14.65"E).

Translating the map's Japanese Kanji, Hiragana and Katakana characters may help uncover the precise locations of where this treasure is buried in a yet unknown river valley somewhere south of Cotabato City.

18.30 The Arsanai Japanese Flag Map Dated 27th August, 1944. Real or Fake?

Ordered by Admiral Forushi, Commanding Naval Chief of Infanta Quezon.

The map shows four separate deposits with the "Balite Tree", not a sallite as stated on the map, as the main geographical reference point. This Japanese to English translation may be a "Balite Tree".
Some Filipinos say that the sallite is similar to a lighthouse. The Japanese flag measures 100 yards by 50 yards. Someone reading this book may recognize where this place is.

The map mentions Pinatayanan Creek and Arsanai Creek, but no other reference to a particular geographical location. If the sallite is a lighthouse, then we must assume that this treasure site must be on the coast somewhere. The Filipino who showed me this map swore it was genuine.

Is it real or fake…you decide.

18.40 Japanese Treasure Map: Location Unknown

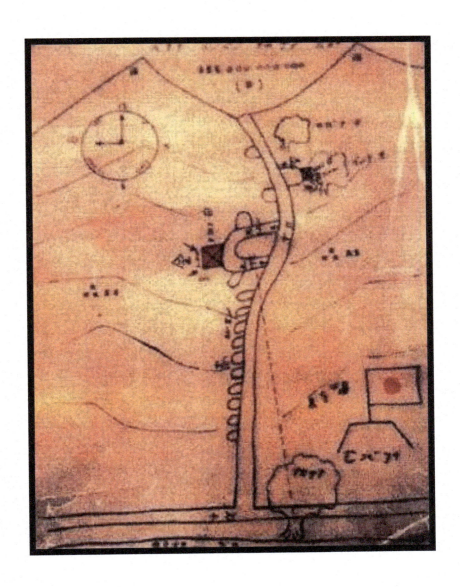

18.50 Another Japanese Treasure Map: Location Unknown

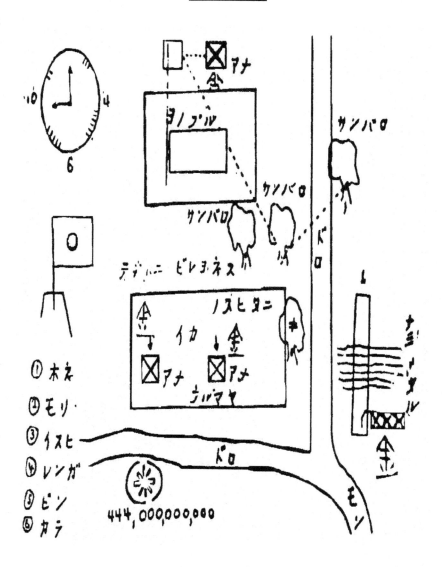

18.60 Imperial Japanese Korean Treasure Symbols 1 For Davao Region Mindanao

Treasure Signs

Y	UNCUT PRECIOUS STONE
‖	MONEY/MANY DEPOSIT
⚘	BURIED GOLD
△	TRIANGLE OBJECT ON CENTER
ᛜ	TREASURE UNDER
=	MANY MONEY
♪	JEWELRIES
⊃	TREASURE UNDER
8	WEALTH UNDER OBJECT
⫯7xH⫯lB	GOLD
⟶	TREASURE ON WATER
✕	TREASURE
⟁	JEWELRIES
XX	DOUBLE FIXED TREASURE
🕊	SUMATRA GOLD
👣	VOLUME OF TREASURE
O or ⚘	GLITTERING DIAMONDS
△	CLEAR DEPOSIT IN 3 CORNERS, STONE OR TREES
□	TREASURE IN BOX
Ɔ	DEPOSIT UNDERNEATH
⧓	SILVER COIN
J	UNDERGROUND DEPOSIT
⊚	UNDER OBJECT
⌒	DEPOSIT ON SIDE
[o]	TREASURE ON THIS SIDE
⻌	UNDER TREE, IN REAR
O	DEPOSIT
·X	TREASURE AT RIGHT
Jeh	COINS
⟟	OBJECT UNDERNEATH
△̲	SILVER
Λ	JEWELRY DEPOSIT

Other Signs

△	BIG ROAD
⊱	CITY
··	SMALL ROAD
⊔	IN BOXES
Z	AT THE BACK
▭	STONE
4K	INSIDE OR SIDE
⋔ƒ3	STOP DIGGING
N	CONTINUATION
†	FAR TO OBJECT
4K	INSIDE OR BESIDES
√	OBJECT POINTING LEFT
:⫯‖	20 YARDS
V	DIG DOWN
=↑	GO DOWN 2 METRES
∕∕	ALONG THE CREEK

18.70 Imperial Japanese Korean Treasure Symbols 2 For Davao Region Mindanao

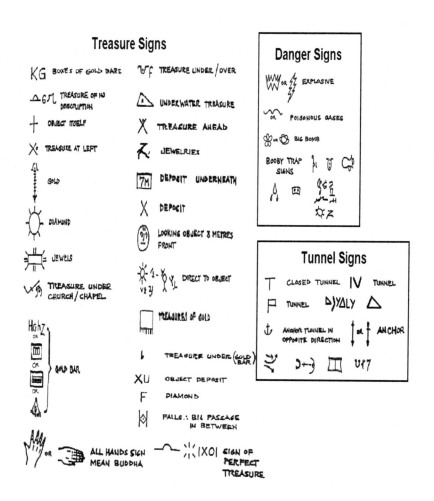

18.80 Japanese Military Map Symbols 1

Japanese Military Map Symbols Circa 1944

Terrain

Cliff	
Coral reef	
Cultivated land	
Grass (pasture) land	
Rice paddy (see below)	
flooded	
dry	
Rocky land	
Sandy land	
Swamp	
Surf	
Spring	
Tidal flats	
Uncultivated land	

Fence Types

bamboo	
earth	
hedge	
wall	

Tree

Bamboo, large	
small (reeds)	
Broad leaf (deciduous)	
Cut over (stumps)	
Jungle	
Orchard	
Palms (cf. bamboo)	
Mulberry	
Pine (conifers)	
Pine (dwarf)	

River And Road

River - intermittent	
Roads - highway (cf. RR)	
country (tree lined, 24 ft)	
impassable for carts	
under construction	
trails - 3 foot hand-cart	
less than 3 foot paths	

18.90   Japanese Military Map Symbols 2

Japanese Military Map Symbols
Circa 1944

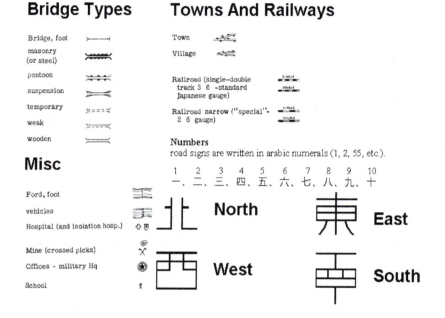

19.00 Japanese Characters For Geographical Features 1

Geographical Features	Kanji Symbols	Hiragana / Katakana
Caves/ Hollow / Cavity	空洞	くうどう
Cave / Den / Grotto	洞	ほら
Cave / Den / Grotto	洞穴	どうけつ
Cave	洞窟	どうくつ
Lake	湖水	こすい
Lake	湖	みずうみ
Mountain		マウンテン
Distant Mountain	遠山	えんざん
Remote Mountain /Mountain Recesses	奥山	おくやま
Peak / Mountain	遠山	たけ
Rocky Mountain	岩山	いわやま
High Mountain / Lofty Peak	高峰	こうほう
Mountain Stream	渓流	けいりゅう
Dead Tree	枯木	かれき
Pine Tree	松	まつ
Large Tree	大木	たいぼく
Camphor Tree	楠	くすのき
Big Tree	巨木	きょぼく
River / Stream	大河	たいが / おおかわ
River / Stream	川	かわ
Stream / Current Flow	流れ	ながれ
Mountain Stream	谷川	たにがわ
Swamp / Marsh	沢	さわ
Muddy Stream	濁流	だくりゅう
Lake	湖 / 湖水	レーク / みずうみ / こすい
Cave	洞窟	どうくつ

19.10 Japanese Characters For Geographical Features 2

Geographical Features	Kanji Symbols	Hiragana / Katakana
Cave / Den / Grotto	洞	ほら
Among Rocks	岩間	いわま
Top Of A Waterfall	滝口	たきぐち
Waterfall / Rapids	滝	たき
Places		
Military Camp	軍営	くんえい]
Military Barracks	屯営	とんえい
Railway Station	停車場	ていしゃば
Airfield	飛行場	ひこうじょう
Prison Of War Camp	捕虜収容所	ほりょしゅうようじょ
Catholic Church	カトリック教会	カトリックきょうかい
Warnings		
Danger	危ない	あぶない
Hazard / Danger	危険	きけん
Harm / Injury	危害	きがい

19.20 General Observations Taken From A Japanese Topographical Map Of 1940

Japanese official topographical maps were published on standard scales of 1 to 10,000, 1 to 20,000, 1 to 50,000, and so on. As the 1 to 50,000 is the most usual, and employs the standard symbols, parts of maps in this scale are here reproduced for illustration. Sometimes the scale will be stated at the bottom as a fraction in Arabic numerals, sometimes not. However, there is a distance scale at the bottom of the sheet in meters and ri, the Japanese "statute mile," actually a one-hour walk, or league, of approximately 2.5 U.S. miles. The meter scale is recognizable by its marking in thousands, and by the Japanese character 米 at the left, which in small print is apt to look like an asterisk. The **meter-scale** is apt to be on top, the ri-scale below. From the meter scale, the mathematical scale of the map may be quickly calculated by the following method: A meter is approximately 39 inches. Therefore, measure off from the metric scale a convenient number of thousand-meter units to correspond with the inch-scale of the ruler, multiply the thousand-meter units so measured by 39,000 and divide by the number of inches spanned. For example, in the scale below, as shown on a Japanese map, the total length of the metric scale, including the fraction-scale to the left of zero, is 4 inches; therefore 5,000 meters equals 4 inches; 1,000 meters equals 39,000 inches; 39 x 5,000 = 195,000; divided by 4 the result is 48,750, or approximately 50,000; hence, the scale is 1 to 50,000.

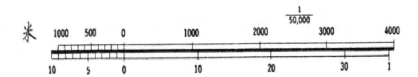

Each dash therefore equals 1 meter or approximately 39 inches. Why is this information useful to us?
The Japanese used these maps to mark strategic military positions, and in some cases the burial positions of buried gold bullion and gem stones.

Rice or tracing paper overlays would be used to mark these important positions and be taken and kept by the commanding officer. The positions were dots and a brief description of what was buried there. If these overlays were later found on a dead Japanese officer, they would be worthless to the Allied American forces unless they knew which topographical map was used and the correct orientation the overlay should be viewed with respect to north in order to fully understand the importance of these dots and strategic positioning on the right scaled map area in the first place.

Assumptions would have to be made that the dead Japanese officer was in charge of defending or attacking a geographical area, and that his overlay would "fit" the topographic map very close to where he died.

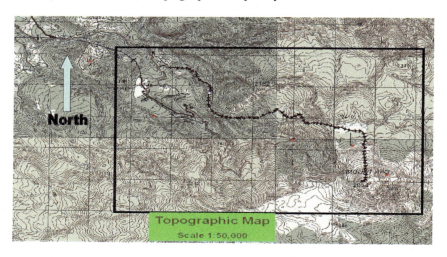

A topographical map of Mount Apo in Mindanao showing dowsed buried treasure locations shown as red dots.

Dowsing for Japanese gold deposits in 2011 by the author resulted in five small soldier or officer deposits being detected. These deposits are awaiting verification and further investigation by local Filipino treasure hunters.

19.30 Treasure Symbols Showing Distance

In this section of the book I have included many of the treasures symbols that describe how far the treasure is located. You will see that both the meter and the yard measurements were used to convey distance.

Symbol	Meaning	Symbol	Meaning
	30 YARDS		2 METERS MORE
	40 YARDS		5 YARDS
	50 YARDS		5 YARDS
	50 YARDS		5 YARDS
	1 YARD MORE		5 YARDS
	2 YARDS MORE		10 YARDS
	3 YARDS MORE		10 YARDS
	4 YARDS MORE		10 YARDS
	5 YARDS		APPROX. 50 YARDS
	5 YARDS		3 METERS MORE
	5 YARDS		4 METERS MORE
	5 YARDS MORE - NORTH		5 METERS MORE
	8 YARDS MORE		5-10 METERS

Treasure Symbols Showing Distance

Symbol	Meaning	Symbol	Meaning
7ǁ	10 YARDS	V⌈	5 METERS
mc∘	50 YARDS	Vǁ	10 METERS
⟶	5 METERS WITH CAVE		GET DOWN TO OBJECT 2 METERS
=	1 TO 30 METERS (MASAKO CODE)	W∘W	5 METERS
/	50 YARDS ARROW WAY (TANAKA CODE)	−▭	LOCATION 2 METERS
V0	50 YARDS (TANAKA CODE)	(∘∘∘∘∘∘∘)	7 METERS RIGHT
☼	11 YARDS (TANAKA CODE)	Mr∘	50 METERS
W	5 YARDS (TANAKA CODE)	∿∘	50 METERS
7"	20 YARDS (TANAKA CODE)	⟶	LONG RANGE UP TO 100 METERS
∩V∘	10 YARDS (TANAKA CODE)	F⊃2	1 FATHOM
∘/ǁ	20 YARDS (KOREAN CODE)	F⊃2	1 FATHOM
ǁǀ∘	50 YARDS (KOREAN CODE)	⌒⌒	5 YARDS
+∘	OBJECT A T RIGHT, 1 METER	⌒⌒	5 YARDS

Treasure Symbols Showing Distance

Symbol	Meaning	Symbol	Meaning
→→	POINTING 1 METER (KOREAN CODE)	⊥	DIRECTLY POINTING TO OBJECT DOWNWARD 2 METERS
→→→	POINTING 2 METERS (KOREAN CODE)	⊥	POINTING TO OBJECT 2 METERS DOWNWARD
→→→→→	POINTING 4 METERS (KOREAN CODE)	✕	TREASURE IN LEFT, 1 METER
W	5 YARDS	:7"	20 YARDS
大	15 YARDS FROM THE ARROW OR ANY OTHER POINTING SIGN	M.	50 YARDS
～	50 YARDS FROM THIS POINT	o→	SHORT RANGE, UP TO 25 METERS
∫=	5 METERS WITH CAVE	o→	SHORT RANGE, UP TO 10 METERS
‖⊤	10 METERS FROM THIS POINT	o→	1 TO 7 METERS
m～	50 YARDS AWAY	o→	1 TO 5 METERS
M	50 YARDS AWAY	o↱	5 METERS WITH CAVE
7⊥	5 YARDS	Ψ	UP TO 7 METERS
Z	THERE, 15 YARDS	↓	UP TO 4 METERS
‖2	10 YARDS	↓	UP TO 3 METERS

Treasure Symbols Showing Distance

Symbol	Meaning	Symbol	Meaning
⇁	5 YARDS DISTANCE	→	50 TO 100 METERS
=	DOUBLE THE DISTANCE OF ONE	→	1 METER TO 50 METERS (MASAKO CODE)
7"	20 YARDS MORE	7//	10 YARDS
+ηve	10 YARDS	↻→	1 TO 7 METERS WITH CAVE
⌐✓¡	5 YARDS OBJECT UNDER	ʃʃ←	TUNNEL TWO METERS DOWN

19.40 Treasure Symbols Showing Direction

Here in this section I have included many of the treasure signs that convey an instruction or a clear direction to the treasure hoard.

元レ	EASTERN PART TREASURE DEPOSIT IN DIVISION FORM		SINGLE SHELL FACING UPARD DEPOSIT UNDER
らレ	TREASURE IN TUNNEL		SHELL UPSIDE DOWN – TRAVEL
レ	IN TUNNEL		RIGHT AT THE BOTTOM
IUレ	STRAIGHT OR IN TUNNEL	三	DIRECTION
| • |	DEPOSIT TREASURE IN THE SPRING		POINTING NORTH
	POINTING OUT WEALTH	Y9	TREASURE
	SOUTHERN PART IN TUNNEL TREASURE		TREASURE

Treasure Symbols Showing Direction

Symbol	Meaning	Symbol	Meaning
↶	DEPOSIT UNDER WATER	739	DON'T
G⌒	DEPOSIT UNDER WATER	M ✹	DOWN WARD
ĀKO	DEPOSIT UNDER STONE	=TZ	THIS
◁9	POINTING DIRECTION	⌐⌐	TREASURE DOWN
F5	TUNNEL REAR	HI	RIVER/WATER
NE	METERS OR MORE	HM	TREASURE UNDER WATER
6	THIS	YB✓	EAST
7	ARROW	YP✓	EAST
7K	INSIDE OR SIDE	⌐◠⌐	EAST
J	AT PLAZA CENTER	□□ b◠◠	WEST
✻	MEETING ANOTHER SIGN OF EQUAL DISTANCE	□□○ ✓	WEST
人⃛/	THERE	□□ □□ ✓	WEST
††ノ	RIGHT	≡7|||	SOUTH

Treasure Symbols Showing Direction

Symbol	Meaning	Symbol	Meaning
	NOT THIS		SOUTH
	NORTHERN PART IN TUNNEL TREASURE		TREASURE DIVIDED IN 4 FORM DEPOSIT
	WESTERN PART IN TUNNEL TREASURE		TREASURE DIVIDED IN 5 FORMS DEPOSIT
	EASTERN PART IN TUNNEL TREASURE		TREASURE DIVIDED IN 6 FORMS DEPOSIT
	POINTING HEAD DIRECTION ON THE TREASURE		POINTING TO DESCRIBED TUNNEL
	NEAR LOCATION		POINTING OUT TREASURE
	TRAVEL TO NEXT SIGN		UNDER STAIR OF THE HOUSE
	IN TUNNEL		TREASURE UNDER TREE
	MINERALS HERE		TREASURE DIVIDED AS SHOWN
	LOOK AROUND TOWARD TREASURE		TREASURE DIVIDED AS SHOWN
	TREASURE DIVIDED AS SHOWN		POINTING DEEP
	NEAR HERE		POINT DIRECTION TO TUNNEL
	COIN DEPOSIT		ARROW WAY

Treasure Symbols Showing Direction

Symbol	Meaning	Symbol	Meaning
°S	MINERAL CLOSE BY	7KO	DEPOSIT UNDER BIG STONE
6	DEPOSIT UNDER WATER	7K	INSIDE
9	OPPOSITE SIDE	~	TREASURE ON OPPOSITE SIDE
③	OPPOSITE SIDE		TRAVEL IN OPPOSITE DIRECTION
XC	STREET	U6	TREASURE UNDER
7	UNDER	△ (with line)	DEPOSIT AROUND BEND, TREE OR ROCK TRIANGLE
<3	ENTRANCE	△	TREASURE TO ONE SIDE OF TREE OR ROCK TRIANGLE
7t	DOWN	+	TREASURE IN WATER
UM	TREASURE UNDER	†	TREASURE BURIED IN CREEK
T	BEHIND	P	TUNNEL TYPE
ɔt	STAIR	y	UNDERGROUND PASSAGE
T	UNDER OR INSIDE	F=o	TREE
7X	DEPOSIT DOWN	△ooo	TREASURE IS DIVIDED INTO THREE POINTS

Treasure Symbols Showing Direction

Symbol	Meaning	Symbol	Meaning
⍉	DEPOSIT UNDER	ꓩ	UNDER
(JY2)	DEPOSIT UNDER WATER	C⚹O	LOOK FOR THE BIG STONE
7⚹O	DEPOSIT UNDER BIG STONE	HC	GOLD OR DEPOSIT CLOSE BY
ЧIZ	INSIDE	ZIG	IN FRONT
ꚁ	DEPOSIT INSIDE	VΛ	DIG UNDER THE SIGN
⊥	NORTH	⌂	UNDER OR INSIDE
⋈	LEFT AND RIGHT DEPOSIT	⌂	DEPOSIT AROUND BIG TREE OR ROCK TRIANGLE
∼∼∼∼ X	TREASURE UNDERNEATH THIS SITE	⊗	CENTER POINT OF HOLE OR CENTRE OF TREASURE SITE
≠	END TUNNEL OR END OF CAVE. TREASURE UNDER WALL	⊃	ROCK ENCLOSED TREASURE
⚒	DEPOSIT IN CAVE OR INSIDE HARD ROCK	IIJ	TREASURE IN CAVE OR MANHOLE
⊤	DEEP DOWN BELOW	◇	TREASURE INSIDE OF ROCK TRIANGLE
Y	HEAD LEFT	ठ	DEPOSIT INSIDE
⋈	UNDER	T5	NORTH

Treasure Symbols Showing Direction

Symbol	Meaning	Symbol	Meaning
⁊	OBJECT UNDER OR TUNNEL	↑	INVERTED DIRECTION
∫	OBJECT IN THE SIDE OF THE CREEK	△ ▽	WEALTH UNDER
∕	TUNNEL OR CREEK	TTU	TREASURE IN SLOPE OR CAVE IN
○	DOT OR HOLE – TUNNEL ENTRANCE	➤→	OPPOSITE SIDE
>⊂⊃	ARROWS	大	DOWN BELOW
ԱՈ	TREASURE UNDER	下	UNDER OR INSIDE
ՍՈ	TREASURE UNDER	⋈	DEPOSIT LEFT AND RIGHT
ՍՈ	TREASURE UNDER	木	TREE
⇇(	TREASURE UNDER CAVE	工	DOWN
†	RICH OBJECT BURIED IN THE CREEK	Y	TREASURE ON CREEK OR 'Y' TUNNEL
†	THE LONG PART POINT TO TREASURE IN WATER	大	OBJECT IN BIG RIVER
♡ﾂ	TREASURE ON THIS SIDE	K>K	OBJECT IN THE WATER
⋈	DEPOSIT DOWN TO NEXT SIDE	⋏	ENTRANCE

Treasure Symbols Showing Direction

Symbol	Meaning	Symbol	Meaning
△ (with dot)	DEPOSIT OF TREASURE IN TREE OR ROCK TRIANGLE	TΣ5A	CAVE
✓	WESTERN PART IN TUNNEL TREASURE	◇	POINTING OUT WEALTH
E-3	STOP, CHANGE DIRECTION, TURN ABOUT	Ɛ3	CHANGE DIRECTION
▭ (with arrow down)	DIG DOWNWARD	/	TUNNEL ON CREEK
⊔⊔	MOUNTAIN	Z71	LEFT
|o|	UNDER THE MAIN ROAD	4	POINTING NORTH
↱	POINTING OUT THE TREASURE	T	INWARD
৬৲	TREASURE UNDER OR OVER THE CAVE	L-17HN	HEAD EAST
3→→o2	OPPOSITE DIRECTION	႕ပ	IN SLOPE OR IN CAVE
/ʃʃ/	RIVER	⊤	UNDER OR INSIDE
7C	DOOR	中	UNDER OR INSIDE

407

Treasure Symbols Showing Direction

Symbol	Meaning	Symbol	Meaning
≋	RIVER GOING UPWARD	下	DOWN BELOW
≋	RIVER GOING DOWNWARD	木	DOWN BELOW
⌒.	TRAVEL ARROW BASE SIGN HERE	F	TREE
↘	POINT OUT TREASURE	木	TREE
川	RIVER OR CREEK	山	MOUNTAIN HILL
Ш	RIVER OR CREEK	東	EAST
(tunnel symbol)	TUNNEL	(center direction symbol)	CENTER DIRECTION
171八1	SOME MORE	不	STRAIGHT DOWN BELOW
(back symbol)	BACK	◎ ◎	LOOKING AT THE TREASURE
(here symbol)	HERE	෧	TREASURE BELOW
4SKP	IN ONE SIDE	≋M≋	DEPOSIT UNDER WATER
(boot left)	STILL DEEP, OR TRAVEL LEFT	⇒	RIGHT DIRECTION TOWARDS THE OBJECT
(boot right)	CEMENTED, OR TRAVEL RIGHT	T	CLOSE

Treasure Symbols Showing Direction

Symbol	Meaning	Symbol	Meaning
⌒	TREASURE UNDER	⌐	SOUTH
Y	TUNNEL	ℐ	UNDERGROUND PASSAGE
～	TREASURE NEAR THE CREEK	C	GATE
◎)◦	POINTING TO THE OBJECT	△	DEPOSIT AROUND BEND TREES OR ROCK TRIANGLE
⊥	TREASURE INSIDE	Z25	NEAR TREE
∴∴	2 OBJECTS AT BOTH SIDES	⊔⊔	WAY ENTRANCE, WAY OUTSIDE
╱	TUNNEL ON CREEK	IV	OBJECT UNDER
W	GO DOWN	∼∽	TREASURE ON OPPOSITE SIDE
♡	TREASURE UNDER	V	V-SIGN IS TUNNEL ALSO AN ARROW
◢	VERY NEAR TO THE OBJECT, CONTINUE DIGGING	>○<	DEPOSIT DOWN TO NEXT SIDE
G∽→	TO THE OBJECT TREASURE	7+	FAR DISTANCE
⊬⊦	OBJECT UNDER	73▢	AT THE BACK
1⌒	UNDER	Z≠	FRONT

Treasure Symbols Showing Direction

Symbol	Meaning	Symbol	Meaning
⊣—	TUNNEL	▷◁	TREASURE UNDER
⌷	DEPOSIT SIGN, POT TYPE UNDER WATER	⟩⟩⟩⟩→	OPPOSITE SIDE
∫	BELOW WATER IMPACT	A̅	GO INSIDE
△	TREASURE TO ONE SIDE OF TREES OR ROCK TRIANGLE	9	OPPOSITE SIDE
4K	INSIDE	7HE	DOOR
ZXI	ROOM	Z	UNDER
7JZ	2 IN TUNNEL FORM DEPOSIT NORTH AND SOUTH	IV	POINTING SOUTH
CS	3 IN TUNNEL FORM DEPOSIT EAST - NORTH AND SOUTH	~~	POINTING EAST
SJ	4 IN TUNNEL FORM DEPOSIT EAST - NORTH - SOUTH AND WEST	⌒	POINTING WEST
↓	POINTING DEEP	爪||	CAVE OR IN TUNNEL
⌒	POINTING OUT WEALTH	(7)	TREASURE DIVIDED IN 2 FORM DEPOSIT
))ո-Ľ	EASTERN PART TREASURE DEPOSIT IN DIVISION FORM	⌐	TREASURE DIVIDED IN 3 FORM DEPOSIT
ո-Ľ	EASTERN PART TREASURE DEPOSIT IN DIVISION FORM	◇	OPEN CLAMP SHELL, OPEN DOOR, UNDER SEARCH

Conclusion

In this book I have tried to give you, the treasure hunter and adventurer, past history and in-depth knowledge of where to look for buried treasure, and also many pages explaining what to look for and how to decipher hundreds of treasure symbols that were used throughout the Philippines and possibly in other parts of Southeast Asia by the Japanese Imperial Forces during the Second World War.

Please remember the past is always very much in the present, especially when we are treasure hunting in the Philippines. Everyone has a treasure story to tell on the islands; some are true, others are false. Always have an open mind, and be wary of "fantastic easy money" stories from local Filipino conmen or treasure groups.

Your independent research is crucial in sifting out fact from fiction. This book has taken me over six years in research and many visits to the Philippines, researching known treasure sites on Luzon and in Mindanao with Filipino groups who needed my help and field-dowsing skills. My research is ongoing and now I find I have enough material to write a second book, which will include even more treasure code books, treasure maps, and true stories of poor Filipinos that have become rich.

My dream is to write a detailed diary of such a treasure expedition. This particular group will start a new treasure recovery project in early 2013. I will detail how the treasure deposit was researched, located and excavated using skills learnt from writing this book, and this story will be included in my second book, together with many photographs of excavating closed tunnels and yes recovered treasure too!

My first book is not supposed to be the "definitive answer" to all the unanswered questions that you may come across regarding your site analysis and recovery activities, but I hope that it will aid you in finding your answers and ultimately result in you successfully recovering a small amount of the thousands of millions of dollars worth of buried gold, gems and artifacts still awaiting to be discovered, either sunk or buried in or around the exotic islands that make up the Philippine islands situated in the South China Sea.

May your God bless you and keep you safe and happy treasure hunting.

Aquila

Bibliography

In Search of Gold by Tomas Cyran: Published by Trafford Press **ISBN 1-4206197-0.**

Gold Warriors by Sterling & Peggy Seagrave: Published by Verso Press **ISBN 1-84467531-9.**

Japanese Special Naval Landing Forces by Gary Nila & Robert A.Rolfe: Published by Osprey Books **ISBN 978-1-84603-100-7.**

Asian Loot by Charles C. Mc Dougald: Published by San Francisco **ISBN 0-940777-08-8.**

Japanese Army in World War II Conquest of the Pacific (1941-42) by Gordon L.Rottman: Published by Ospery books **ISBN 978-1-84176-789-5.**

Japanese Archives: Honbo, Tokyo Japan.

Treasure Hunters Association of the Philippines 1970 data source.

Webster's New World: Japanese Dictionary **ISBN 0-02-861725-8.**

The Successful Treasure Hunter's Essential Dowsing Manual by David Villanueva: Published by True Treasure Books **ISBN 0-9550325-0-4** (www.truetreasurebooks.com).

Successful Treasure Hunter's Secret Manual: Discovering Treasure Auras in the Digital Age by David Villanueva **ISBN 978-0-9550325-5-4** (www.truetreasurebooks.com)

The Marcos Dynasty by Sterling Seagrave: Published by Harper & Row **ISBN 0-06-015815-8**

The Gold of the Sun (Robert Curtis)

The Marcos Legacy Revisited: Raiders of the Lost Gold (Erick San Juan)

The World Atlas of Treasure (Derek Wilson)

The Yamamoto Dynasty (Sterling Seagrave)
Tracing Marcos' Gold - The True Story of the Yamashita's Treasure (D.Ahl Umali)

Appendix

Concrete Breaking Solutions (Non Explosive Demolition Agent)

Bristar, Address: BASF Philippines, Inc.11/F Hanjinphil Corporation Building 1128 University Parkway, North Bonifacio, Global City, Taguig, Metro Manila, 1634, Philippines. E-Mail **lie.chico@basf.com** Phone (63-2) 811 – 8000 (63-2) 811 – 8000 Telefax: (63-2) 838 - 1025

Bristar: (non-explosive demolition agent) (more or less 2,000 pesos per 5 kg/bag) Address: Condeck Sales Center, Room 201, Torimar Bldg., 370 Escolta St. Sta. Cruz, Manila, Philippines. Tel: (632) 2425647 / 2418201 1269 Makati City Phone +63 2 845 29 81Telefax: +63 2 845 29 93

Ter-Mite (Non Explosive Demolition Agent)
Dextec Oy Ltd.
Otsolahdentie 7
FI- 02110 Espoo
Finland
Fax +358 9 8565 7261
Website link:
http://www.ter-mite.com/?gclid=CPCi1raFia8CFQITfAodNWCt-Q#

Zhejiang Top king Chemical Co., Ltd., (Non Explosive Demolition Agent)
Tel: 0086-579-84416678
Fax: 0086-579-82855290 Mobile: 0086-15205896321
Email: info@breakag.com
Address: No.558, Binwang Road, YiwuCity, Zhejiang Province, China.
Website links: http://www.breakag.com and
http://www.breakag.com/BREAKAG.html

Dexpan Non Explosive Blasting:

Website link: http://www.dexpan.com
How to use Dexpan video:
http://www.youtube.com/watch?v=YlDQvgM4pKM&feature=related

Concrete Dissolving Solutions:

See Website link:
www.romixchem.com/romix_cart/proddetail.php?prod=10001BST005PL

Molecular Cement Dissolver: Website link:
http://www.romixchem.com/romix_cart/back_set.php

Muriatic Acid for Concrete Etching: Website link:
http://www.nycoproducts.com/products.asp?pid=81

Concrete Cutting Solutions:

Core Drilling:
www.coredrillcity.co.uk/masonry.php?osCsid=b269um62q432dvdutle1thd4t2

Petrol Disc Cutters: www.tooled-up.com/Product.asp?PID=143003

Diamond Drill Bits: Concrete and marble:
www.discountdiamondbits.com/3prosecobit.html

Gold Prices:

www.metalprices.com/FreeSite/metals/gold/gold.asp

www.goldprice.org/

www.cooksongold.com/metalprices/

www.livecharts.co.uk/MarketCharts/gold.php

www.taxfreegold.co.uk/goldpriceslive.html

Ground-Penetrating Radar and Electromagnetic Induction Instruments

Applications

- Excellent for locating septic tanks
- Lost Utility Pipes
- Wells
- Cellars
- Secret Tunnels
- Hidden Rooms
- Buried or Hidden Objects
- Cemetery Surveys
- Aircraft Wreckage
- Can be used in a boat to locate sunken vessels or vehicles
- See through walls to locate hidden rooms or voids
- Locate and Identify ferrous and non ferrous
- Finds Gold and Silver

See:
Geophysical: www.geophysical.com
Geofizz: www.geofizz.co.uk/p
Geomatrix: www.geomatrix.co.uk

Internet Treasure News Groups

www.treasurenet.com
www.THunting.com
www.ukdetectornet.co.uk
alt.treasure.hunting
www.tseatc.com/ww2loot.html

Metal Detector Manufactures

Accurate Locators: www.accuratelocators.com
Deep Search (Gold Scan 5 meters) Metal Detectors
http://ktselectronic.com
Fitzgerald Detectors: www.treasurenow.com
Search and Recovery Service:
www.treasurenow.com/html/SearchAndRecovery.html
Garrett Metal Detectors: www.garrett.com
Metal Detector Sales: www.kellycodetectors.com
Minelab International Ltd: www.minelab.com

Metal Detector Manufactures (continued)

OKM 3D Image Gold Detectors:
www.okmmetaldetectors.com/index.php?lang=en#
Rangertell Long Range Detectors:www.rangertell.com/indexcc.htm
Electroscope Long Range Detectors: www.electroscopes.com/
Whites Electronics (UK) Ltd: www.whites.co.uk

Self Breathing Equipment For Hazardous Places

Website links:
http://multimedia.3m.com/mws/mediawebserver?mwsId=66666UuZjcF SLXTtlXTVMXMVEVuQEcuZgVs6EVs6E666666—
http://www.wormald.com.au/fire-products/breathing-apparatus/selfcontained-breathing-apparatus-scba
http://www.labsafety.com/refinfo/ezfacts/ezf193.htm

SBE And Communication Equipment

http://www.honeywellsafety.com/americas/respiratoryprotection/?tid=1231&bid=179&hid=113&iid=0

Thermal Image Cameras

www.thethermalimagingcamera.com
www.isgthermalsystems.co.uk
www.flir.com/gb/thermal-imaging/#

Underwater Cutting Equipment

www.broco-rankin.com/broco/underwater.cfm

Useful Contacts:

Casio "Pro Trek" Sports Watches: www.casio.com
Clark Development Corporation: www.clark.com.ph
Colorado Gold Dowsing Sticks: www.coloradogoldsticks.com
DENR (Philippine treasure permits): www.denr.gov.ph
Gas Masks And Ventilation Systems: www.scottint.com
Sarin Gas Detectors: http://www.detcon.com/xgas-sarin01.htm
Useful Contacts (continued)

Methane Gas Detectors: http://www.detcon.com/xgas-methane01.htm
Hydrogen Cyanide Detectors: http://www.detcon.com/xgas-hydrogencyanide01.htm
Mustard Gas Detectors: http://www.detcon.com/xgas-mustard01.htm
If you are not sure of the Karat content of the gold, purchase an M24 Stock# TES-170.00: This device will assay gold ranging from 9-24-Karat.

See: http://www.shorinternational.com/TestGold.htm
Gold Buying Station: *Security Plant Complex, Bangko Sentral ng Pilipinas,. East Ave*. Diliman *Quezon City*, Tel. No. 929-7071 loc. 337-925-7179.
See link:
http://www.bsp.gov.ph/downloads/regs/08%20Security%20Plant%20Complex.pdf

The process you need to follow in order to sell your gold to Security Plant Complex based in Quezon City is that you must supply the following information:

1. Letter of Delivery and Sale (LDS)
2. Letter of Authorization with ID picture and Residence Certificate (For first time seller/change of representative)
3. Enrollment to BSP checkless payment process
(For first time seller/if changes are made in the account to be credited)
See link:
http://www.bsp.gov.ph/downloads/regs/08%20Security%20Plant%20Complex.pdf

GPS Units: www.garmin.com

Laser Thermometers:
www.testersandtools.com/Infrared-Laser-Thermometer.php

Wells Fargo Old U.S. Notes Exchange (Makati, Luzon)

Wells Fargo Old U.S. Notes: Buyer contact: Mr Zach Anderson on: 0908-531-1521 or email address: zma@alumni.rice.edu
(English only please).

Subic Bay:

http://www.cocktaildivers.com/en/cocktaildivers-subic-wracks.htm

Coron Wrecks:

The Japanese wrecks are a result of an air attack by U.S. fighters and bombers from a U.S. Navy aircraft carrier, carried out on the 24th September, 1944. There was a fleet of twenty-four Japanese supply ships at anchor around Coron.
Coron is a small fishing and trading town on Busuanga Island, in the Calamian Islands, to the southwest of Manila and is well off the regularly travelled tourist path. It is both stunning yet so beautiful you will never forget this place. See: http://coronwrecks.com/sites.htm

Desperate Race for Vast Riches…A Dream?

www.geocities.com/filipinoculture/treasure.html
If you are tempted to take up the Yamashita challenge in the Philippines, read this article from a San Francisco newspaper, which tells how one seventy-four-year-old lost his life savings by investing in a scheme to dig up buried Japanese treasure.

Philippine WWII History link:

http://fourthmarinesband.com/photos_fall.htm
http://www.thelifeofadventure.com/yamashitas-gold/

For the children of the Philippines may God bless you all, you are hope and the future and the true treasure of this great land that is the Philippines.

CPSIA information can be obtained
at www.ICGtesting.com
Printed in the USA
BVOW05s1627031216
469292BV00009B/184/P